SAVING THE SOULS OF MEDIEVAL LONDON

Church, Faith and Culture in the Medieval West

General Editors
Brenda Bolton, Anne J. Duggan
and Damian J. Smith

Other titles in the series:

Edited by Martin Brett and Kathleen G. Cushing
Readers, Texts and Compilers in the Earlier Middle Ages
Studies in Medieval Canon Law in Honour of Linda Fowler-Magerl

Greta Austin
Shaping Church Law Around the Year 1000
The *Decretum* of Burchard of Worms

Edited by John Doran and Damian J. Smith
Pope Celestine III (1191–1198)
Diplomat and Pastor

Edited by Bruce C. Brasington and Kathleen G. Cushing
Bishops, Texts and the Use of Canon Law around 1100
Essays in Honour of Martin Brett

Edited by Éamonn Ó Carragáin and Carol Neuman de Vegvar
Roma Felix – Formation and Reflections of Medieval Rome

Edited by Louise Bourdua and Anne Dunlop
Art and the Augustinian Order in Early Renaissance Italy

Christine Walsh
The Cult of St Katherine of Alexandria in Early Medieval Europe

Michael E. Goodich
Miracles and Wonders
The Development of the Concept of Miracle, 1150–1350

Saving the Souls of Medieval London

Perpetual Chantries at St Paul's Cathedral, c.1200–1548

MARIE-HÉLÈNE ROUSSEAU

Routledge
Taylor & Francis Group

LONDON AND NEW YORK

First published 2011 by Ashgate Publishing

2 Park Square, Milton Park, Abingdon, Oxfordshire OX14 4RN
52 Vanderbilt Avenue, New York, NY 10017

Routledge is an imprint of the Taylor & Francis Group, an informa business

First issued in paperback 2020

British Library Cataloguing in Publication Data
Rousseau, Marie-Hélène.
  Saving the souls of medieval London : perpetual chantries at St Paul's Cathedral, c.1200–1548.
  – (Church, faith and culture in the medieval West) 1. Chantries–England–London–History–
  To 1500. 2. St. Paul's Cathedral (London, England)–History–To 1500. 3. Church of England–
  Clergy–History–To 1500. 4. Church of England–Benefices–History–To 1500. 5. London
  (England)–Church history. 6. Church history–Middle Ages, 600–1500. I. Title II. Series
  262'.03421-dc22

Library of Congress Cataloging-in-Publication Data
Rousseau, Marie-Hélène.
  Saving the souls of medieval London : perpetual chantries at St. Paul's Cathedral, c.1200-1548
  / Marie-Helene Rousseau.
    p. cm. — (Church, faith, and culture in the medieval West)
  Includes bibliographical references and index.
  ISBN 978-1-4094-0581-8 (hardcover : alk. paper)
  (ebook) 1. St. Paul's Cathedral (London, England)—History. 2. Chantries—England—
  London. 3. London (England)—Church history. I. Title.
BX5195.L7R68 2010
246'.9595094212—dc22

                                                                        2010042014

ISBN 978-1-4094-0581-8 (hbk)
ISBN 978-0-367-60240-6 (pbk)

Contents

List of Figures and Tables

Figures

Tables

Acknowledgements

This adventure began more than ten years ago when I first set foot in London to undertake a doctoral degree at the University of London under the direction of Caroline Barron. I wish sincerely and truly to thank her for accompanying me and guiding me throughout this journey. Neither the thesis nor the book version would have seen the light of day had it not been for her expertise, mentorship, constant availability and never-ending encouragement. I will be grateful in perpetuity. I also want to express my gratitude towards Clive Burgess, my academic advisor, and Elizabeth New for their generous help and support throughout the years, and towards my PhD *viva* committee, Virginia Davis and Nicholas Orme, who were instrumental in my pursuit of further research, and especially Professor Orme, who pushed me to publish my work. I am also indebted to David Lepine, who kindly agreed to read my manuscript: his insightful suggestions considerably improved the end product, and to John Schofield, who generously shared his map of St Paul's precinct that he prepared for his report to be published by English Heritage in 2011. Thanks are owed to Denise Angers, John Barron, Ann Bowtell, Joyce Coleman, Matthew Davis, Jessica Freeman, Martin Gravel, Stephanie Hovland, Hannes Kleineke, Jennifer Ledfords, John McEwan, Clementine Oliver, Eleanor Quinton, Joel Rosenthal, Christian Steer, Robert Tittler, June Vayo and Scott Wells for discussing my project, answering specific queries, or encouraging me in pursuing my research. I also want to acknowledge the constructive comments that I have received from often anonymous historians when presenting my work at conferences and seminars in London and in North America, and also the judicious feedback that I got from the participants of the California Medieval History Seminar who read two of my book chapters and offered me such a warm welcome.

I would like to express my gratitude towards the archivists and librarians of the Guildhall Library, the Corporation of London Records Office, the Institute of Historical Research, London Metropolitan Archives, the National Archives and St George's Chapel Archives, who, during my many years of research, were eager to provide me with assistance. Special thanks are due to the staff and the readers of the Huntington Library in California, where I converted the thesis into a book. I could not have wished for a better work environment. I would also like to acknowledge the Social Sciences and Humanities Research Council of Canada for the generous doctoral and post-doctoral scholarships that I received in 1999–2003 and 2003–2005. The editors of the series and the staff at Ashgate, especially Emily Yates, deserve my gratitude for being so patient and understanding, and for making this publishing experience such a pleasant one. I would also like to thank the anonymous reader who commented on my thesis, and whose comments helped me transform it into a better book. Any errors and faults remain my own.

In the decade spent working on this project I incurred debts of gratitude towards a great number of friends. They should know that their unconditional support and good humour enabled me to carry on my project throughout the years. I am particularly thankful to my neighbours at Goodenough College, the friends of the BWMA in Pasadena, and fellow long-distance runners who helped me decompress after solitary days spent in libraries and archive centres. From close and afar their continued interest in my work kept me on track. Special thanks are owed to Kim Segel and Paul Darnell, Bronwyn Thorburn and Andrew Riseley, Devon Curtis and Audrée-Isabelle Tardif, who in addition to being great friends, hosted me for extended periods of time. I would also like to thank Felice Botts and Nicola Wilkins for providing me with more than their share of moral support. By proofreading parts of my work, many of my friends have learnt more than they ever wished about medieval chantries: I am especially grateful towards Paige Randall, who read through the whole manuscript.

Perhaps involuntarily but with good spirit, my family has accepted that my life will be spent in far- away lands. I would like to thank my parents, my three sisters (especially my twin Mélanie) and their families, for the love and support they consistently give me. I also want to thank my in-laws for their warm welcome and kind interest in my various endeavours. Finally, a word for my loving husband Robert Ward, who has walked next to me in this long but exciting journey, at times motivating me, pushing me and challenging me, but never letting me give up: merci!

List of Abbreviations

Alumni	John Venn and J.A. Venn, *Alumni Cantabrigienses. A Biographical List of All Known Students, Graduates and Holders of Office at the University of Cambridge from the Earliest Times to 1900* (3 vols, Cambridge, 1922–1954)
BRUC	A.B. Emden, *A Biographical Register of the University of Cambridge* (Cambridge, 1963)
BRUO	A.B. Emden, *A Biographical Register of the University of Oxford to 1500* (3 vols, Oxford, 1957–1959)
BRUO, 1501–1540	A.B. Emden, *A Biographical Register of the University of Oxford A.D. 1501 to 1540* (Oxford, 1974)
CCR	*Calendar of Close Rolls*
Chamber Accounts	Betty R. Masters (ed.), *Chamber Accounts of the Sixteenth Century*, London Record Society, 20 (London, 1984)
CPR	*Calendar of Patent Rolls*
CSPD	C.S. Knighton (ed.), *Calendar of State Papers, Domestic Series, of the Reign of Edward VI (1547–1553) Preserved in the Public Record Office* (London, 1992)
Dugdale	Sir William Dugdale, *The History of St. Paul's Cathedral. With a continuation and additions by H. Ellis* (London, rep. 1818)
Fasti I	John Le Neve, *Fasti Ecclesiae Anglicanae 1066–1300*, vol. I: *St Paul's, London*, compiled by Diana E. Greenway (London, 1968)
Fasti II	John Le Neve, *Fasti Ecclesiae Anglicanae 1300–1541*, vol. V: *St Paul's, London*, compiled by Joyce M. Horn (London, 1963)
Fasti III	John Le Neve, *Fasti Ecclesiae Anglicanae 1541–1857*, vol. I: *St Paul's, London*, compiled by Joyce M. Horn (London, 1969)
GL	Guildhall Library, London
HC	Husting Court

Hennessy				George Leydon Hennessy, *Novum Repertorium
					Ecclesiasticum Parochiale Londinense* (London, 1898)

Kitching				C.J. Kitching (ed.), *London and Middlesex Chantry
					Certificate, 1548*, London Record Society, 16
					(London, 1980)

Letter-Book				R.R. Sharpe (ed.), *Calendar of Letter-Books Preserved among
					the Archives of the Corporation of the City of London at the
					Guildhall* (11 vols, London, 1899–1912)

Letters & Papers			*Letters and Papers, Foreign and Domestic, of the Reign of
					Henry VIII* (21 vols, London, 1862–1932)

LMA					London Metropolitan Archives

McHardy				A.K. McHardy (ed.), *The Church in London, 1375–1392*,
					London Record Society, 13
					(London: The Society, 1977)

Newcourt				Richard Newcourt, *Repertorium Ecclesiasticum Parochiale
					Londinense* (2 vols, London, 1708–1710)

ODNB					*Oxford Dictionary of National Biography*
					(Oxford, 2004)

Sharpe				R.R. Sharpe (ed.), *Calendar of Wills proved and Enrolled in
					the Court of Husting, London, 1250–1688*
					(2 vols, London, 1889–1890)

Sudbury				R.C. Fowler and Claude Jenkins (eds.), *Registrum Simonis
					de Sudbiria Diocesis Londoniensis, AD 1362–75* (2 vols,
					London, 1927, 1938)

TNA					The National Archives, UK

Wriothesley				Charles Wriothesley, *A Chronicle of England during the
					Reigns of the Tudors from A.D. 1485 to 1559.* Edited by
					William Douglas Hamilton, Camden, 11, 20
					(2 vols, Westminster: Nichols, 1875–1877)

Introduction

St Paul's Cathedral stood at the centre of religious life in medieval London.[1] From the time of its foundation in 604, its community of secular clergy offered continual rounds of worship for the glory of God. The cathedral served as the bishop of London's principal seat and the mother church of the diocese, acting as a flagship in liturgy, music and visual splendours for all other religious institutions of the diocese of London.[2] Historical circumstances had denied St Paul's a metropolitan status, but because of London's particular standing as the kingdom's nucleus of economic and political activities, the cathedral's prestige extended beyond the borders of the diocese.[3] The Dean and Chapter counted among the principal landowners in the capital and surrounding countryside, and the cathedral, over 600 feet in length and one of Europe's greatest Gothic churches, functioned as the theatre for the enactment of events of national importance. Every day Londoners and visitors from the kingdom and abroad entered the cathedral for a myriad of pious, professional, entertainment and educational purposes.[4] The medieval cathedral also played yet another role: St Paul's served as a powerhouse of commemoration and intercession, where prayers and requiem masses were offered on a vast scale for the salvation of the living and the dead.

This spiritual role of St Paul's was carried out essentially by the numerous chantry priests working and living within its precinct. Unlike other members of the cathedral staff, whose services at St Paul's were supported by the cathedral's original endowment and whose positions were part of its bureaucracy and personnel, these chantry priests drew their livelihoods exclusively from private

---

[1]   St Paul's has been the subject of a magisterial study undertaken under the editorship of Derek Keene, Arthur Burns and Andrew Saint (eds), *St Paul's. The Cathedral Church of London, 604–2004* (New Haven/London, 2004).

[2]   The medieval diocese of London covered the city of London, the counties of Middlesex and Essex and the Hertfordshire deanery of Braughing.

[3]   Pamela Taylor, 'Foundation and Endowment: St Paul's and the English Kingdoms, 604–1087', in Keene, Burns and Saint, *St Paul's*, pp. 5–16, esp. p. 5.

[4]   For a discussion of the various roles and functions of St Paul's in the Middle Ages, see Derek Keene, 'From Conquest to Capital: St Paul's c.1100–1300', in Keene, Burns and Saint, *St Paul's*, pp. 17–32; and Caroline M. Barron and Marie-Hélène Rousseau, 'Cathedral, City and State, 1300–1540', in *ibid.*, pp. 33–44.

funds bequeathed to the cathedral by individual donors. Convinced of the general and specific benefits of the celebration of the Eucharist, these donors invested large sums of money, farm lands or city properties expressly to increase the number of priests at the cathedral celebrating daily masses. In return for their financial contributions, the donors were recognised as founders and main beneficiaries of the religious services performed by these priests, and were given the opportunity to determine the priests' selection process, define their duties and responsibilities, and appoint the patrons who would oversee their chantry foundations.[5] At least eighty-four individual chantries were established in the cathedral from the late twelfth century onwards with the intent that they would last in perpetuity.[6] Although a minority disappeared and others were amalgamated, these perpetual chantries contributed substantially to the daily life of the cathedral by enhancing its liturgical services, increasing the numbers of priests, and intensifying the relations with the city of London.

Chantries owed their existence to a combination of Christian tenets that had long-established roots in the Middle Ages. The teachings of the Church held that while Christ's ultimate sacrifice on the Cross made atonement for man's original sin, it did not redeem Christians from the venial or minor sins they committed during their lifetimes. Unless they atoned for these sins, Christians would be steered away from the gates of heaven towards the fires of hell, where they were doomed to languish for eternity. The Church through its dispensation of the sacraments, however, offered avenues for salvation. The sacrament of penance, especially, enabled the reconciliation of sinners with both God and the Church.[7] While absolution had to be achieved on earth, satisfaction could be undertaken in the next life, if not entirely fulfilled in the course of this one.[8] The place where sins could be atoned and souls cleansed was purgatory: a 'third place' between heaven and hell.[9] Although collectively depicted as

---

[5]   The key study on these foundations in England remains Kathleen Wood-Legh, *Perpetual Chantries in Britain* (Cambridge, 1965).

[6]   In addition there were temporary chantries where incumbents celebrated masses at St Paul's for a specific number of years. These are not included in this study, since these incumbents did not become members of the cathedral clergy.

[7]   Kenan Osborne, 'Reconciliation', in Richard P. McBrien (ed.), *The Harper-Collins Encyclopedia of Catholicism* (New York, 1995) pp. 1083–7.

[8]   Clive Burgess, '"A Fond Thing Vainly Invented": An Essay on Purgatory and Pious Motive in Later Medieval England', in S.J. Wright (ed.), *Parish, Church and People. Local Studies in Lay Religion, 1350–1750* (London, 1988), pp. 56–84, esp. p. 63.

[9]   For a historical account on the theological development of the concept of purgatory, see Jacques Le Goff, *The Birth of Purgatory*. Transl. by Arthur Goldhammer (Chicago, 1984). Le Goff argued that since the noun *purgatorium* did not exist before the late twelfth century, purgatory as a place was not yet born. R.W. Southern places the development of the idea of

hell with agonising fires, purgatory came to embody an extension of earth and likewise an expansion of this lifetime.[10] The length and intensity of torments varied according to the sins perpetrated. It was possible to ease post-mortem agony by carrying out good works on earth. These could take many different forms, including prayers, almsgiving, fasting, and the sacrament of the altar (the mass).[11] The development of another Catholic tenet, the Communion of Saints, also offered assistance.[12] The prayers and suffrages of Christians on earth could be directed towards gathering the intercession of the saints to help Christian souls in purgatory. The three components of the Church were interlinked: the Church militant on earth, the Church suffering in purgatory and the Church triumphant in heaven, and their contacts were reciprocal.[13] Alongside prayers and suffrages, the offering of the Eucharist soon became the preferred instrument for the cult of the dead, and anniversaries provided privileged occasions to intercede for them. In 211 Tertullian alluded to the observance of the anniversary day of the departed, and St Cyprian recorded the offering of the Eucharist for the repose of the soul of a recently deceased Christian.[14] St Augustine and Gregory the Great both contributed greatly to the practice of praying for the dead by asserting the mutual solidarity of all Christians, the living as well as the dead.[15] Because priests were the only ones authorised to celebrate mass, the Church soon dominated the domain of intercessory commemoration, which contributed to its increasing prosperity.[16] Hope for spiritual returns prompted countless pious foundations and donations to the Church in the Middle Ages. Kings and magnates founded great abbeys throughout Christendom to redeem their sins by channelling continuous prayers performed by monks.[17] Although monasteries were especially associated with the cult of the dead, they never enjoyed a monopoly over intercessory practices. The same intention accounted

---

purgatory about a century earlier; see his review of Le Goff's work, 'Between Heaven and Hell', *Times Literary Supplement*, 18 June 1982, pp. 651–2.

[10]   *Ibid.*, p. 652.

[11]   Le Goff, *Birth of Purgatory*, p. 266; Burgess, '"A Fond Thing Vainly Invented"', p. 66.

[12]   For the importance and development in the Middle Ages of the concept of communion of saints, see Brian Patrick McGuire, 'Purgatory, the Communion of Saints, and Medieval Change', *Viator*, 20 (1989), pp. 61–84.

[13]   *Ibid.*, p. 67.

[14]   Le Goff, *Birth of Purgatory*, p. 47; Wood-Legh, *Perpetual Chantries*, p. 2.

[15]   McGuire, 'Purgatory, the Communion of Saints', pp. 70, 73; Le Goff, *Birth of Purgatory*, pp. 66–9, 90–93.

[16]   Le Goff, *Birth of Purgatory*, p. 135.

[17]   Clive Burgess, 'London Parishes: Development in Context', in Richard Britnell (ed.), *Daily Life in the Late Middle Ages* (Stroud, 1998), pp. 151–74, esp. p. 156; R.W. Southern, *Western Society and the Church in the Middle Ages* (London, 1970), Chapter 6.

for the founding of numerous colleges and benefactions within parish churches staffed by secular priests.[18] The less well-off in society also made contributions to the Church: in numerous religious institutions, small landowners and townsmen financed the provision of lights and lamps in return for spiritual benefits.[19] They could also join guilds, whose members, men and women, lay and religious, were bound together by religious duties. Found in England from at least the late tenth century, these guilds provided funeral rites and commemorative masses for their members after death.[20]

This quest for continuous prayers for the living and the dead shaped the religious landscape of medieval London.[21] By the late twelfth century, in addition to St Paul's Cathedral and a parochial network of more than one hundred churches encompassed within a square mile area, London housed St Martin le Grand, a pre-Conquest collegiate foundation, the English headquarters for two crusading orders (the Knights Templar and the Knights Hospitaller), and a number of Augustinian houses, such as the priories of Holy Trinity, St Bartholomew, St Katherine by the Tower, and St Mary Bishopsgate, which were all served by canons. The thirteenth century witnessed London's enthusiastic reception of the newly created orders of friars and the installation of six mendicant communities. In the fourteenth and fifteenth centuries, wealthy Londoners endowed colleges, such as Pountney's College and Whittington's College, where secular priests prayed for them and performed complementary good works. While these various foundations reflected changing trends in devotional practices, they nevertheless responded to a common goal: to increase the liturgical provisions generated in the city while funnelling some of that devotional energy towards the salvation of the founders' souls. Others shared the same ambitions as these founders, but rather than establishing new houses, they invested in existing ones to support their liturgical activities. In return for donations, these benefactors were commemorated by religious services, such as anniversaries or obits that re-enacted funeral masses, usually on the anniversary dates of the founders' deaths.

---

[18]　For a reappraisal of collegiate churches, see Clive Burgess, 'An Institution for All Seasons: The Late Medieval English College', in Clive Burgess and Martin Heale (eds), *The Late Medieval College and Its Context* (Woodbridge, 2008), pp. 3–27.

[19]　David Postles, 'Lamps, Lights and Layfolk: "Popular" Devotion before the Black Death', *Journal of Medieval History*, 25 (1999), pp. 97–114, esp. p. 105.

[20]　Gervase Rosser, 'The Anglo-Saxon Gilds', in J. Blair (ed.), *Minsters and Parish Churches: the Local Church in Transition, 950–1200* (Oxford, 1988), pp. 31–4, esp. p. 31.

[21]　The following is based on Barron's excellent introduction in Caroline M. Barron and Matthew Davies (eds), *The Religious Houses of London and Middlesex* (London, 2007), pp. 5–24.

By the late twelfth century, the first chantries were established at St Paul's Cathedral. By the mid-thirteenth century they were also founded in several monastic, collegiate and parochial churches in the capital, and became a characteristic feature of London's religious panorama in the later Middle Ages.[22] Their emergence and popularity were the result of interlinked developments. On the one hand, by the twelfth and thirteenth centuries theological doctrines about the notion of purgatory, the sacrament of penance, and the belief in the efficacy of prayers increased the demand for the celebration of intercessory masses; while on the other hand, the availability of very large endowments required to found a religious house was declining. The appeal of chantries was not, however, due only to their affordability: while being within the means of a larger segment of the population, chantries were also the pious projects of magnates and kings who could and did fund other religious institutions. It has recently been proposed that it was the monastic incapacity to cope with the high demand for intercessory practices that propelled the chantries to the top rank of pious foundations.[23] Burdened by the weight of their obligations, monastic orders began regrouping the celebration of anniversaries and post-mortem commemorations. In response, founders explored other venues for pious provisions, especially by endowing chantries.[24] Because they were served by secular priests who, unlike monks, were not bound by monastic vows, chantries offered more flexibility to founders to shape their foundations according to their preferences. In addition to the daily celebration of liturgical tasks, they could add supplementary duties to the incumbents, such as distributing alms, teaching children, helping with the cure of souls and participating in the choir services. These extra-liturgical activities varied according to the founders' wishes, and the needs of the religious establishments and communities in which they were founded. The private and collective benefits of chantries were interlinked: while chantries appealed to the founders' preoccupations with their own salvation, they were additionally intended to contribute to the general welfare of society by securing grace on earth.[25] Accordingly, long after founders had died and their

---

[22]   Examples can be found in *ibid.*, pp. 80, 199; and in Sharpe, vol. 1, pp. 10, 14, 21, 23, 29.

[23]   Howard Colvin, 'The Origin of Chantries', *Journal of Medieval History*, 26 (2000), pp. 163–73.

[24]   David Crouch, 'The Origin of Chantries: Some Further Anglo-Norman Evidence', *Journal of Medieval History*, 27/2 (2001), pp. 159–80. Crouch discusses the tradition of magnates patronising secular churches, such as collegiate churches, and sees them as precursors to chantry foundations.

[25]   For a discussion of this, see Clive Burgess, 'St George's College, Windsor: Context and Consequence', in Nigel Saul (ed.), *St George's Chapel, Windsor, in the Fourteenth Century* (Woodbridge, 2005), pp. 63–96; *idem*, 'London, the Church and the Kingdom', in Matthew

memory was fading, chantries were maintained because of the contributions they made to society.

The sheer number of perpetual chantry foundations established at St Paul's offers a unique opportunity to scrutinise the contributions made by chantries, how they were influenced by, and in turn shaped, the cathedral, the roles played by the chantry priests within the cathedral church and precinct, and the efforts made over several centuries to maintain them. By the late twelfth century, when the earliest chantries were established in St Paul's, the cathedral was already a venerable institution, observing its own customs and rules based on the *institutio canonica* written by Chrodegang, Bishop of Metz (c.755).[26] St Paul's was one of the nine secular cathedrals of England that were staffed by secular clerics.[27] The bishop of London had his palace in the precinct and, throughout the centuries, many bishops played an active role in the affairs of the cathedral. The cathedral was organised on a prebendal system, with thirty canons who were granted part of the cathedral endowment, in the form of estates or parish churches, or in a fixed cash sum, to support them.[28] Only a small minority of these canons, however, were permanently resident at the cathedral. The daily management of the cathedral was the responsibility of the four dignitaries: the dean had cure of souls for the cathedral personnel, the treasurer was in charge of the plate and vestments, the precentor was responsible for the choir and the song-school, and the chancellor was the keeper of the seal and archives of St Paul's as well as the *magister scholarum*. By the twelfth century, the chancellor himself was not expected to teach; he had been replaced by a schoolmaster, but the supervision of the grammar school and the theology school remained his prerogative. By custom these last three offices – the treasurer, the precentor and the chancellor – ranked below the archdeacons of London, Essex, Middlesex and Colchester in the cathedral hierarchy. Although ranked immediately after the dean in terms of prestige, these four archdeacons exercised no authority within the cathedral. Junior officers, such as the sacristan, succentor, almoner and chamberlain, assisted

---

Davies and Andrew Prescott (eds), *London and The Kingdom. Essays in Honour of Caroline M. Barron. Proceedings of the 2004 Harlaxton Symposium* (Donington, 2008), pp. 98–117.

[26]   Kathleen Edwards, *The English Secular Cathedrals in the Middle Ages. A Constitutional Study with Special Reference to the Fourteenth Century* (Manchester, 1949), p. 9; Christopher Brooke, 'The Earliest Times to 1485', in W.R. Matthews and W.M. Atkins (eds), *A History of St Paul's Cathedral and the Men Associated with it* (London, 1957), pp. 1–99, esp. p. 12.

[27]   The other eight were Salisbury, Lincoln, York, Exeter, Hereford, Lichfield, Chichester and Wells. In addition to these there were ten cathedrals served by monks and one by Augustinian canons.

[28]   On the cathedral personnel and organisation, see Keene, 'From Conquest to Capital', pp. 17–32.

the four main officers in their tasks. The major part of the *opus Dei* was assumed by the minor clergy, whose organisation was unique to St Paul's.[29] There were thirty vicars choral, who were first appointed at the cathedral to act in the choir as deputies to the absent major canons. Earliest mentions of them date from the twelfth century and, having evolved into a formal body, by 1273 they lived in a common hall. Although in clerical orders, these vicars were not required to be ordained priests; thus they did not celebrate mass. This task was fulfilled instead by a body of twelve minor canons, whose origins were probably contemporary with the vicars. Chosen by the dean, the subdean had the leading position, and was followed by two minor canons bearing the unusual title of senior and junior cardinals in charge of disciplining their fellow minor canons and monitoring the choir services. At their induction, chantry chaplains joined the ranks of the minor clergy. Because they were priests, they were placed above the vicars choral in the cathedral hierarchy but below the minor canons, whose ancient origins gave them precedence.[30] None of these groups were members of the cathedral chapter, which was formed exclusively of the resident major canons.

The chantries at St Paul's merit a new investigation, not least because the main studies of these institutions were undertaken in the seventeenth century by Sir William Dugdale and in the nineteenth century by William Sparrow Simpson.[31] The Guildhall Library now houses the cathedral archives, which contain numerous documents relating to chantries, such as foundation ordinances, accounts, tenement sales, inventories and records of chaplain appointments. Most are still in their original form, usually individual rolls of parchment, but some chantry documents were transcribed in cartularies.[32] Unfortunately they were never copied into a single manuscript, a *liber cantariarum*, such as the one that exists for Lincoln Cathedral.[33] Moreover, these chantry documents do not cover the whole period in a consistent way. Post-thirteenth-century foundations are generally better documented than their earlier counterparts, but

---

[29]   See Virginia Davis, 'The Lesser Clergy in the Later Middle Ages', in Keene, Burns and Saint, *St Paul's*, pp. 157–61.

[30]   William Sparrow Simpson (ed.), *Registrum Statutorum et Consuetudinum Ecclesiae Cathedralis Sancti Pauli Londinensis* (London, 1873), pp. 138–9.

[31]   Dudgale, pp. 18–28, 354–8, 391–2. William Sparrow Simpson, 'On a Newly-Discovered Manuscript Containing Statutes Compiled by Dean Colet for the Government of the Chantry Priests and Other Clergy in St Paul's Cathedral', *Archaeologia*, 52 (1890), pp. 145–74. Repr. in *idem, S. Paul's Cathedral and Old City Life* (London, 1894), pp. 97–124. St Paul's chantries were also studied in an MA dissertation by Nichola Gear, 'The Chantries of St Paul's Cathedral' (Royal Holloway, University of London, 1996).

[32]   GL Ms 25501; Ms 25502; Ms 25504; Ms 25505.

[33]   Dorothy Owen, 'Historical Survey, 1091–1450', in Dorothy Owen (ed.), *A History of Lincoln Minster* (Cambridge, 1994), pp. 112–63, esp. p. 149.

inconsistently: several documents relate to a single chantry, while others, founded in the same period, may be barely recorded. At different times, beginning in the mid-thirteenth century, the cathedral authorities drew up lists of chantries that provide details such as names of founders, places of worship, chaplains' names and wages, and endowments.[34] Information on the day-to-day managerial tasks carried out by the Dean and Chapter can be found in the surviving medieval Chapter Act Book covering the years 1411 to 1448.[35] For chantries on the eve of the Reformation, Dean Sampson's register (1536–1560) is a key source.[36] The registers of the bishops of London also refer to chantry foundations within their gift, as do London civic records for those in the mayor's care.[37] In addition, the wills of some founders and chaplains survive. Those of founders often contain regulations for the chantries they wished to found at St Paul's. These instructions should be treated with caution, however, as they testify to the founders' intentions, and not to their success in actually achieving their aims.[38] For example, Henry de Guldeford (d.1313) asked for a chantry of three priests, but his executors provided for only one chaplain.[39] In other instances, the projected chantries seem never to have seen the light of day. Although Dean Thomas Lisieux (d.1456) left provision for the establishment of a chantry to be endowed with the money he was owed by Henry VI, the chantry was never set up, presumably because the king never repaid his debt.[40] Royal sources also supply information about St Paul's chantries. In 1279, Edward I issued the statute *De viris religiosis*, usually known as the mortmain statute, which aimed to put an end to any unauthorised transfer of properties to institutions, called 'dead hands' because when lands or properties were given into them, the Crown could no longer levy feudal dues. Although the legislation was not exclusively aimed at the Church, it was the principal target.[41] From 1299 onwards, royal licences were granted to by-pass this regulation. Chantry founders then sought

---

[34]   GL Ms 25121/1954, Ms 25502, fols 100–101; Ms 25504, fols 93–93v., 127v.; Ms 25505, fols 65v.–66; Dugdale, pp. 310–36; Cambridge, University Library, Ms Ee 5.21.

[35]   GL Ms 25513.

[36]   GL Ms 25630/1.

[37]   GL Ms 9531; Letter-Books (1272–1509), Journals (1416–1548) and Repertories (1495–1550) now kept at LMA.

[38]   The limitations of the information to be obtained from wills are discussed in Clive Burgess, 'Late Medieval Wills and Pious Convention: Testamentary Evidence Reconsidered', in Michael Hicks (ed.), *Profit, Piety and The Professions in Later Medieval England* (Gloucester, 1990), pp. 14–33.

[39]   Sharpe, vol. 2, p. 233; GL Ms 25121/1754.

[40]   TNA PROB 11/4, fols 56–58 and Brooke, 'Earliest Times', pp. 96–7.

[41]   Sandra Raban, *Mortmain Legislation and the English Church 1279–1500* (Cambridge/New York, 1982), p. 14.

these licences to alienate endowments to support their pious provisions, and there are surviving mortmain licences for eighteen chantries at St Paul's. More were presumably sought, but were not enrolled or have been lost.[42] On the other hand, a handful of licences were granted for chantries for which there is no other evidence.[43] As with wills, mortmain licences may reveal intention rather than actual foundation.

This book investigates the chantries and their impact on the life, services and clerical community of the cathedral. The evidence assembled here demonstrates the flexibility and adaptability of these pious foundations, and explores the contributions they made to the clerical and lay communities in which they were established. For the first time some light is shed on the men who played roles that, until the abolition of the chantries in 1548, were seen to be crucial to the spiritual well-being of medieval London.

---

[42] In the foundation deed of 1386 (GL Ms 25121/1925), it is stated that John of Beauchamp had received a licence from Edward III to found a chantry at St Paul's, but the licence has not survived, nor is it enrolled.

[43] *CPR, 1377–1381*, p. 499; *CPR, 1422–9*, p. 269; *Letters & Papers, Henry VIII*, vol. 1, part 1, p. 827, no. 1804 [40].

Chapter 1

Founding Chantries

As intercessory foundations, chantries had their roots in a system of beliefs and customs strongly established by the late twelfth century. Well before they took their place in the spectrum of commemorative options, endowments provided intercession to lessen the sufferings of souls in purgatory, in the forms of monastic prayers, anniversary masses, corporate masses, guild masses and even daily masses.[1] Chantries evolved from these customary practices sometime in the late twelfth century. The spontaneous and simultaneous nature of this evolution, however, renders it hard to pinpoint their first manifestations with any accuracy. Wood-Legh, the pioneer of chantry studies, suggested the college of four chaplains established at Marwell in Hampshire by Henry of Blois (d.1171), bishop of Winchester, as her candidate for the first chantry ever established on English soil.[2] Endowments provided for contemporary foundations at the cathedrals of Paris, Amiens, Rouen and Lichfield in the 1180s and 1190s.[3] At St Paul's Cathedral, the close of the twelfth century was also the period when the earliest chantry foundations were established: the first was founded presumably in the 1180s with the money that Richard Foliot, former archdeacon of Colchester (d.1181), bequeathed to the Dean and Chapter for the maintenance of a chaplain who would pray for him and for all the faithful departed; while three others date from the 1190s.[4] During his episcopacy (1189 × 1198), Richard Fitz Neal established a chantry of two chaplains to commemorate all the kings of England and the bishops of London.[5] He also set up an altar dedicated to the Merovingian Queen

---

[1]   Crouch, 'Origin of Chantries', p. 163; Colvin, 'Origin of Chantries', pp. 163–73.

[2]   Wood-Legh, *Perpetual Chantries*, p. 4. Crouch suggested that this particular foundation should be seen as a prototype rather than a full-fledged chantry foundation, but agrees that the late twelfth century was the period when chantries first took form; 'Origin of Chantries', pp. 174–7.

[3]   Colvin, 'Origin of Chantries', p. 165; Crouch, 'Origin of Chantries', p. 177; Grégoire Eldin, 'Les chapellenies à Notre-Dame de Paris (XIIe–XVIe siècles). Recherches historiques et archéologiques' (Thesis, École nationale des chartes, 1994), vol. 1, p. 44.

[4]   GL Ms 25121/160.

[5]   Gibbs, Marion (ed.), *Early Charters of the Cathedral Church of St. Paul*, Camden, 3rd series, 58 (London, 1939), no. 186.

Radegund, whose offerings provided for a chaplain who prayed for his soul.[6] In 1199, less than a year after becoming bishop of London, Fitz Neal's successor, William of Ste-Mère-Eglise, set up a chantry of one chaplain. From then until the Reformation at least eighty-four perpetual chantries were established at the cathedral, although not all coexisted: some were amalgamated, and a minority disappeared.[7] This chapter explores the identity of the individuals who founded these commemorative services, the types of arrangements they made with the cathedral authorities and the nature of the endowments that provided financial support to maintain them.

Founders

The Angevin royal family played a leading role in the emergence of chantries. They endowed daily masses in perpetuity on both sides of the channel, including the commemoration of Young King Henry (d.1183) at the Cathedral of Rouen.[8] At the Cathedral of Notre-Dame, their French rival, King Philip, instigated the earliest chantry endowments.[9] At St Paul's it was men attached to the cathedral who stood behind the earliest foundations, although one of the chantries provided prayers especially for the souls of all English kings and bishops of London.[10] As mother churches of dioceses, cathedrals were flagships in liturgical developments.[11] The cathedral's high-ranking clergy would have been acquainted with the development of the various options in commemorative practices and many of them would have had the financial means to participate in their development. At St Paul's Cathedral, one archdeacon and two bishops were responsible for the first four foundations, while between 1200 and 1250 the cathedral clergy established all but one of the foundations.[12] Although their monopoly of chantries at St Paul's did not last more than a few decades, the predominance of higher-ranking clerics as chantry founders remained unchallenged throughout the centuries. Until the dissolution of the mid-

---

[6] GL Ms 25502, fols 100–101; Ms 25504, fols 93–93v.

[7] For details of each foundation, see Appendix. When the date of foundation could not be found, the date of the founder's death has been taken as the approximate date of the chantry establishment.

[8] Crouch, 'Origin of Chantries', p. 177.

[9] Eldin, 'Les chapellenies', vol. 1, p. 44.

[10] Gibbs, *Early Charters*, no. 186.

[11] On the liturgy at St Paul's, see Alan Thacker, 'The Cult of Saints and the Liturgy', in Keene, Burns and Saint, *St Paul's. The Cathedral Church of London*, pp. 113–22.

[12] For the identification of founders, see Appendix.

sixteenth century, more chantries were founded by or for men associated with the cathedral than for any other group in society (see Table 1.1).

Table 1.1   Chantry founders at St Paul's Cathedral

Founders	1150–1199	1200–1249	1250–1299	1300–1349	1350–1399	1400–1449	1450–1499	1500–1548	Total
Bishops	3	2	4	2	1	–	2	1	15
Deans	–	3	1	–	1	3	–	1	9
Major canons	1	6	7	13	1	1	–	2	31
Minor clergy	–	–	3	2	–	–	–	–	5
Non members of the cathedral	–	1	6	9	3	2	–	–	21
Mixed foundation	–	–	–	–	1	1	–	–	2
Unknown identity	–	1	–	–	–	–	–	–	1
Total	4	13	21	26	7	7	2	4	84

The predominance among chantry founders of bishops, deans, major canons and even a few members of the minor clergy is clearly a result of their special relationship with the cathedral. Not only was the cathedral their place of work, and the place of their daily worship; it was also the physical symbol of the large clerical community of which they were part. Not surprisingly, such men invested their fortunes in St Paul's. More than just interceding for the salvation of their souls, their chantries contributed to the embellishment of the physical setting of their cathedral and to the enrichment of its liturgy.[13]

---

[13]   The positive impacts of chantries are discussed in Chapter 2 and Chapter 3. For a defence of the communal benefit of the parish chantries, see Clive Burgess, '"For the Increase of Divine Service": Chantries in the Parish in Late Medieval Bristol', *Journal of Ecclesiastical History*, 36 (1985), pp. 45–65; *idem*, 'Strategies for Eternity: Perpetual Chantry Foundation in Late Medieval Bristol', in Christopher Harper-Bill (ed.), *Religious Belief and Ecclesiastical Careers in Late Medieval England. Proceedings of the Conference held at Strawberry Hill, Easter 1989* (Woodbridge, 1991), pp. 1–32.

This close relationship between chantry and working environment is even clearer in the case of chantries founded by members of the cathedral's lesser clergy. These clerics were those who ensured the daily celebration of the *opus Dei* at the cathedral and performed the private services at the side altars. For instance, in 1275 a chantry was established for John de Braynford, who had served John le Romeyn's chantry in 1261.[14] In one case, there was a clear correlation between the chantries that these men served in life and the focus of their post-mortem pious bequests. Walter de Blockele (d.1307) had been chaplain of Roger de La Legh's chantry, for which he developed a very strong attachment. Not only did he personally contribute to its welfare by increasing its endowment and by providing lodging for its chaplain; he also requested that his own chantry chaplain should serve at the same altar where he had himself celebrated the daily mass for many years as chaplain of de La Legh's chantry.[15] Apart from these two foundations, only three other chantries were founded by minor clergy of St Paul's: Godfrey de Acra in the 1260s, Godfrey of St Dunstan in the 1290s, and Nicholas Husband in the late 1340s, all minor canons at the cathedral.[16] This small representation of minor clergy among chantry founders is presumably a result of the heavy financial investment involved in chantry foundation. Only those who had an inheritance or other substantial income could provide an endowment, because the customary annual wages earned by the minor clergy were insufficient to fund a perpetual chantry. In the late thirteenth century, St Paul's chantry chaplains were earning on average six marks per annum.[17] Relying on such a salary alone, it would have been impossible for individual priests to accumulate sufficient capital to endow a perpetual chantry. For this reason, the majority of the lesser clergy had to content themselves with more provisional and cheaper foundations.[18] The precarious chantry of chaplain Simon de Herlyng, rescued by Robert le Seneschal, minor canon, in 1298, less than three years after its foundation, was probably of such a temporary kind, and so is omitted from this survey.[19] On the Continent, especially in Germany, clerics often solved the problem of the financial cost of a permanent chantry by designating themselves as the first

---

[14]　GL Ms 25121/1482, 1934.

[15]　GL Ms 25271/48.

[16]　GL Ms 25121/339; Sharpe, vol. 1, pp. 209, 496–7.

[17]　GL Ms 25504, fol. 127v.

[18]　For discussion on the chaplains' wages, see Chapter 2, pp. 59–60; and on the chaplains' pious foundations, see Chapter 5, especially p.173.

[19]　GL Ms 25271/10. The foundation deed of the chantry did not survive, but in 1295 Simon de Herlyng was serving the chantry of Fulk Basset's parents; Dugdale, p. 335.

incumbents of their newly created chantry.[20] By reducing the original costs, this practice made the foundations more affordable for chantry priests. Although no definite examples of this practice have been found in England, it appears that St Paul's authorities may have facilitated chantry founding by priests by restoring to the founders during their lifetime the properties with which they had endowed their chantries. Between 1262 and 1268 the Dean and Chapter granted to minor canon Godfrey de Acra, for the term of his life, the houses and the rent that he had given to them and to the chaplain celebrating masses for him and his benefactors in the chapel of St James.[21] In York, between 1330 and 1390, the chantries were not exclusively patronised by the most powerful members of the city oligarchy.[22] At St Paul's Cathedral a comparable 'popularisation' of chantries occurred half a century earlier, but with only five perpetual chantries founded by members of the minor clergy, it was limited. The founding of chantries remained the preserve of the most prosperous members of society in general, and St Paul's clergy in particular.

At the same time as chantries became, to a certain extent, available to cathedral members of more restricted means, they also became the pious focus of some lay people and clerics who had no direct connections with the cathedral. By as early as c.1215–1219, a chantry had been established for Alice, daughter-in-law of William Marshall, earl of Pembroke.[23] By the mid-thirteenth century, this type of founders became more common. For instance, chantries were established for John le Romeyn (d.1256), treasurer of York Minster; John Lovel (1297), justice of the king; William de Hareworth (d.1301), rector of West Tilbury; and Henry de Guldeford (d.1313), clerk.[24] Their attachment to the mother church of the diocese, relations to one of its members, or their links with royal government probably lay behind their foundations. For example, John

---

[20] Kathleen Wood-Legh, 'Some Aspects of the History of Chantries in the Later Middle Ages', *Transactions of the Royal Historical Society*, 4th series, 28 (1946), pp. 47–66, esp. pp. 51–2.

[21] GL Ms 25121/339; Ms 25121/343.

[22] R.B. Dobson, 'The Foundation of Perpetual Chantries by the Citizens of Medieval York', in G.J. Cuming (ed.), *The Province of York. Papers read at the Fifth Summer Meeting of the Ecclesiastical History Society*, Studies in Church History, 4 (Leiden, 1967), pp. 22–38, esp. p. 34.

[23] Gibbs, *Early Charters*, nos 221–2. Her husband also provided for a light burning above her tomb in the cathedral. The omission of this chantry from the lists drawn up in the thirteenth and fourteenth centuries suggests that her chantry lasted only for a few years, although the chantry was mentioned in the alphabetical list of c.1440; Cambridge, University Library, Ms Ee 5.21, fols 143–148.

[24] GL Ms 25501, fol. 47. John Le Neve, *Fasti Ecclesiae Anglicanae 1066–1300*, vol. VI: *York*, compiled by Diana E. Greenway (London, 1999), p. 24; *ODNB*, 'Romanus, John'; GL Ms 25241/24; Sharpe, vol. 1, pp. 135–6; GL Ms 25121/1754.

Lovel specified that his chaplain was also supposed to pray for Bishop Richard.[25] Lay Londoners, usually among the most powerful and prosperous citizens, also showed an interest in the cathedral. Between the 1270s and the 1370s, twelve chantries were established by Londoners, of whom five had held prestigious civic offices, and two were women, both members of prominent London families.[26] Such foundations demonstrate that Londoners contributed to the enrichment of the cathedral's liturgical services.[27] In many instances, however, St Paul's was not their sole object of devotion: they also desired to be remembered in their parish churches. In addition to their foundations at St Paul's, Roger Beyvin (d.1278) left tenements for a chantry in the church of St John Zachary, Hamo Chigwell (d.1333) for a chantry in the church of St Matthew Friday Street, and John Pulteney (d.1349) for the College of St Laurence.[28] Likewise John Grantham, who augmented the original endowment of William de Haverhull's chantry in 1330, asked in his will that a chantry be established in the parish church of St Antonin.[29] It is noteworthy that some of these London chantries were sited together at St Paul's Cathedral: three of them were situated in the chapel of the charnel house.[30] Nevertheless, if this regrouping of chantries was a general trend, it was not an absolute rule. The chaplain of Mayor Nicholas de Farndone's chantry (d.1334) shared the altar of St Dunstan with the chaplain serving the chantry of Reginald de Brandon, late major canon of St Paul's.[31]

Thus between c.1270 and c.1370, St Paul's chantries lost some of their exclusive character. Far from commemorating only the cathedral dignitaries, masses were now celebrated for the lesser clergy as well as for the higher clergy, for lay people as well as for clergymen, for women as well as for men. This 'openness' of chantry foundation came to an end in the late fourteenth century. After the passage of the Black Death, the number of new chantries fell dramatically. Whereas twenty-six foundations were established within the first half of the fourteenth century alone, only twenty new ones were created from

---

[25]   GL Ms 25121/427.

[26]   Hamo Chigwell, Nicholas de Farndone, John Pulteney, Walter Neel, John Hiltoft, Aveline of St Olave (de Basing) and Isabelle Bukerel; see Appendix.

[27]   Professor Dobson noted the general indifference to York Minster of the laity, who preferred their parish churches; 'Foundation of Perpetual Chantries', pp. 25–6. Andrew Brown came to a different conclusion regarding Salisbury, *Popular Piety in Late Medieval England. The Diocese of Salisbury 1250–1550* (Oxford, 1995), pp. 49–55.

[28]   Sharpe, vol. 1, pp. 29–30, 42, 382–3, 609–10. For more information on John Pulteney's foundation, see H.B. Wilson, *A History of the Parish of St Laurence Pountney* (London, 1831), pp. 25–72.

[29]   Sharpe, vol. 1, pp. 475–6.

[30]   On the charnel house, see Chapter 3, pp. 74–7.

[31]   GL Ms 25121/635.

the mid-fourteenth to the mid-sixteenth century. Economic and demographic factors contributed to this drop in foundation number. A dramatic decline in population and an economic depression accompanied the onset of endemic plague and impeded the maintenance of the pre-plague foundation rate. Moreover, the general loss of property value and shortage of priests affected the running of existing chantries at the cathedral. In c.1370 nine chantries were said to be vacant, presumably due to lack of income, and difficulties in finding incumbents. These general financial difficulties experienced by chantries prompted the major amalgamations carried out by Robert de Braybroke, bishop of London, in 1391 (see Figure 1.1).

The amalgamations followed a visitation which Bishop de Braybroke undertook to St Paul's Cathedral.[32] He acknowledged that the original endowments of many chantries had lost so much value that they could not sustain the chaplains' wages, inflated as these were by both the shortage of priests and the rising cost of living.[33] De Braybroke sought royal permission, which he obtained, to rearrange the needy chantries into twenty-seven groups.[34] Presumably in response to these financial difficulties experienced by chantries, the cathedral authorities from then on restricted foundations to the wealthiest and most powerful members of society, who could secure properly endowed chantries. From the late fourteenth century onwards, two chantries were the work of aristocrats and one chantry was a collective establishment by lay and ecclesiastic founders.[35] A chantry was established for a rich London merchant before being lavishly enlarged by a canon of St Paul's, and in 1408 the chantry for Beatrice de Roos, a wealthy widow from the Yorkshire nobility, was the last lay foundation at St Paul's.[36] The other founders were cathedral members who occupied senior positions in its hierarchy. Three chantries were founded for major canons, four for deans and three for bishops of London. The general reduction in the number of foundations from the late fourteenth century until

---

[32] Rosalind Hill, "*A Chaunterie for Soules*": London Chantries in the Reign of Richard II', in F.R. Du Boulay and Caroline M. Barron (eds), *The Reign of Richard II. Essays in Honour of May McKisack* (London, 1971), pp. 242–55.

[33] *Ibid.*, p. 243.

[34] *CPR, 1388–1392*, pp. 421–2.

[35] See Beauchamp, of Gaunt, and 'Albrygton, Boyes, de Braybroke, and Hampden' in the Appendix. For a study of the involvement of the aristocracy in cathedrals, see Joel Rosenthal, *The Purchase of Paradise. Gift Giving and the Aristocracy 1307–1485* (London, 1972), esp. p. 35.

[36] See de Bury and Holme, and de Roos in the Appendix. Matthew Davies and Ann Saunders, *The History of the Merchant Taylors' Company* (Leeds, 2004), p. 25. For information on Adam de Bury, see Caroline M. Barron, *Revolt in London: 11th to 15th June 1381* (London, 1981), pp. 1–24.

Figure 1.1   A number of the cathedral's chantries were amalgamated in 1391 by Robert de Braybroke, bishop of London

the Reformation should not been seen as reflecting a decline in the belief in the value of chantries, but rather reflects a decline in the number of people able to afford them.[37] At York Minster, the fifteenth-century chantry foundations were also limited to a smaller group of prosperous founders.[38]

The fact that the Dean and Chapter authorised the establishment of only securely endowed chantries brought another direct change in the general features of chantry foundation: an increase in their size. Whereas in the past the more numerous, but less generously endowed, chantries usually provided for one chaplain, in the later Middle Ages the number of chantries for two or more chaplains increased significantly. Hitherto only two founders established chantries for more than two chaplains.[39] Fulk Basset initially established a chantry of two chaplains in his lifetime (c.1252) and then, in 1261, his executor established a separate chantry of three chaplains.[40] This first chantry came to be known as the chantry for the souls of his parents, Alan and Aveline Basset, and the second as Fulk Basset's chantry.[41] John Pulteney's chantry of three chaplains was linked with his college attached to the parish church of St Laurence.[42] The largest foundation ever endowed at St Paul's Cathedral dates from the late fourteenth century. Adam de Bury (d.1386), the former mayor of London, originally intended his chantry to be served by three chaplains, but when his executor Roger Holme, major canon and chancellor, made the final arrangement with the Dean and Chapter, he increased the number of chaplains to seven.[43] A close friendship with Adam de Bury presumably motivated Roger Holme's decision to share de Bury's chantry rather than to found his own.[44] Roger Holme also founded a college for his chaplains and laid down rules for them to follow.[45] A few years later, in 1403, another chantry college was established for the two chaplains serving the chantry of John of Gaunt, Duke of Lancaster.[46]

---

[37] Dobson, 'Foundation of Perpetual Chantries', p. 35. He disagrees with Professor Jordan's suggestion that prayers for the dead had fallen into disrepute. See W.K. Jordan, *Philanthropy in England 1480–1660* (London, 1959), p. 306.

[38] Sarah McManaway, 'Some Aspects of the Foundation of Perpetual Chantries in York Minster' (MA dissertation, University of York, 1981), p. 79.

[39] For the number of chaplains serving each chantry, see the Appendix.

[40] GL Ms 25504, fols 93–93v.; Ms 25122/286.

[41] GL Ms 25502, fols 100–101.

[42] Sharpe, vol. 1, pp. 609–10.

[43] Sharpe, vol. 2, pp. 254–5; GL Ms 25145.

[44] Adam de Bury bequeathed to Holme all his lands and possessions situated in Calais.

[45] GL Ms 25146.

[46] GL Ms 25121/1941. J.B. Post, 'The Obsequies of John of Gaunt', *Guildhall Studies in London History*, 5 (1981), pp. 1–12, esp. 6–7. Before the establishment of this chantry,

In short, clergy who had served the cathedral in their lifetime constituted the great majority of chantry founders at St Paul's. The preponderance of cathedral dignitaries among chantry founders was not unique to St Paul's: similar proportions can be found in other cathedrals. At Exeter, twenty of the twenty-four chantry founders had been bishops, deans and canons of the cathedral. Only three chantries were established for the local aristocracy and there was one chantry which was a mixed foundation, similar to Holme's College.[47] Salisbury Cathedral had a slightly higher input of lay people, where seven chantries out of thirty-four were founded by them.[48] Because they were staffed by monks, who had taken vows of poverty and therefore would not have had the means to establish chantries, monastic cathedrals had a higher percentage of lay foundations. At the monastic cathedral of Norwich, six were for bishops and five for members of the provincial aristocracy.[49] The exceptional feature of St Paul's is the fact that for a limited period members of the lesser clergy were able to endow their own perpetual masses, for in no other secular cathedrals can the minor clergy be seen to have participated in chantry foundation in this manner. These chantries reflect the relative wealth of St Paul's minor clergy, as well as the relatively affordable price of chantry foundation during the late thirteenth and early fourteenth centuries.

Founding Process

From the late twelfth century until the Reformation, chantry foundation at St Paul's Cathedral had a direct impact on the material and financial assets of the Dean and Chapter. As the founders were liable for all the costs incurred by their chantries, including the celebrants' salaries, the supply of vestments, and the regular provision of bread, wine and wax, even the most modest chantry foundation involved a substantial endowment. To ensure that these endowments provided sufficient income to maintain their chantries, founders concluded different types of agreements with the cathedral authorities.

Kathleen Wood-Legh distinguished three categories of agreements or funding processes. The earliest arrangement took the form of a *gift*, whereby the

two salaried chaplains may have been employed in St Paul's to sing for the soul of Blanche of Lancaster (d.1369).

[47] Nicholar Orme, *The Minor Clergy of Exeter Cathedral, 1300–1548. A List of the Minor Officers, Vicar Choral, Annuellars, Secondaries and Choristers* (Exeter, 1980), pp. 133–7.

[48] Brown, *Popular Piety*, p. 53.

[49] Rachel Ward, 'Chantries and Their Founders in Late Medieval Norwich' (MPhil thesis, University of Cambridge, 1994), p. 13.

chantry founder gave to a religious institution sufficient property to maintain a chaplain.[50] Rather than being administered separately, the property conferred in this way was usually merged with the general possessions of the recipient house. Furthermore, the practicalities of the chantry foundation, the selection of the chaplain and the setting of his wages were left to the discretion of the recipient house. The advantages of this kind of arrangement lay principally in the large degree of autonomy accorded to the recipients in the management of the pious foundation and, where the chantry founders were concerned, on their stability and reliability. Even if the original endowment no longer provided a sufficient income to sustain a chaplain, the religious recipient was obliged to maintain the chantry. In return, however, founders had to accept the loss of control over their foundation, and the chaplains were left dependent upon the goodwill of their religious hosts. To meet these drawbacks, founders developed another kind of chantry arrangement, a full ecclesiastical *benefice*.[51] The first chaplain and his successors became the legal owners of the original endowment granted to them by chantry founders, which conferred on them a legal status. In return the chaplains had to follow the regulations laid down by the founders. Their possession was made official by a formal institution by the bishop, and was henceforth as secure as a rectory or perpetual vicarage. This kind of arrangement became the most popular form in England, yet it conferred little protection against progressive dilapidation of the endowments as a result of mismanagement, neglect or greed on the part of the chaplains. The third form of chantry arrangement, the *service*, thus aimed to reduce the probabilities of loss of income by granting the original properties to a body of trustees who, as well as being responsible for the management of the endowment, were in charge of hiring and supporting the chaplains. Corporations such as the mayor and the commonalty of a town, or the Dean and Chapter of a cathedral, could act as trustees.[52] With this kind of arrangement the chaplains lost the protection conferred by a canonical institution. Chantry founders were not necessarily confined to one of these three forms and they could include characteristics of more than one form in their pious foundations, which makes the categorisation of chantry foundations sometimes a difficult task.[53]

---

[50] Wood-Legh, *Perpetual Chantries*, p. 8.

[51] *Ibid.*, pp. 11–15.

[52] *Ibid.*, p. 16.

[53] *Ibid.*, p. 27. In his study of Bristol chantries, Clive Burgess demonstrates how the popularity of one form of arrangement over the others depended on the ease with which chantry founders could secure mortmain licences for their pious foundations; 'Strategies for Eternity', pp. 6, 12.

However useful this categorisation is, it unfortunately cannot be adopted wholesale as a framework for the classification of St Paul's chantries because it does not take account of the particular context of chantry foundation within a specific religious institution such as a secular cathedral.[54] In this environment some elements of chantry foundation seem to have been fundamental, thus curtailing freedom of chantry founders, as most chantry foundations at St Paul's entailed a canonical institution and ecclesiastical jurisdiction. One chantry, however, can be described as a *service*, founded for Thomas Carleton (d.1389).[55] In this instance, endowments were given to the fraternity of St John the Baptist of the Merchant Tailors, which in return had to support the chantry chaplain at St Paul's. This chantry, most unusually, did not involve a canonical institution, and seems to have been excluded from cathedral jurisdiction.[56] Not surprisingly, the chantry is never mentioned in the cathedral archives and we know of its existence only through the founder's will and records from the Merchant Tailors.[57] In this case the cathedral served only as a place of worship and the celebrations took place in St John the Baptist's Chapel, the use of which was granted to the fraternity by Bishop Sudbury.[58] The Dean and Chapter did not record the chaplains' appointments, nor did the chaplains apparently live at the *Presteshous* with the other chantry chaplains.[59] Presumably because of the lack of control over the chaplain of Carleton's chantry, Carleton's 'experience' may not have been satisfactory to the Dean and Chapter. When other chantries were founded in partnership with city companies, such as de Roos's chantry in 1408, the Dean and Chapter were involved in the chantry organisation, and as for all other chantry priests, the company chaplains were placed under the jurisdiction of the Dean and Chapter.[60]

---

[54]   McManaway experienced the same difficulties when trying to categorise chantry foundation at York Minster; 'Some Aspects', p. 10.

[55]   Sharpe, vol. 2, pp. 272–3. For more information on Thomas Carleton, see Hannes Kleineke, 'Carleton's Book: William FitzStephen's "Description of London" in a Late Fourteenth-Century Common-Place Book', *Bulletin of the Institute of Historical Research*, 74 (2001), pp. 117–26.

[56]   Because this chantry was not placed under the jurisdiction of the Dean and Chapter, it was not included in the Appendix.

[57]   Matthew P. Davies, 'The Tailors of London and their Guild, c.1300–1500' (PhD thesis, University of Oxford, 1994), p. 18. It is possible that other company chantries were founded at St Paul's, but for which no references survive in the cathedral archives, such as John Patesley's chantry, which was managed by the Goldsmiths; *CPR, 1549–1551*, pp. 386–401.

[58]   Davies and Saunders, *Merchant Taylors' Company*, p. 23.

[59]   Discussion of the chaplains' residence takes place in Chapter 3, pp. 77–83.

[60]   The appointments of its chantry chaplains were recorded in the Chapter Act Book, GL Ms 25513, fols 54, 115v., 135, 218.

By definition, all chantries at St Paul's, except for Carleton's, correspond to *benefices*, because they entailed a canonical institution. However, rather than grant the endowments to the first chaplain and his successors, founders tended to give them to the Dean and Chapter, a typical characteristic of the *gift*. But these chantry foundations do not quite correspond to the *gift*, for instead of merging with the communal possessions of the cathedral, the endowments were generally managed separately. Consequently, this categorisation cannot be applied exactly to chantry foundation in St Paul's. It can, however, furnish the basic criteria with which we can establish a new classification. As all chantry chaplains shared the same clerical status, the foundations have to be distinguished solely by the designated recipients of the endowments. To adopt this terminology in this new classification, the *gift* corresponds to endowments given to the Dean and Chapter of St Paul's in exchange for a chantry creation. The *benefice* designates endowments granted in the name of the first chaplain and his successors to hold in perpetuity, and the *service* endowments entrusted to feoffees. For the sixty-four chantries for which some information survives regarding their endowments, we can identify forty-nine *gifts*, endowments in the form either of tenements or rents given directly to the Dean and Chapter of St Paul's. In these cases the Dean and Chapter were the recipients of the endowment and had to fulfil their obligation to maintain a chaplain as long as the endowment yielded sufficient income. Ten chantry foundations correspond to *benefices*, where the founders granted to the first chaplains the original endowments. In the fifteenth century two foundations of this kind acquired full corporate status, with the explicit right bestowed on the chantry chaplains to sell and acquire lands, plead in court and have a chantry seal.[61] Only one chantry can be described as a *service*; that is, the chantry endowment was given to a body of feoffees, although the chantry, that of Thomas Kempe, still involved a canonical institution.[62] Three foundations combined elements of more than one form. The chantries of Godfrey de Acra, Richard and Stephen de Gravesend and Lancaster College were as much a *gift* as a *benefice*, for the chantry endowments were given both to the Dean and Chapter and to the chantry chaplains.[63] The chantry of John Pulteney (d.1349) has not been included in this classification because it was exceptional: Pulteney's chantry was an extension of his college established at the parish church of St Laurence, and the master of the college inherited the obligation to meet all chantry expenses at St Paul's.[64] The high percentage of *gifts*, in comparison with *benefices* and *services*, illustrates the particular context of the cathedral where the

---

[61] Thomas More's and Walter Sherrington's chantries.
[62] TNA PROB 11/8, fols 226v.–228v.; Brooke, 'Earliest Times', p. 92.
[63] GL Ms 25121/343; Ms 25121/1941, 1957.
[64] GL Ms 25271/35.

Dean and Chapter represented a secure body to which founders could entrust their endowments. At York Minster, chantry endowments were often assigned to the corporation of the vicars choral, who inherited the costs of administering the properties as well as the duties of appointing the chantry chaplains.[65] The chantry endowments at York were either managed separately or merged into the communal funds of the vicars choral. At St Paul's Cathedral, by contrast, the chantry endowments were never made over to the college of the twelve minor canons or to the vicars choral, although many minor canons acted as chantry chaplains or as chantry patrons.[66]

Endowments

The types of endowments put in the hands of the Dean and Chapter and chantry chaplains varied during the three and a half centuries in which chantries were founded at St Paul's, illustrating, on the one hand, the great flexibility given to the founders by the cathedral authorities and, on the other hand, the founders' desire to explore all possibilities to secure the most sustainable and enduring endowments. The earliest founders, especially, resorted to different kinds of endowments since chantry foundations were a novelty and so open to experimentation. Instead of being endowed with rents or lands, one of the chantries of Richard Fitz Neal (d.1198), bishop of London, received its income from the offerings at the altar of St Radegund, where a chaplain celebrated intercessory masses for his soul.[67] The chantry was last mentioned in the list of c.1370, when it was said to be vacant.[68] By then, there was a chapel dedicated to St Radegund situated in the cathedral crypt, kept by a warden appointed by the Dean and Chapter.[69] References to appointments and exchanges recorded in the Chapter Act Book in the fifteenth century suggest that the position of warden of St Radegund's Chapel in the crypt was highly coveted.[70]

Only a very small number of chantry founders followed Bishop Fitz Neal's example in endowing their chantries with revenues linked to the cathedral.

---

[65] McManaway, 'Some Aspects', pp. 52–3. One-third of all chantry endowments at York Minster in the fourteenth century took this form.

[66] The participation of the minor canons is discussed in Chapter 2, pp. 38–40 and Chapter 5, pp. 122, 127–8.

[67] See above, pp. 11–12.

[68] The list does not mention any income related to this chantry, as for six other chantries out of nine said to be vacant; GL Ms 25121/1954.

[69] GL Ms 25121/1940.

[70] GL Ms 25513, fols 47, 172v., 222v., 229.

The chaplain of Dean William de Sanctae Mariae Ecclesia's chantry received a stipend in kind: fourteen white bread loaves, seven brown bread loaves and thirty portions of beer every week from the cathedral's brewery and bakery, along with an annual income of two marks.[71] If the chaplain did not receive his pittance in kind, he was to receive a stipend of £5 from the treasury. Fulk Lovel's chantry endowment relied on rents from the prebend of Portpool, while Thomas Kempe's chantry was associated with the position of penitentiary, before being financed by the appropriation of the parish church of Chigwell.[72] Presumably these founders compensated the cathedral for these revenues. In the case of William de Sanctae Mariae Ecclesia's chantry, the Dean and Chapter received the sum of 120 marks from the dean's executors to cover the chantry expenses. Presumably the Dean and Chapter hoped that by investing this sum they would get a high return that would enable them to meet the various chantry expenses.

Other founders of the late twelfth and early thirteenth centuries relied on other kinds of endowments. The chantry of Chesthunt, also established by Bishop Richard Fitz Neal (1189 × 1198), was endowed with a quit-rent of eight marks issuing from the church of Chesthunt, and from which the chantry derived its name.[73] Canon Roger the Chaplain endowed his chantry with his houses in Milk Street and Ivy Lane, London.[74] Richard de Umfraville imitated him by leaving tenements in the parish of St Mildred Poultry.[75] Martin of Pattishall's chantry was sustained by income issuing from a marsh in the parish of Bures in Essex.[76] All these different kinds of endowments in rents, lands and emoluments from churches provided patterns from which subsequent founders could select and adapt their own endowments. Quit-rents and tenements in the city of London were by far the most common sources of endowments.[77] As a result, chantries contributed significantly to making the Dean and Chapter of St Paul's one of the most important landowners of the city of London in the later Middle Ages.[78]

---

[71] GL Ms 25121/1947.

[72] GL Ms 25121/605; TNA PROB 11/8, fols 226v.–228v. For more details about the office of penitentiary, which consisted of hearing confessions, see R.M. Haines, *Ecclesia Anglicana: Studies in the English Church of the Later Middle Ages* (Toronto, 1989), Chapter 3.

[73] GL Ms 25122/1432.

[74] GL Ms 25501, fol. 25.

[75] GL Ms 25501, fol. 31.

[76] GL Ms 25157.

[77] See the Appendix.

[78] Derek Keene and Vanessa Harding, *A Survey of Documentary Sources for Property Holding in London before the Great Fire* (London, 1985), pp. 39–51, esp. 47. Less significantly, the chantries also increased the estates of the Dean and Chapter outside London; Brooke, 'The Earliest Times', pp. 60–65.

As for the chantry of Chesthunt, several founders obtained quit-rents from religious institutions to endow their chantries. This form of endowments had the advantage of eliminating the hazard of possible dilapidation of the tenements. For instance, the chantry of Henry de Wingham (d.1262) relied on a quit-rent from the abbey of Beeleigh by Maldon, Essex.[79] Although the foundation deed of John le Romeyn's chantry (d.1256) refers to the donation of houses in London to the Dean and Chapter, later documents suggest that the chantry was in fact endowed with a quit-rent paid by the prior of St Mary's Hospital without Bishopsgate for a marsh called Lobwerbe in the parish of Little Benflete in Essex.[80] In the 1370s the chaplain William Bridbroke petitioned the prior for arrears of his stipend.[81] The documentation on Nicholas Husband's chantry also reveals a change from the original intentions. While the first licence in 1313 enabled him to alienate in mortmain three messuages and eight shops in the parish of St Sepulchre without Newgate to the Dean and Chapter of St Paul's, the second licence obtained in 1315 authorised him to alienate the same tenements to the Prior and Convent of St Bartholomew, Smithfield, in return for providing his chantry.[82] This transfer is the more striking given the fact that Nicholas Husband was a minor canon at St Paul's. His chantry seems not to have been set up immediately after he had obtained this licence: it was omitted from the c.1320 survey and the foundation is reiterated in his will, written in 1347.[83] In return for the donation of tenements, the Prior and Convent of St Bartholomew were bound to provide the Dean and Chapter of St Paul's with a quit-rent of eight marks and two doves in a wooden box each year to maintain a chaplain. Likewise in 1423 John Westyerd's executors organised Thomas Stowe's chantry by providing an annual quit-rent of fourteen marks to be paid to the Dean and Chapter by the Priory of St Bartholomew, Smithfield, in return for tenements in the parish of St Nicholas Shambles.[84] By the late fourteenth century, chantry founders made similar financial agreements with city companies to endow their foundations: in exchange for a sum of money or tenements, the city companies provided annual quit-rents to fund the chantries. The Goldsmiths managed the chantry of John Hiltoft (d.1370), while in addition to the chantry of Thomas Carleton (d.1389), the Merchant Tailors provided income for the chantry of

---

[79]   See Chapter 2, p. 54.
[80]   GL Ms 25501, fol. 47.
[81]   GL Ms 25122/1081.
[82]   *CPR, 1307–1313*, p. 557; *CPR, 1313–1317*, p. 366.
[83]   GL Ms 25502, fols 100–101; Sharpe, vol. 1, pp. 496–7.
[84]   Sharpe, vol. 2, pp. 434–6.

Beatrice de Roos (1408) and the later foundation of Richard FitzJames (1529).[85] The guild of St Katherine of the Haberdashers and the craft of the Saddlers were involved in the chantries of John Dowman (1525) and of John Withers (1535) respectively, for which they provided quit-rents to the Dean and Chapter.[86]

Although the forms of endowments varied, the result remained the same: chantry foundations deposited considerable capital in the hands of the Dean and Chapter. Thanks to the chantry lists drawn up by the cathedral authorities, it has been possible to calculate the total value of the chantries at different periods.[87] In c.1253 their annual value amounted to £49 10s 8d.[88] Less than twenty years later this sum had increased to £87 8s 4d.[89] By c.1320 the amount had almost doubled, £158 8s 4d, and in c.1370 it reached £279 18s.[90] Finally, a decade before the dissolution, the *Valor ecclesiasticus* calculated the value of chantries at £410, which represented almost 20 per cent of the total value of the cathedral properties.[91] At the time of the dissolution in 1548, once the chaplains' wages and other costs associated with the celebration of masses were deducted, the Dean and Chapter appear to have made an annual profit of £200.[92] Although the management of chantries entailed other expenses, such as endowment repairs and maintenance, there can be no doubt that the chantries contributed to the general wealth of the cathedral before they were swept away and their endowments transferred into the king's hands.[93]

In order to establish their chantries, founders either achieved the necessary finances and property transfers in their lifetime, or relied on their executors to accomplish them after their deaths. These transactions and transfers were not always straightforward: they could entail long negotiations or provoke subsequent complications. Because the Dean and Chapter had a direct interest, they kept meticulous records of these transactions and, in some cases such as de Swereford's chantry, we can follow the different stages of the negotiations

---

[85]   The respective roles of the Dean and Chapter and of the city companies in the chantry organisations are discussed in Chapter 2. Lisa Jefferson (ed.), *Wardens' Accounts and Court Minute Books of the Goldsmiths' Mistery of London* (Woodbridge, 2003), p. 187; Davies and Saunders, *Merchant Taylors' Company*, p. 23.

[86]   For information on the Haberdashers and on the Saddlers, see Ian Archer, *The History of the Haberdashers' Company* (Chichester, 1991), esp. pp. 16, 34; and John W. Sherwell, *The History of the Guild of Saddlers of the City of London* (London, 1889, rep. 1956).

[87]   This is a minimum total, for the value of some chantries was not always given.

[88]   GL Ms 25504, fols 93–3v.

[89]   GL Ms 25504, fol. 127v.

[90]   GL Ms 25502, fols 100–101; Ms 25121/1954.

[91]   Keene, 'From Conquest to Capital', p. 24.

[92]   Kitching, p. xxx.

[93]   See Chapter 6, pp. 160–64.

necessary to consolidate the chantry endowment.[94] Lancaster College was entangled in legal procedures in the 1400s, which generated additional costs.[95] The executors of John of Gaunt, duke of Lancaster, including Thomas Langley, bishop of Durham, made prolonged visits in London to forward the negotiations.[96] Consolidating an endowment could entail the amalgamation of different sources of revenues. Roger Holme gathered three endowments that had been conferred on the cathedral and attached them to Adam de Bury's chantry in c.1390.[97] Holme incorporated John de Wengham's chantry (d.1305), presumably set up in addition to the provision of an obit established in 1292.[98] Simultaneously, Holme consolidated the revenues issuing from eight tenements in the parish of St Martin Ludgate, built by William de Navesby, late major canon, and given to the cathedral.[99] Finally he annexed the income issued from a tenement called 'Le Red Door' in the parish of All Hallows Barking, left by Thomas de Northflete (d.1317), late canon of St Paul's, for the maintenance of his obit.[100] Roger Holme's own financial contribution, as he specified in his foundation deed, was to pay for the repair of the tenements of John de Wengham and William de Navesby.[101] The original contributors were not forgotten as a result of Holme's intervention: an obit was celebrated for Thomas de Northflete's soul until the Reformation, and de Navesby and de Wengham were included in the list of beneficiaries for whom the chantry priests were to pray.[102]

From the fifteenth century onwards, an important feature of chantry foundations is the significant number of chantries established by Londoners, often in their capacity as executors, for the benefit of clerics associated with the cathedral,[103] and in some cases many years after the death of the beneficiary.[104]

----

[94]   GL Ms 25501, fols 42–43.

[95]   GL Ms 25152.

[96]   R.L. Storey, *Thomas Langley and the Bishopric of Durham, 1406–1437* (London, 1961), p. 5.

[97]   GL Ms 25145.

[98]   *BRUO*, vol. 3, pp. 2014–15. The chantry was only recorded in the list of c.1370.

[99]   The purpose of the donation remains unknown, for no documentation survives relating to Navesby's bequest.

[100]   *Fasti II*, p. 28; GL Ms 25271/19.

[101]   GL Ms 25145.

[102]   Kitching, no. 112; GL Ms 25145.

[103]   John Westyerd, vintner, founded a chantry for Dean Thomas Stowe; John Drayton, goldsmith, for Bishop Roger Walden; William Vale, cutler, for Dean William Say; William Barbe, fishmonger, for Canon John Dowman; Henry Hyll, haberdasher, for Bishop Richard FitzJames; and Robert Brokel, baker, for Canon John Withers: see Appendix, pp. 186–8.

[104]   The chantry for Thomas Stowe (d.1405) was officially established in 1423, while the chantry of Roger Walden (d.1406) was founded in 1456/57. The chantry for William Say

These chantries were not the first of this type, however. Margaret, widow of William de Bigott and heir of Robert de Sutton, had founded a chantry for Dean Martin of Pattishall (d.1229) in 1239.[105] Foundation by lay people for ecclesiastics was probably the result of previous arrangements between the beneficiary and an 'administrator', in which the former entrusted sufficient properties to the administrator in order to establish a chantry.[106] The high proportion of this type of foundation in the later period reveals the trust that the clerics placed in the merchant class of London and in their ability to take care of the financial aspects of their foundations.[107]

Another feature of chantry foundations was the additional donations or 'top-ups' that existing chantries received from later benefactors. In 1309/10 Thomas de Bredestrete left tenements to augment the chantry of Godfrey of St Dunstan, late minor canon of St Paul's.[108] Likewise in 1335 William Flambard de Wykys left all his houses in the city of London for the maintenance of Richard de Newport's chantry (1309).[109] Did these Londoners associate themselves with these existing chantries to honour the original founder, or to save them from financial difficulties? For example, in 1330 John Grantham, pepperer and citizen of London, came to the rescue of de Haverhull's chantry, which was experiencing financial difficulties. In exchange for prayers and masses, Grantham renovated, at his own expense, a tenement near Dowgate that formed part of the original endowment.[110] In some instances, the donations were so large that the names of the subsequent benefactors coexisted with those of the original founders, as with de Bury/Holme and de Haverhull/Grantham. One of the most famous augmentations was that carried out by John Carpenter for the welfare of the soul of Richard Whittington. In 1430 the king granted Carpenter a licence to increase the endowment of Beyvin's chantry situated in the chapel of St Mary over the charnel house in St Paul's churchyard.[111] The chaplain was to pray for the soul of the original founder, Roger Beyvin, and for the soul of Richard

---

(d.1468) was established in 1503.

[105] GL M 25127.

[106] Dobson also found an example of this kind of arrangements at York Minster: the mayor and citizens of York administered the chantry for Treasurer Thomas Haxey (d.1426). Dobson, 'Foundation of Perpetual Chantries', p. 27.

[107] Wood-Legh also concluded that the ecclesiastics entrusted their chantries to the town's control: *Perpetual Chantries*, p. 178.

[108] Sharpe, vol. 1, p. 209.

[109] *Ibid.*, p. 403. He was presumably related to Simon Flamberd, one of Richard de Newport's executors.

[110] GL Ms 25121/535.

[111] *CPR, 1429–1436*, pp. 56–7.

Whittington. Religious fraternities also supported chantries in need. By 1379, a fraternity had already been established to support the charnel house's chapel.[112] In 1453 another fraternity, the guild of St George of the Armourers' Company of London, may have been associated with Wokyndon's chantry, founded in 1321, for both the guild and the priest of Wokyndon's chantry worshipped in the Chapel of St George located in the east end of the New Work's north aisle.[113]

These examples of subsequent endowments highlight two important features concerning chantries. First, they illustrate the variety of strategies employed to secure their survival. These initiatives, taken by individuals or by the cathedral authorities, demonstrate that the fate of chantries mattered.[114] It may be that there was a reduction in the number of chantries founded in the fifteenth century because many people were already involved in the upkeep of existing chantries, whether by way of patronage, or by successive donations, or by association with a guild.[115] Second, these examples reveal how Londoners contributed to the cathedral chantries' survival, since most subsequent endowments were the gifts of lay Londoners.[116] They not only rescued chantries founded by Londoners, as in the cases of Beyvin's chantry and Wokyndon's, but also those established by members of the cathedral clergy, such as de Newport's and St Dunstan's. Similarly, in 1434 Walter Caketon, an arrowsmith, enlarged the chantry of Dean Thomas More (d.1421) from three to four chaplains, while in 1444 John Stile, vintner, left tenements for the augmentation of Dean de Eure's chantry.[117] Likewise, Roger Merssh (d.1459) asked to be buried in Sherrington's chapel

---

[112] See Chapter 3, p. 76. For cathedral fraternities, see Elizabeth New, 'Fraternities in English Cathedrals in the Later Medieval Period', in Tim Thornton (ed.), *Social Attitudes and Political Structures in the Fifteenth Century* (Stroud, 2000), pp. 33–51. For parish fraternities, see H.F. Westlake, *The Parish Gilds of Medieval England* (London, 1919) and Caroline M. Barron, 'The Parish Fraternities of Medieval London', in Caroline M. Barron and Christopher Harper-Bill (eds), *The Church in Pre-Reformation Society: Essays in Honour of F.R.H. Du Boulay* (Woodbridge, 1985), pp. 13–37.

[113] *CPR, 1416–1422*, p. 11; *CPR, 1452–1461*, p. 105. The Chapel of St George replaced the altar of St Thomas Becket where the chantry was previously located. Thacker, 'Cult of Saints', p. 121.

[114] For instance, in 1475, John Wood, major canon, left £10 to rescue whatever chantry was in financial difficulty, TNA PROB 11/6, fols 159–160.

[115] Dobson, 'Foundation of Perpetual Chantries', p. 37.

[116] In addition to the examples already mentioned, Mathilda de Staunford (d.1322) bequeathed a house to St Paul's for the maintenance of chantries at the cathedral, and William Wodehall of Henele (d.1357) and Thomas de York (d.1361), vintner, made bequests to the college of secular priests of St Paul; Sharpe, vol. 1, p. 299; vol. 2, pp. 6, 39.

[117] Sharpe, vol. 2, pp. 467–8, 503–4; another example is the provision for an obit for Dean Thomas Lisieux by William Wodehous, barber, in 1472, GL Ms 25271/69.

and endowed the chantry with London properties,[118] and Geoffrey Meleman (d.1499), a London mercer, left tenements to the four chaplains serving Holme's College to increase their stipends.[119]

The eighty-four perpetual foundations established at St Paul's were not evenly distributed throughout the centuries. More than sixty chantries were established before the mid-fourteenth century: four at the close of the twelfth century, thirteen in the first half of the thirteenth century, twenty-one in the second half and twenty-six in the first half of the fourteenth century.[120] Only twenty chantries were post-plague foundations. This chantry pattern is not specific to St Paul's. In most English secular cathedrals, the peak period in chantry foundation was the late thirteenth and early fourteenth centuries.[121] At the national level, the golden age of the early fourteenth century was followed by a post-plague decline.[122] These figures are, however, somewhat misleading, for they do not reflect the additional contributions made throughout the centuries to support or augment existing chantries. Furthermore, it appears that the cathedral authorities had observed a deliberate policy from the later fourteenth century onwards of restricting chantry foundations to those very generously endowed, thus limiting the pool of potential founders, in order to prevent future financial difficulties. The Dean and Chapter had learned from past experience that modestly endowed foundations might not generate sufficient income to support chantry priests. In 1345 the mayor of London had complained to the Dean and Chapter about the fact that some chantries were vacant.[123] In the later fourteenth century the shortage of priests and the economic depression jeopardised the survival of some chantries.[124] It took the intervention of the episcopal authorities

---

[118] Sharpe, vol. 2, pp. 539–40. As Sherrington's executor, Merssh established Sherrington's chantry; see Thomas Hearne (ed.), *The History and Antiquities of Glastonbury. Added with The Endowment and Orders of Sherington's Chantry, founded in Saint Paul's Church, London* (Oxford, 1722), pp. 161–223. The original documents are part of the archives of St Stephen Walbrook's parish, GL Mss 3067; 3068 (the author did not have the chance to have a look at them).

[119] Sharpe, vol. 2, p. 599. The number of chaplains serving Holme's College had by then been reduced, even though William Brewster, major canon, had left a bequest to the college, GL Ms 25121/1488.

[120] See Table 1.1.

[121] Edwards, *English Secular Cathedrals*, p. 288.

[122] Alan Kreider, *English Chantries: The Road to Dissolution* (Cambridge, Mass., 1979), p. 72.

[123] H.T. Riley, *Memorials of London and London Life in the XIIIth, XIVth and XVth Centuries* (London, 1868), pp. 224–5.

[124] This situation was observed at Exeter Cathedral by Nicholas Orme, 'The Medieval Chantries of Exeter Cathedral, Part 1', *Devon and Cornwall Notes and Queries*, 34 (1981–2), pp. 319–26, esp. p. 320; and in the diocese of Norwich by Rachel Ward, 'The Foundation

at the end of the fourteenth century to remedy this situation by dramatically reducing the number of existing chantries. The 1391 major amalgamations alongside the additional lay contributions demonstrate that continuous efforts were deployed to save the existing chantries rather than to found new ones. It was perhaps because chantries were seen as communal endeavours that benefited the whole community, rather than solely private affairs, that they managed to attract additional and continuous support.

---

and Functions of Perpetual Chantries in the Diocese of Norwich, c.1250–1547', (PhD thesis, University of Cambridge, 1998), p. 19.

Chapter 2
Managing Chantries

Chantry chaplains were considered to be integral members of St Paul's clerical community and were placed under the jurisdiction of the Dean and Chapter. Therefore all new foundations had to be sanctioned and authorised by the cathedral officials. Conforming to general cathedral principles did not, however, sacrifice the chantries' distinctive characteristics. There was room for founders to establish their foundations the way they saw fit. Consequently, once founders had guaranteed sufficient income to maintain their chantries, agreements about the details of the chantry management and daily functioning were concluded between the Dean and Chapter and the founders in order to guarantee that the personal desires of the latter would be respected.[1] Founders were aware that the success of their chantries depended on two major factors: their financial security, and the quality and constancy of services assumed by the chantry chaplains. First, founders wanted to ensure that the properties with which they endowed their chantries were well managed and generated sufficient income over long periods to meet any costs. To try to avoid any loss of income they established complex systems of supervision and possible sanctions for inefficient administration. Second, since their salvation was at stake, founders wanted to ensure the quality of their pious foundations by regulating the selection of the chaplains and detailing their religious duties. By specifying requirements, they could express personal devotions.[2]

In total, instructions in wills or foundation deeds survive for approximately sixty-five of St Paul's perpetual chantries from the late twelfth to the early sixteenth century.[3] These instructions regulated at least three components: the selection of chaplains, their religious and devotional duties, and the chantry

---

[1]   Examples of chantry foundation deeds are printed in R.N. Swanson, *Catholic England. Faith, Religion and Observance before the Reformation* (Manchester, 1993), pp. 229–41.

[2]   R.B. Dobson 'Citizens and Chantries in Late Medieval York', in *Church and Society in Medieval North of England* (London, 1996), pp. 267–84, esp. p. 268.

[3]   When the chantry was a post-mortem foundation, the responsibility for concluding an agreement with the Dean and Chapter was left to executors. In this context, the expression 'founders' refers to the beneficiary or to his executors, as appropriate.

management and financial organisation.[4] Chantry ordinances were devoted to these practical purposes and founders tended not to use them as a forum for eschatological speculation. Exceptionally, in 1436, John Carpenter prefaced the deed by which he increased the endowment of Beyvin's chantry located in the charnel house with the following:

> It should be the fervent desire and solicitous care of the prudent and devout man to provide advantageously for the increase of divine service in perpetuity, especially through the continual celebration of the solemnities of masses in which for the well-being of the living and the repose of the dead to God the Father His only begotten Son is offered in the Host by the hands of the priest.[5]

With time, founders generally became more sophisticated in their requests.[6] With some exceptions, instructions for the earliest chantry foundations are far more concise than later ones. Obviously founders, as time went by, became more aware of the potential difficulties that chantries might encounter and, as a result, developed different systems of supervision and control in order to diminish the risks. From the fourteenth century onwards they introduced elaborate provisions regulating the appointment of chaplains and the tasks for which they would be responsible. Simultaneously there was a general progression towards the inclusion of standardised requirements about participation in the choir, length of vacancies, and the chaplains' various administrative duties. Furthermore, as foundation ordinances became more elaborate, founders devoted more detail to personalised instructions. Perhaps the most striking example is Roger Holme, who left a series of detailed, although conventional, instructions to his chaplains in the late fourteenth century.[7] He enumerated all the specific masses that his seven chaplains were to celebrate on a daily basis, included a long list of benefactors, dead or alive, for whom the chaplains were to pray, and left specific instructions to his chaplains regarding almsgiving in London.

A prototype for almshouse foundation came into use in the mid-fifteenth century.[8] At St Paul's a standard chantry foundation model was adopted only in the sixteenth century and used for the chantries of John Dowman in 1525, of Richard FitzJames in 1529 and of John Withers in 1535.[9] Not only did these

---

4   Wood-Legh, 'Some Aspects', p. 52.
5   GL Ms 25513, fol. 156. Translated by Wood-Legh, *Perpetual Chantries*, p. 306.
6   McManaway, 'Some Aspects', pp. 41, 58.
7   GL Ms 25145.
8   John Goodall, *God's House at Ewelme. Life, Devotion and Architecture in a Fifteenth-Century Almshouse* (Aldershot, 2001), Appendix 1.
9   GL Ms 25271/73; LMA HC roll 240(28), HC roll 241(18).

chantries use the same prototype with very few deviations; they also shared many similar characteristics. First of all, these chantries were founded *for* cathedral members, but *by* citizens of London. William Barbe, fishmonger, established the chantry of the major canon John Dowman. Bishop FitzJames's chantry was organised by Henry Hyll, haberdasher, and, likewise, Robert Brokel, baker, set up the chantry for John Withers, another major canon. The most striking similarity between these three chantries, however, concerns the involvement of a city company: the fraternity of St Katherine of the craft of the Haberdashers for Dowman's chantry, the fraternity of St John Baptist of the craft of the Merchant Tailors for FitzJames's, and the craft of the Saddlers for Withers's chantry. It is worth noting that the professions of these administrators did not correspond to the company with which these chantries were associated.

The Selection of Chaplains

One of the principal instructions enumerated in chantry ordinances, not surprisingly, relates to the process of selecting chantry chaplains. Founders relied on two complementary approaches for ensuring that their chantries would always be in safe hands, guaranteeing future good conduct. First of all they entrusted the right of appointing the chaplains to trustworthy men, relying on their judgement to select the best candidates. Second, they indicated the qualities that celebrants should possess.[10] Given that the decision ultimately remained subjective and was at the patrons' discretion, chantry founders in general described the qualities that the chaplains should exhibit very succinctly. In twenty-one cases, they simply stipulated that they should be 'suitable' [*ydoneus*], which left patrons plenty of room for interpretation.[11] Four founders sought 'honest' or 'honest and suitable' chaplains. In one foundation deed 'honesty' was joined to 'competence' and in another with 'good conversation'. Because of the weight of their administrative duties, the chaplains of Thomas More's chantry were to be both '*habiles*' and '*capaces*'.[12] The frequency of the term 'suitable' suggests perhaps some degree of influence exerted among founders, or exercised by the cathedral authorities, during the writing up of these instructions. The results of a national inquiry

---

[10]   Chantry foundation charters give an indication of lay expectation of ideal priests; see Robert Swanson, 'Problems of the Priesthood in Pre-Reformation England', *English Historical Review*, 105 (1990), pp. 845–69, esp. p. 849.

[11]   These requirements are listed in Marie-Hélène Rousseau, 'Chantry Foundations and Chantry Chaplains at St Paul's Cathedral, London c.1200–1548' (PhD thesis, University of London, 2003), Appendix D.

[12]   GL Ms 25121/1933; Lambeth Palace Ms 2018, fol. 1v.

on priesthood demonstrate that it was more common to seek the attribute '*honestas*'.[13] The qualitative 'suitable', as well as the designations 'sufficient', 'fit' and 'able', however, also included moral considerations.[14] Only for the chantries of Richard de Newport and Ralph de Baldock, established in 1309 and 1320, were the chaplains to be competent both in reading and in singing.[15] All chaplains, however, because they were priests, were expected to have a minimum of literacy and be able to read Latin.[16] This scarcity of any specific educational requirement before the mid-fifteenth century suggests that founders judged the moral qualities of their priests more significant than their scholarly knowledge.[17]

Two requirements were introduced in the fifteenth century regarding the selection of chaplains. First was the particular request made in 1447 by Walter Sherrington, and repeated by the last three chantry founders of St Paul's, that the chaplains serving their chantries were to be Englishmen.[18] This singular restriction seems to suggest disquiet regarding the intrusion of foreigners in the church community or in the city of London in general, rather than to reflect the presence of foreigners among chantry chaplains.[19] Walter Sherrington's chantry also introduced the requirement to choose chantry chaplains from among university graduates.[20] The requirement was also included in the instructions for Say's and Dowman's chantries in 1503 and 1525 respectively.[21] Not surprisingly, these founders had direct links with universities and/or the world of learning. Walter Sherrington's foundation also included a library, and his two chaplains were required to act as librarians, although Sherrington was not a graduate. William Say attended New College, Oxford, and John Dowman was a Cambridge fellow.[22] Dowman endowed five scholarships for poor scholars to attend St John's College, Cambridge, founded in 1512 by Bishop Fisher, and he requested that his chaplains be chosen from among St John's scholars.[23] Records

---

[13]   Peter Marshall, *The Catholic Priesthood and the English Reformation* (Oxford, 1994), pp. 51–2.

[14]   *Ibid.*, p. 52.

[15]   GL Ms 25121/741; Ms 25501, fol. 96.

[16]   For a discussion on priestly knowledge, see Haines, *Ecclesia Anglicana*, Chapter 8.

[17]   This conclusion corresponds to Marshall's; *Catholic Priesthood*, p. 52.

[18]   Hearne, *History and Antiquities*, p. 183.

[19]   An inquiry into the chaplains' origins shows that they were all Englishmen, with the exception of a few Welsh priests; see Chapter 5, pp. 112–13.

[20]   Hearne, *History and Antiquities*, p. 183.

[21]   GL Ms 25518; Ms 25271/73.

[22]   *BRUO*, vol. 3, pp. 1649–50; *BRUC*, pp. 192–3.

[23]   GL Ms 25271/73; Cambridge, St John's College, Ms K54.

from the college prove that his wish was respected.[24] Dowman's foundation at St Paul's can be seen as an extension of his scholarly endowment. In the later Middle Ages, a crisis of patronage forced university graduates to seek lower positions within the church hierarchy as competition for rectories and vicarages intensified, and many clerical positions were founded exclusively for graduate chaplains to promote some 'old-boy networks'.[25] Furthermore, the wages offered for these chantries allocated to graduate chaplains did not differ from the wages given in other chantries established at the same time. For example, both Dowman's chantry (1525), which specifically required a graduate chaplain, and Withers's chantry (1535), which did not, paid an annual stipend of £8 to the incumbent. Founders who desired graduate chaplains did not have to resort to higher wages as an incentive to attract them. The job market was working in their favour.

Disquiet regarding pluralism first appears in the early fourteenth-century foundation agreements. Overall twenty founders felt it necessary to stipulate that their chaplains should be barred from holding another benefice in addition to their chantry.[26] This prohibition corresponded to the Canon Law statute *Ad Excitandos* that forbade priests from celebrating more than one mass a day.[27] Surprisingly, perhaps, these prohibitions were often formulated by clerics who were themselves pluralists. It is noteworthy that founders appear to have felt the need to repeat this ban on pluralism from the 1320s onwards, probably following the publication in 1317 of the papal constitution *Execrabilis*, which forbade clerks to hold more than two benefices simultaneously.[28] The repetition of the ban resulted perhaps from the general non-observance of this prohibition. Pluralism was probably a necessary evil caused by the general devaluation of the chaplains' stipends, and ecclesiastical authorities recognised that chaplains needed other sources of income to sustain them.[29] Nevertheless, there was a fear that the chantries would be neglected if city clergy served them.[30] Bishop de

---

[24]   See Chapter 5, pp. 114–15.

[25]   Robert Swanson, 'Universities, Graduates and Benefices in Later Medieval England', *Past and Present*, 106 (1985), p. 53.

[26]   Rousseau, 'Chantry Foundations', Appendix D.

[27]   Lyndwood's *Provinciale*, Lib. III, tit. 23, cap. 1., rprt in J.V. Bullard and H. Chalmer Bell (eds), *Lyndwood's Provinciale* (London, 1929), p. 94.

[28]   Nicholas Bennett, 'Clerical Non-Residence in the Diocese of Lincoln in the Fourteenth Century', in Nicholas Bennett and David Marcombe (eds), *Thomas de Aston and the Diocese of Lincoln. Two Studies in the Fourteenth-Century Church* (Lincoln, 1998), pp. 4–31, esp. p. 21.

[29]   On an inquiry into pluralism at St Paul's, see Chapter 5, pp. 130–31. C.J. Godfrey, 'Pluralists in the Province of Canterbury in 1366', *Journal of Ecclesiastical History*, 11 (1960), pp. 23–40.

[30]   Brooke, 'The Earliest Times', p. 75.

Braybroke forbade beneficed clerics from holding chantries within the cathedral, although he exempted the minor canons, who were entitled to occupy a chantry even if they were already beneficed.[31]

Since the requirements for occupying a chantry position at St Paul's were largely unspecific, many priests would have been able to meet the requirements. So how were the chantry chaplains actually chosen? Ties of friendship and family connections may have played an important role at the time of selecting chaplains, although few examples specifically refer to family members. Walter de Blockele (d.1307) stated in his will that his chantry could be given to his nephew, if he desired it.[32] His nephew managed Walter de Blockele's post-mortem affairs, but he seems not to have taken up the offer.[33] This was not the only case of a chantry being allocated to a family member. Chaplain John de Braynford served the chantry of his namesake and uncle in the late 1290s.[34] Similarly, in c.1370, a chaplain named John Hiltoft was serving the chantry of John Hiltoft, goldsmith.[35] The paucity of such examples, however, suggests that the tendency observed in Germany – where founders created chantry positions for the benefit of clerical members of their family – was less marked in England than elsewhere.[36]

Obviously friends and acquaintances could also have benefited from patronage. At York, merchants founded chantries to provide income for clerics who had worked for them and gained their favour.[37] At St Paul's, clergy who held a position in the cathedral enjoyed an advantage since they already had their 'foot in the door'. Nicholas Husband, himself a minor canon, reserved the position in his chantry for a fellow minor canon.[38] John de Ware also allocated the chantry positions to fellow minor canons while establishing the chantry of Walter and Alice Neel, and re-endowing the chantry of Mayor Nicholas de Farndorn.[39] As cathedral members of high rank also formulated the request, it

---

[31] Simpson, *Registrum Statutorum*, p. 149.

[32] GL Ms 25271/48.

[33] GL Ms 25121/459.

[34] Dugdale, p. 334.

[35] GL Ms 25121/1954.

[36] This observation was also made by Wood-Legh, 'Some Aspects', p. 50; and Marshall, *Catholic Priesthood*, p. 53. In the Comté of Avignon family members of the founders frequently served their chantries: Jacques Chiffoleau, *La comptabilité de l'Au-delà: Les hommes, la mort et la religion dans la région d'Avignon à la fin du Moyen Âge (1320–1480)* (Rome, 1980), pp. 247–8.

[37] Dobson, 'Foundation of Perpetual Chantries', p. 37.

[38] GL Ms 25271/32. In contrast, Walter de Blockele (d.1307), himself a chaplain, prohibited minor canons from occupying his chantry: Sharpe, vol. 1, pp. 184–5.

[39] GL Ms 25121/635.

may have reflected a kind of brotherhood between higher and lesser clergy.[40] In time twelve specific chantries (or groups of chantries when these had been amalgamated) became associated with the minor canonries.[41] Only one chantry at St Paul's, that of Thomas Kempe, was exclusively allocated to a major canon. This exceptional association dates not from the original foundation, but results from an *ad hoc* intervention by Kempe. In 1467 Bishop Kempe assigned his newly founded chantry as well as the office of penitentiary to a faithful servant, John Barvile.[42] In 1474 he sought a royal licence to appropriate the prebend of St Pancras to the office of the penitentiary, in this way combining his chantry with a major canonry of St Paul's.[43] At Barvile's death in 1482 his successor, Thomas Dultyng, received the rectory of the parish church of Chigwell as a source of income, in addition to the combined package.[44] Kempe's chantry remained in the hands of a major canon until the dissolution of 1548.

In terms of ensuring the quality of celebrants in a situation where a large number of priests were available, the role and discretion of the designated patrons were obviously of paramount importance. In the case of foundations by laymen, the right of nomination usually stayed within the family.[45] The male descendants of the earl of Warwick inherited the privilege of presenting chaplains to John Beauchamp's chantry.[46] The heirs and descendants of John of Gaunt, however, did not inherit the right of appointment to his chantry. After the death of his executors, the right was, uniquely, transferred to the dean of St Stephen's College, Westminster, an institution founded by Edward III and intimately connected with the royal family.[47] When founders were ecclesiastics, they usually nominated members of the cathedral hierarchy to act as chantry patrons. On the whole, the Dean and Chapter inherited the task for at least twenty-six chantries, but on some occasions the task was given to specific members of the cathedral. For instance, the cathedral treasurer and the archdeacon of Colchester acted as patrons of de Swereford's and de Meleford's chantries, respectively.[48] When founding chantries at St Paul's, bishops of London unsurprisingly conferred the

---

[40] GL Ms 25121/1958.

[41] See Chapter 5, p. 127 and Chapter 6, pp. 152–3.

[42] GL Ms 9531/7, fol. 102v.

[43] *Fasti II*, p. 55.

[44] GL Ms 9531/7, fol. 185v.

[45] Details on appointment rights are listed in Rousseau, 'Chantry Foundations', Appendix D.

[46] GL Ms 25121/1925.

[47] GL Ms 25121/1941.

[48] GL Ms 25501, fols 42–43; LMA HC roll 64(127).

right of nomination on their successors.[49] Minor canons, such as the sacristan and the cardinals, bore responsibility for five chantries established by major canons, revealing the trust that the higher clergy had in members of the minor clergy.

Cathedral members did not, however, enjoy a monopoly in appointing chantry chaplains. The right of nomination could also be given to lay authorities, as in the case of Henry de Guldeford's chantry for which the mayor and the chamberlain of London received an annual fee of 20s for appointing chaplains.[50] This agreement appears to have overruled a previous decision to assign the responsibility to the mayor of London to intervene only if the Dean and Chapter failed to appoint a chantry chaplain after fifteen days.[51] This was unusual, but not exceptional. The mayor of London also received an annual fee of one mark for presenting a suitable chaplain to Beyvin's chantry, serving in the chapel of the charnel house.[52] In 1436, when John Carpenter re-founded this chantry, he gave the presentation right jointly to the mayor and the chamberlain of London, who were to exercise their right in turn.[53] In 1348 John Pulteney had also conferred the right of appointment on the mayor of London: the mayor was to choose two chaplains, and the master of St Laurence's College the third one.[54] City companies also inherited nomination rights. The wardens of the Goldsmiths' company were given the responsibility for appointing chaplains to Hiltoft's chantry, while the Merchant Tailors appointed chaplains to the chantries of Carleton and de Roos.[55] In the case of John Dowman's chantry, the master and wardens of the fraternity of St Katherine kept the right of appointment, although they had to select a fellow from St John's College.[56]

Thus it seems that each founder gave the right of appointment to the agent whom he judged most suitable to select appropriate chaplains. The nomination first occurred at the chantry foundation, then at each vacancy caused by the chaplain's death, retirement or resignation. Obviously founders tried to avoid any extended vacancy, since this would have undermined all the purposes of the foundation. They therefore tended to be precise as to the time allowed for selecting a new chaplain. This varied from one chantry to another, from three to forty days. Should the agent with responsibility for nominating fail to fulfil

49   Bishops of London were the patrons of at least six chantries.

50   GL Ms 25121/1754.

51   *Letter-Book E*, pp. 30–31.

52   Sharpe, vol. 1, pp. 29–30.

53   GL Ms 25513, fols 156–159.

54   GL Ms 25271/35.

55   Lisa Jefferson (ed.), *Wardens' Accounts and Court Minute Books of the Goldsmiths' Mistery of London* (Woodbridge, 2003), p. 187; Sharpe, vol. 2, pp. 272–3; Dugdale, pp. 354–7.

56   GL Ms 25271/73.

his task, it was to be transferred to another party. In many cases the bishop of London was appointed to take over if the Dean and Chapter of St Paul's showed any sign of negligence in this respect.[57] Why did the founders feel the need to establish such systems of supervision? It has been demonstrated that the mayor of London and the members of the city guilds who were responsible for nominating chaplains did so conscientiously.[58] Similarly, it may be argued that cathedral members had more to lose than to gain from an extended vacancy, for their reputation was at stake.[59] As a result, any trend towards increasing care should not be seen as denoting lack of confidence in chantry patrons, but rather seems to indicate a realisation that founders could, with confidence, maintain some control over their foundation. Once nominated, the chaplains might not enter their chantry immediately. First they had to be admitted by the Dean and Chapter. The ceremony took place in the chapter house and the new chaplains appear to have been expected to pay for all induction charges.[60] Then, after they had proven their proficiency as singers, they had to swear an oath of obedience and fidelity to the Dean and Chapter.[61] This oath included a promise to observe the cathedral statutes and to fulfil their chantry duties.[62]

Religious Duties

The chantry chaplains' primary function was to celebrate intercessory masses for the founders' souls. Such practice emanated from the belief that a mass celebrated expressly for the soul of named individuals attenuated the punishment that they had to endure for the redemption of their sins. A liturgy meant to procure the beneficial effects of prayers for the dead was codified by St Benedict of Aniane at the beginning of the ninth century.[63] This liturgy included the recitation of the

---

[57] Bishops generally inherited the right of presentation for rectories and vicarages, when the designated patron failed to present a candidate; see Peter Heath, *The English Parish Clergy on the Eve of the Reformation* (London/Toronto, 1969), p. 31.

[58] Hill, '*Chaunterie for Soules*', p. 249. Other historians made the same observations; see Burgess, 'Strategies for Eternity', pp. 4–5; E.F. Jacob, 'Founders and Foundations in Later Middle Ages', *Bulletin of the Institute of Historical Research*, 35 (1962), pp. 29–46, esp. p. 33.

[59] Records show that the right of appointment was taken seriously; see Chapter 4, pp. 94–5.

[60] GL Ms 25157; Ms 25513, fols 162–162v.

[61] Edwards, *English Secular Cathedrals*, p. 291.

[62] *Ibid.*, p. 292. Dean Lisieux transcribed the oath in his compilation of the cathedral statutes: Cambridge, University Library, Ms Ee.5.21., fol. 4.

[63] Dom David Knowles, *The Monastic Order in England. A History of Its Development from the Times of St Dunstan to the Fourth Lateran Council, 940–1216* (2nd edn, Cambridge, 1963), pp. 25–30.

seven penitential psalms with litanies and an office of the dead, which became the usual service celebrated at funerals and, by extension, at anniversaries, the annual commemoration of a particular death. It comprised three canonical hours, known by the word with which they began, *placebo* for the vespers, *dirige* for the matins and *commendatio* for the lauds.[64] Chantry chaplains were often required to recite the office of the dead on a regular basis, before celebrating the mass of Requiem. The mass of Requiem, named for the first words of the entrance antiphon *Requiem aeternam dona eis Domine*, was developed especially for the departed no later than the sixth century. Because it was deemed to be particularly efficacious in assisting souls in purgatory, it became popular among chantry founders.[65]

Faithful to this established tradition, founders at St Paul's required their chaplains to celebrate religious services to expedite the salvation of their souls. The formula of a daily mass and the office of the dead formed the basis on which they then elaborated to satisfy, or promote, personal devotional aspirations. Founders varied the frequency of the recitation of the office of the dead. This might be a daily recitation, as for Roger de La Legh's chantry in 1278, or a weekly celebration, as for Dowman's chantry (1525).[66] Other founders used their foundation deeds to specify particular prayers. In 1325, Roger de Waltham specified the special collects that his chaplain was to recite during his lifetime, and others that were to be used after his death.[67] In 1436 John Carpenter requested that before mass his chaplain had to recite on his knees [*flexis genibus*] the *Pater Noster* and the *Ave*, with special prayers for Roger Beyvin (the original chantry founder), for Richard Whittington (the re-founder) and for other benefactors, including John Carpenter himself.[68] The chaplains serving Lancaster College had to celebrate masses with prayers after communion for the welfare of King Henry IV when alive, and then for his soul and for the souls of his parents, John of Gaunt and his wife Blanche.[69]

---

[64]   Wood-Legh, *Perpetual Chantries*, pp. 296–8.

[65]   A. Cornides and R. Snow, 'Requiem Mass', in Thomas Carson and Joann Cerrito (eds), *New Catholic Encyclopedia* (Washington, DC, 2003), vol. 12, pp. 134–6; Wood-Legh, *Perpetual Chantries*, p. 284.

[66]   GL Ms 25121/1936; Ms 25271/73.

[67]   The 'unusually detailed liturgical prescriptions' are presented and discussed in Lucy Sandler, 'The Chantry of Roger of Waltham in Old St Paul's', in Janet Backhouse (ed.), *The Medieval English Cathedral. Papers in Honour of Pamela Tudor-Craig. Proceedings of the 1998 Harlaxton Symposium* (Donington, 2003), pp. 168–90.

[68]   GL Ms 25513, fols 156–159.

[69]   GL Ms 25121/1941.

Chantry founders were at liberty to express personal devotional preferences; this is at its most obvious in their ability to select and specify the celebration of different masses. In 1349, the three chaplains of John Pulteney's chantry were required to say the mass of the Virgin and the office of the dead.[70] Most notably, Roger Holme took full advantage of the opportunities open to a chantry founder. When formulating the ordinances for his seven chantry chaplains in c.1390, he specified the es to be celebrated by each one (Table 2.1).[71]

Table 2.1   Masses to be celebrated by Holme's chantry chaplains

Mass	Days of the Week						
	Sunday	Monday	Tuesday	Wednesday	Thursday	Friday	Saturday
1st	Holy Spirit	Holy Spirit	Holy Spirit	Holy Spirit	Holy Spirit	Holy Spirit	Holy Spirit
2nd	Mass of the day	Mass of the day	Mass of the day	Mass of the day	Mass of the day	Mass of the day	Mass of the day
3rd	Holy Trinity	Angels	Office of Salus Populi	St Mary	Corpus Christi	Holy Cross with Music	St Mary
4th	St Mary	St Mary	St Thomas the Martyr	Requiem	St Mary	St Mary	Requiem
5th	Requiem	Requiem	St Mary	St John the Baptist	Requiem	Requiem	Unspecified
6th	Feast	Feast	Feast	Feast	Feast	Feast	Feast
7th	All Saints	All Saints	All Saints	All Saints	All Saints	All Saints	All Saints

Table 2.1 illustrates Roger Holme's zeal to regulate every aspect of his chantries. Most founders observed well-established conventions: on Sunday, the mass of the Trinity; on Monday, the mass of the Angels; on Tuesday, the mass of St Thomas the Martyr; on Wednesday, the mass of All Saints; on Thursday, the mass of Corpus Christi; on Friday, the mass of the Cross; and on Saturday, the mass of the Blessed Mary.[72] Holme's arrangements were not, therefore, peculiar – he simply took more trouble than most to specify his requirements. Holme's instructions nevertheless suggest that he had a particular devotion to the Holy Cross: not only was the mass of the Holy Cross sung (*cum nota*) on Friday, but also his chantry chapel was located near the rood of the north door.[73] Later chantry

---

[70]   GL Ms 25271/35.
[71]   GL Ms 25145.
[72]   Wood-Legh, *Perpetual Chantries*, p. 288.
[73]   For the location of altars, see Chapter 3, pp. 70–73.

founders of St Paul's seem not to have promoted the new cults introduced in the late fifteenth century, such as the 'Name of Jesus' and the 'Five Wounds', which were both, for example, advocated by Margaret, Lady Hungerford (d.1478) at her chantry foundation at Salisbury Cathedral.[74] The presence of a particular fraternity dedicated to the Holy Name of Jesus, already promoting this cult in St Paul's, may explain why founders seem not to have seen any need to prescribe this mass.[75]

Bishop Richard Clifford's ordinance of 1414, which made the Use of Sarum obligatory at the cathedral, suggests that St Paul's chantry chaplains followed the Use of Sarum at least from the beginning of the fifteenth century, while the choir was still officiating according to the ancient Use of St Paul's.[76] Clifford introduced the new Use stating that those officiating in the choir were saying their offices according to the Use of St Paul's, while those outside the choir were conforming to the Use of Sarum, presumably referring to chantry and obit celebrations as opposed to the *opus Dei*. Only the ordinance for Sherrington's chantry (1447), however, refers explicitly to the Use of Sarum by requiring that the chaplains celebrate the commemoration of the dead according to the Use of Sarum.[77] Other specific references to the Salisbury Use in the context of chantry foundation are the possession of a *portiforium* of the Use of Sarum by the chaplains of Lancaster College, and the receipt of a missal according to that Use by de Baldock's chaplains in the fifteenth century.[78] Even in Sherrington's chantry ordinances, the Use of Sarum did not totally eclipse the Use of St Paul's. In regard to the canonical hours, the chaplains were left with the choice of following the Sarum Use or the Pauline Use.

A lot of ink has been spilled over the question of the significance of the increased demand for intercessory masses in the later Middle Ages. Some

---

[74] Michael Hicks, 'The Piety of Margaret, Lady Hungerford (d.1478)', *Journal of Ecclesiastical History*, 38 (1987), pp. 19–38, esp. p. 31. For a survey of new cults, see R.W. Pfaff, *New Liturgical Feasts in Later Medieval England* (Oxford, 1970).

[75] On this topic, see Elizabeth New, 'The Cult of the Holy Name of Jesus in Late Medieval England, with Special Reference to the Fraternity in St Paul's Cathedral' (PhD thesis, University of London, 1999).

[76] William Sparrow Simpson, 'A Mandate of Bishop Clifford superseding the Ancient Use of St Paul's Cathedral Church by the Use of Sarum', *Proceedings of the Society of Antiquaries of London*, 2nd series, 14 (1892), pp. 118–28. For more information on Sarum Use, see Terence Bailey, *The processions of Sarum and the Western Church* (Toronto, 1971).

[77] Hearne, *History and Antiquities*, p. 181.

[78] GL Ms 25154; Ms 25122/3. One chaplain, Henry Welewes, also rector of St Nicholas Olave, received in heritage a *portiforium* of the Use of Sarum in 1361, while minor canon Martin Elys bestowed in 1394 his *portiforium* with music of the Use of St Paul to the parish church of St Faith; Sharpe, vol. 2, pp. 49–50, 304–6.

historians have interpreted this as a manifestation of a nascent privatisation in religious practices, while others have insisted on the communal components of this pious practice.[79] Scholars studying chantry foundations have generally argued that these institutions, and their services, were to the benefit of the whole community rather than just their founders.[80] The celebration of private masses in itself embodied collective benefits: not only did chantry founders often include a number of named beneficiaries in their foundations, but they also intended their masses to be for the salvation of all the faithful departed.[81] The chantry foundations within St Paul's Cathedral were part of this trend. They required that their chaplains should celebrate the mass for the benefit of their souls, those of family members, those of benefactors and also for the souls of all the faithful deceased. In addition they often required them to undertake other liturgical duties in the choir, especially on feast days. Named beneficiaries sometimes seem to reconstruct entire communities. Roger Holme, for instance, drew up a long list of his kinsmen, friends, chantry patrons and benefactors for whom prayers were to be offered.[82] He enumerated some benefactors still alive. They included Bishop Robert de Braybroke, Dean Thomas de Eure, and five major canons: Adam Holme, William Coloyne, William de Wenlock, Laurence Allerthorp and Guy Mone. The list also contains two secular acquaintances, John Lord Cobham, a member of the royal household, and Henry Yevele, mason and citizen of London.[83] Five other benefactors are only identified by their Christian names, of whom one can tentatively be identified as the sacristan Reginald Spaldyng. But daily prayers were also to be offered for dead benefactors, including the first founder Adam de Bury, major canons John de Wengham and William de Navesby, a relative Walter Holme, and other friends identified by their Christian names. Joan, princess of Wales, was also remembered. Holme's list of chantry beneficiaries may have been particularly exhaustive, but it was not unique. Walter Sherrington provided his chantry chaplains with a tablet to be placed

---

[79] This subject has prompted lively debate, notably between Colin Richmond, 'Religion and the Fifteenth-Century English Gentleman', in Barrie Dobson (ed.), *The Church, Politics and Patronage in the Fifteenth Century* (Gloucester, 1984), pp. 193–208; and Christine Carpenter, 'The Religion of the Gentry in Fifteenth-Century England', in D. Williams (ed.), *England in the Fifteenth Century* (Woodbridge, 1987), pp. 53–74.

[80] Burgess, 'Increase of Divine Service', pp. 46–65 and Ward, 'Foundation and Functions', Chapter 4.

[81] John Bossy, 'The Mass as a Social Institution 1200–1700', *Past and Present*, 100 (1983), pp. 29–61.

[82] GL Ms 25145.

[83] Architect Yevele worked on various occasions for John Lord Cobham and built tombs at St Paul's Cathedral; see John H. Harvey, *Henry Yevele c. 1320 to 1400. The Life of an English Architect* (London, 1944); Sharpe, vol. 2, pp. 346–7.

over the altar as an aide-mémoire, listing all the names of the benefactors, alive or dead, for whom they were to pray. Presumably the list was too long for them to learn it by heart.[84]

Historians have highlighted how chantry foundation, by the 'increase of Divine Service', contributed to the daily attendance at mass by multiplying the number of services offered in any one church.[85] Chantry masses were either celebrated early in the morning, at daybreak or before sunrise, or celebrated successively, presumably to accommodate a wide audience.[86] In secular cathedrals, chantry masses were celebrated in such number that specific arrangements became necessary. At Lincoln, the cathedral authorities scheduled them to be celebrated from 6 am until 11 am, in order to avoid potential chaos.[87] At St Paul's, a list of c.1295 entitled *Ad horas subscriptas debent capellani infrascripti celebrare pro defunctis in ecclesa Sancti Pauli*, refers to chantry masses to be celebrated before or after the mass of the Apostles, *mane in pulsacione prime*, at daybreak at the ringing of Prime, or simply *in mane*, at daybreak.[88] The allocation of different times for the celebration of specific masses raises the question whether a congregation might have attended chantry masses in cathedral churches. Although the distribution of alms to the poor during anniversaries may be taken as evidence of a lay presence during these commemorative ceremonies, attendance at chantry mass on a regular basis is more difficult to prove from the historical record.[89] A reference in a founder's will, however, suggests that a lay congregation was expected. Nicholas de Farndone (d.1334) requested that his chantry be located at the altar of St Dunstan in the New Work, *per la vewe de mes prochains*, so that it could be witnessed by his neighbours.[90]

If the chaplains automatically became members of the cathedral, they did not, however, immediately become members of the cathedral choir. If founders intended them to participate in the main cathedral services, they usually

---

[84]   Hearne, *History and Antiquities*, p. 181.

[85]   Duffy, *Stripping of the Altars*, p. 99. On the importance of the elevation of the Eucharist during mass, see Miri Rubin, *Corpus Christi. The Eucharist in Late Medieval Culture* (Cambridge, 1991), pp. 73–4.

[86]   Wood-Legh, 'Some Aspects', p. 49.

[87]   Margaret Bowker, *The Secular Clergy in the Diocese of Lincoln, 1495–1520* (Cambridge, 1968), p. 177.

[88]   GL Ms 25505, fols 65v.–66.

[89]   On almsgivings see below, pp. 62–3.

[90]   LMA HC roll 62(102). At Exeter the gates of the close were opened at the same time of the celebration of the first chantry mass, so that lay people could attend the celebration; see Nicholas Orme, 'The Medieval Clergy of Exeter Cathedral, 1. The Vicars and Annuellars', *Report and Transactions of the Devonshire Association for the Advancement of Science, Literatures and Arts*, 113 (1981), pp. 79–102, esp. p. 93.

specified choir obligations in their chantry ordinances. The chaplain serving de Haverhull's chantry was asked to attend the choir, as were the other clerics.[91] In 1309 Richard de Newport, then archdeacon of Middlesex, stipulated that his chaplains had to take an oath before the Dean and Chapter that they would participate in the choir during the day and night offices. One chaplain was to take the place of the archdeacon of Middlesex in the choir and the other to take the place opposite him.[92] As for the chaplain of Richard Grene/de Gravesend, he had to follow the choir at least on the major canonical hours on the feasts of nine lections and during the night office on double feasts, for the fulfilment of which he was provided with lodging.[93]

Some founders left it up to their chaplains whether or not they participated in the canonical offices with the cathedral choir. Margaret de Bigott specified in her agreement that chaplains serving Pattishall's chantry should not be obliged to attend these services (see Figure 2.1).[94]

This specific instruction seems to suggest that participation in choir offices was not considered compulsory. In fact, the omission of choir instructions in chantry ordinances may have caused some conflicts. In 1324, Henry Bray, the chaplain serving the chantry of Dean William de Sanctae Mariae Ecclesia, complained to the Dean and Chapter that he had unreasonably been asked to attend services in the choir, since this duty was not stipulated in the chantry ordinances.[95] Further evidence clearly corroborates the argument that not all chantry chaplains of St Paul's were expected to participate in the cathedral choir, and that their participation depended on instructions left in chantry regulations. In an inquiry into pluralism, probably undertaken at the same period as Bishop Simon Sudbury's inquiry of 1366, four minor canons holding chantries testified that their chantry duties did not include participation in the choir.[96] These chantries corresponded to Dean William de Sanctae Mariae Ecclesia's, to Martin of Pattishall's, to Richard Grene/de Gravesend's, and to Nicholas Husband's. Moreover a fifth minor canon serving two chantries, that of Reginald de Brandon and that of Richard de Wendover, attested that he had choir obligations for the first chantry, but not for the second. These five testimonies do indeed correspond to their respective chantry regulations.[97]

91 GL Ms 25121/710.
92 GL Ms 25121/741.
93 GL Ms 25121/1962.
94 GL Ms 25157.
95 GL Ms 25121/1947.
96 GL Ms 25121/1908.
97 GL Ms 25121/732, 1920, 1947, 1962; Ms 25271/32; Ms 25517.

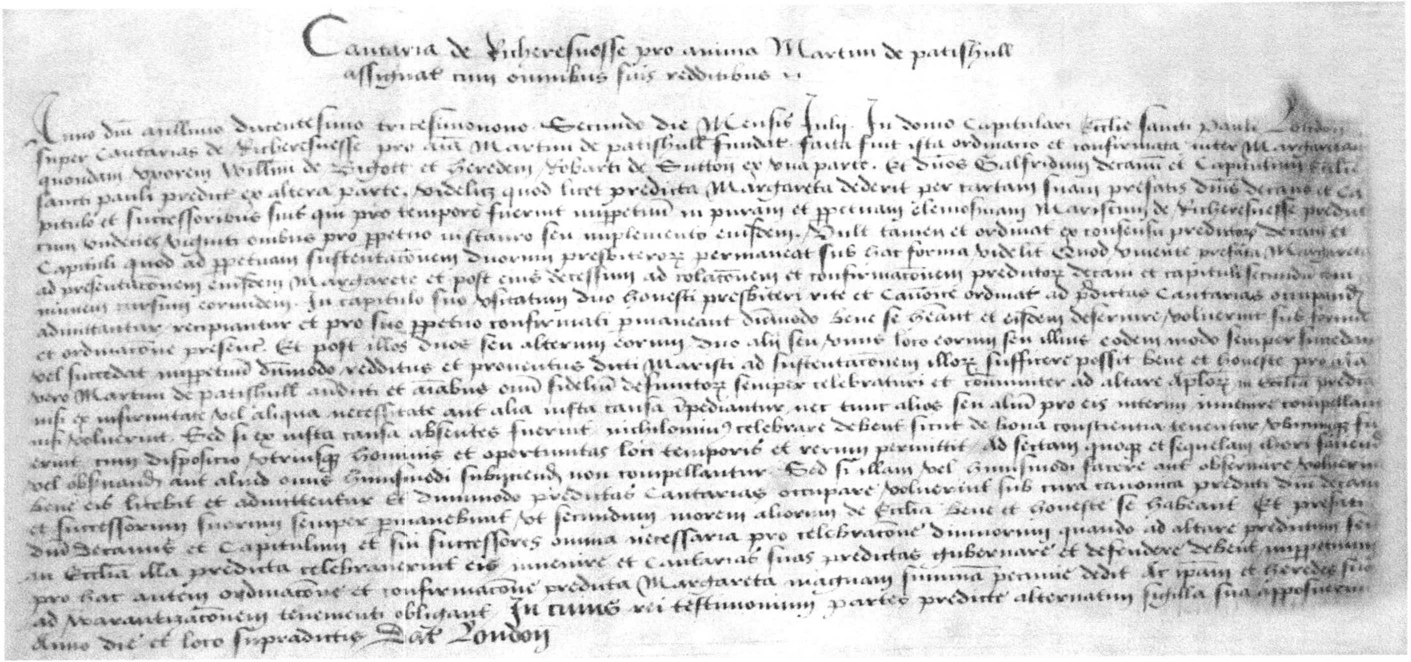

Figure 2.1 Copy of agreement between Margaret de Bigott and the Dean and Chapter for the establishment of the chantry of Martin de Pattishall (Dean of St Paul's, 1228–1229), 1239

The complaint of 1324 presumably prompted subsequent founders to be more specific about participation in the choir. In 1328, Roger de Waltham required that his chaplains were to be present in the choir for at least one principal hour every day, three times a week at matins and, during the solemn feasts, at the three principal services: that is High Mass, matins and vespers.[98] More generally, absence from the choir might lead to expulsion. In 1386 John Beauchamp's executors, in an exceptional move, discharged the chaplain John Godefrey from his regular choir duties, except during principal feasts, but even then the chaplain was to be present in the choir only during the day, and not at night.[99] He was also required to participate in all general processions in the cathedral and in the city of London, performed on Sunday and on other feast days. His successors, however, did not enjoy the same privileges; they were to participate in the choir at all times. It is clear from these instructions that the executors wanted to underline the unique and exceptional character of John Godefrey's exemption.

Thomas de Eure specified choir obligations for his chantry chaplains that varied according to the date.[100] On Sunday and at double feasts, the chaplain was to participate in the choir at prime, High Mass and vespers. On all other days his obligations were reduced to only one canonical hour. He was asked, however, to take part in all processions within or outside the cathedral church. While the presence of William Say's chaplain in the cathedral choir was required during only one principal hour on Sundays, double feasts and during processions, the chaplain did however have to participate each time the dean judged his presence appropriate.[101] In short, later founders apparently reduced the part their chaplains played in the choir by specifying the services that the chaplains had to attend. In this way their wishes were more likely to have been observed. But even by reducing the number of hours, it would have been difficult to ensure that the chaplains faithfully attended all the specified divine services. Lateness and early departure could have been tempting.[102] This might explain why John Withers's chantry chaplains seem to have enjoyed some latitude in this respect: one was 'kepe and be present at the beginning of the High Mass unto the last endyng, and the other at the beginning of evensong to the latter endynge of complayne'.[103] Thus the chaplains might share the duties among themselves.

---

[98]   GL Ms 25121/1650.
[99]   GL Ms 25121/1925.
[100] GL Ms 25138.
[101] GL Ms 25518.
[102] See Chapter 4, pp. 99–100.
[103] LMA HC roll 241(18).

It has been argued that choir duties imposed on the chantry priests raised liturgical standards in medieval parishes, since they had to be present in the choir at matins, evensong and other Divine Services, wearing surplices.[104] Daily participation seems normally to be required even if it was not specifically stipulated. Study of more informative evidence generated in a cathedral tends to support and expand this point.[105] Most chantry founders, themselves often being St Paul's members, wanted their chantry foundation to increase divine worship within the cathedral church. Their numbers would have meant that chantry chaplains would have made a significant difference to cathedral services. Thus the regulations written by Bishop de Braybroke in 1391 reminded the chaplains of their choir duties: 'to attend choir offices day and night, and to take part in processions, funeral rites, and the like'.[106] If fulfilled conscientiously, these tasks would have been heavy. These requirements filled the day:

> The day began with matins. Often this is described in the cathedral statutes and customaries as being in the middle of the night ... Lauds was immediately after matins. Then there was an interval filled by the successive chantry masses until the mass of the Virgin in the Lady Chapel at about nine a.m. The bell for prime was rung as soon as the Lady Mass was over ...Tierce was said while the celebrant was preparing for high mass at ten a.m. ... On ordinary days sext and nones were said after mass, and concluded the morning offices at about eleven a.m. The midday breakfast was followed by a break in the early afternoon. Evensong was said at three p.m.; on obit days it included vespers for the dead in choir. Then came vespers of the Blessed Virgin Mary, and compline was soon afterwards.[107]

The choir instructions left to the chaplains of Lancaster College depart from the norm. Conforming to the custom at St Paul's, the chaplains had to attend the choir for the processions, masses, vespers and compline on all principal feasts and other feasts, and in the processions, vespers and compline on Sundays.[108] The two chaplains, however, celebrated the canonical hours every day in their chapel. Similarly, the chaplain serving the chapel of the Virgin Mary in the charnel

---

[104] Clive Burgess, '"By Quick and by Dead": Wills and Pious Provision in Late Medieval Bristol', *The English Historical Review*, 405 (1987), pp. 837–58, esp. p. 850; *idem*, 'For the Increase', pp. 52–3.

[105] Clive Burgess suggests that *it is* cathedral practice that determined urban practice. Cathedrals were flagships. Personal discussion, June 2003.

[106] Simpson, *S.Paul's Cathedral and Old City Life*, p. 100.

[107] Edwards, *English Secular Cathedrals*, pp. 56–7.

[108] GL Ms 25121/1941.

house had to celebrate all canonical hours within that chapel.[109] The chaplains of Thomas More's chantry also celebrated canonical hours in their private chapel, and were thereby exempted from choir obligations.[110] Their presence was however requested during processions on Sundays and other special days, when they had to wear the chaplain's garb. Otherwise these chaplains were not expected to take part in the choir. Rather than reducing divine worship within the cathedral, these chantries enhanced it, multiplying the locations of worship within the cathedral precinct.

Musical development in the later Middle Ages was marked by the introduction of polyphony, to which secular cathedrals and colleges made an important contribution. St Paul's led the way in England by adopting the new music in the early thirteenth century.[111] The cathedral's focus on musical innovation might have attracted chantry founders to select St Paul's for their pious enterprises. Mayor John Pulteney (d.1349) left a sum of money to the almoner to provide a summer habit for the choristers of St Paul's every year.[112] In return the choristers had to sing [*cum nota*] an anthem of the Virgin in the chapel of St John the Baptist, before the image of the glorious Virgin Mary, followed by the recitation of some prayers and the intonation of specific psalms, including the *De profundis*. Undoubtedly John Pulteney was both a great admirer and promoter of the cathedral liturgy, for he also required the chaplains serving his collegiate foundation at St Laurence Pountney to wear the same vestments and to observe the canonical hours as members of the cathedral choir.[113]

Chantry founders were well aware that, for a variety of reasons, chaplains might find it impossible to discharge their religious duties as prescribed. In order to minimise any interruption of services, they inserted in their ordinances provisions for chaplains to be absent. In case of prolonged absence from the cathedral, some chaplains were obliged to find substitute chaplains, while others might be authorised to perform their services in another church.[114] If needed, the chaplains of Holme's College were allowed to perform their duty elsewhere and, in the case of illness or other handicap, another chaplain had to replace the chaplain who found himself incapable of fulfilling his obligations.[115] Attendance

---

[109] GL Ms 25513, fols 156–159.

[110] Lambeth Palace Ms 2018, fol. 2.

[111] Keene, 'From Conquest to Capital', p. 24. On polyphonic music, see Roger Bowers, *English Church Polyphony. Singers and Sources from the 14th to the 17th Century* (Aldershot, 1999).

[112] GL Ms 25271/35.

[113] Wilson, *History of the Parish*, pp. 54–7.

[114] GL Ms 25121/1650; Ms 25157.

[115] GL Ms 25145.

at services was essential for a chantry, and thus absence was not to be tolerated. Any chaplain who had no legitimate reason for absence was to be fined 2d.

Some foundation ordinances made allowance for absence. In the case of Lancaster College, each chaplain was permitted to leave the chapel for forty days, either consecutively or with intervals, each year, as long as the two chaplains were not absent at the same time.[116] They needed, however, to obtain official authorisation beforehand from the dean or from a senior resident canon. If the chaplains absented themselves for more than the days allotted to them, they were fined 1d per day, and twenty days' illicit absence would deprived them of their chantry.[117] They were not, however, to be expelled if their absence were involuntary, as in a case of sickness or other weaknesses. If they were unable to discharge all their responsibilities, they were at least to pray for the souls of the founders and compensate for their weakness by devotional prayers and other works of piety.[118] The chaplain serving FitzJames's chantry enjoyed established annual leaves of absence. He could take time off once or several times during the year as long as this did not exceed six weeks in all.[119] The two chaplains of Dowman's chantry could also absent themselves as long as their absence did not exceed one month, unless they obtained a special licence from the Master and Wardens of the guild of St Katherine of the Haberdashers, patrons of the chantry.[120]

As full members of the clergy, chantry chaplains were placed under the jurisdiction of the Dean and Chapter of St Paul's Cathedral, who judged all matters of discipline and misbehaviour. Some founders nevertheless specified behaviour they deemed unacceptable and the procedures to be followed if their chaplains transgressed. For example, the chaplains of Lancaster College were to be punished for fornication, misbehaviour through drinking and eating habits, excess in gesture and appearance, anger and so on.[121] They were to be interrogated by the Dean and Chapter. If the chaplains were found guilty three times, they were to be deprived of their positions. Likewise, the chaplains of More's chantry were to be punished for any violence and abusive language against fellow chaplains and fined 12d, which sum was to contribute to the chantry funds.[122] The Chapter Act Book and Dean Sampson's register refer to a

---

[116] GL Ms 25121/1941.
[117] The fines were to go to the chest of the New Fabric of the cathedral.
[118] GL Ms 25121/1941.
[119] LMA HC roll 240(28).
[120] GL Ms 25271/73.
[121] GL Ms 25121/1941.
[122] Lambeth Palace Ms 2018, fol. 5v.

number of cases of misconduct, but on the whole the chaplains appear to have been well behaved.[123]

Administrative and Managerial Duties

The foundation and maintenance of chantries required founders to endow them with sufficient assets to cover all recurring expenses, which included the chaplains' wages, the provision of bread, wine and wax, and the financing of the optional annual obit. Moreover, some chantries entailed the funding of additional charitable and educational provisions, which were also to be supported by the original endowments. Chantry founders were naturally careful to make detailed records concerning their endowments and specific instructions about their management plans.

Just as the provisions for selecting chaplains evolved over time, so did the instructions determining managerial strategies. Founders became increasingly precise in defining management duties and elaborating systems of supervision to minimise all risks of maladministration. In contrast to later foundation deeds, the earliest ones are remarkably succinct. For example, the foundation deed for Martin of Pattishall's chantry (1239) contains only the clause that the endowment should not be converted to other uses. Likewise the foundation charter for de Haverhull's chantry (1253 × 1257) prohibits the misappropriation of the endowment *sub interminatione anathematis*.[124] Fulk Basset's ordinances (1261) introduced the first provision for reversion should the chantry arrangement not be respected; if the Dean and Chapter failed to pay the chaplains, the bishop of London was to take over the endowment and responsibility for providing for charitable works.[125] By exploring the possibilities offered to them, founders gradually elaborated other sanctions and layers of supervision.

As discussed in Chapter 1, chantry endowments took a plurality of forms, either in rents, lands or tenements, and, depending on these forms, chantry founders elaborated different managerial practices.[126] When the original asset took the form of quit-rents issuing from a religious institution, the administrative responsibilities allocated to the Dean and Chapter were minimised: they funded the chaplains' wages and covered other maintenance costs from the given rent. For example, in return of a quit-rent provided by the Prior and Convent of St Bartholomew, Smithfield, the Dean and Chapter disbursed the annual

---

[123] See Chapter 4, pp. 101–7.
[124] GL Ms 25121/710.
[125] GL Ms 25122/286.
[126] See Chapter 1, pp. 24–7.

salary of the chaplain serving Husband's chantry and financed the celebration of his anniversary.[127] When the original asset consisted of tenements or rents issuing from tenements, the management duties allocated either to the Dean and Chapter or to the chaplains (according to the founder's preference) were far greater. They included the collection of rents, the maintenance of the tenements and the keeping of accounts.

For chantries belonging to the first category of endowments, that is, quit-rents obtained from an external institution, the cessation of payments by the 'host' institution to the cathedral authorities constituted the main danger feared by founders. In an attempt to ensure that the institution would respect its financial responsibility, founders included provisions for reversion in their instructions. In case of non-payment, the cathedral authorities were entitled to take action against the institution to recover the original endowment that had been given by the founders to that institution. Although a foundation deed for the chantry of Henry de Wingham (d.1262) does not survive, it may be assumed that such a clause was included in a similar manner to Husband's chantry charter. In 1451 the Dean and Chapter complained to the abbot of Beeleigh by Maldon in Essex regarding the delay in the payments to maintain the two chantry chaplains and de Wingham's obit.[128] They reminded him that an original endowment of 360 marks had been given by the chantry founder to the abbey in exchange for an annual rent to be paid to the Dean and Chapter. By 1424 the chaplain, William Wetwam, had already appeared before the Dean and Chapter to request compensation in lieu of salary pending payment, and this was agreed.[129] The complaint of 1451 seems to have been futile, for no subsequent reference to de Wingham's chantry was ever recorded in the cathedral archives, although his obit was celebrated until the dissolution.[130] In 1537/38, presumably following a delay in payments for Pulteney's chantries, an agreement was reached between the Dean and Chapter of St Paul's and the Master of the College St Laurence Pountney, in which the latter promised to pay one hundred marks to the former.[131]

---

[127] GL Ms 25271/32.

[128] GL Ms 25121/1919; see R.C. Fowler, 'The Abbey of Beeleigh By Maldon', in William Page (ed.), *Victoria History of the Counties of England. A History of Essex* (London, 1907), vol. 2, pp. 172–6. Fowler suggested that because many lawsuits are recorded between the cathedral and the abbey on matters of payment, the abbey never fulfilled its obligations to pay the annual rent. Nevertheless it appears from St Paul's chantry lists that chaplains were praying for de Wingham from 1271 onwards.

[129] GL Ms 25513, fol. 149.

[130] Kitching, no. 111; GL Ms 25206.

[131] GL Ms 25121/1179. A previous settlement of debts was concluded in 1446/47 between the same parties: GL Ms 25121/1174.

The right of reversion was not always allocated to the Dean and Chapter. While leaving instructions for Thomas Stowe's chantry in 1423, John Westyerd specified that if the Prior and Canons of St Bartholomew's Priory failed to fulfil their obligations towards Stowe's chantry, the right of ownership of the chantry endowment and the responsibility for meeting the associated charges were to be transferred to the wardens of the fraternity of SS Mary and Giles, located in the church of St Giles, Cripplegate.[132] It was only in the case of further failures that the Dean and Chapter were to inherit the original endowment. Presumably this arrangement was chosen because, by involving the interests of different parties, the risks that the endowment might be devoted to unintended uses were reduced. Chantry founders also resorted to reversion when the Dean and Chapter were put in direct charge of managing the original endowment. In these instances, founders allocated the right of reversion to a third party according to their preference. Dean Gilbert de Bruera authorised his chantry chaplain, the mayor of London or any alderman to take action against the Dean and Chapter of St Paul's if mismanagement showed any sign of imperilling the upkeep of St Katherine's chapel or if the maintenance of chantry tenements displayed any sign of incompetence.[133] The Dean and Chapter were then to bear the cost if they were responsible for any loss of value. On the other hand, if there had been no negligence, then the costs of the chantry were to be diminished in proportion to the loss in the tenements' value. The instructions left for John Beauchamp's chantry are similar.[134] In exchange for tenements and rents in the parish of St Mary Aldermanbury in London, the Dean and Chapter were to cover the various chantry expenses, which included the chaplain's stipend of ten marks, the wine and wax, and the annual anniversary valued at 40s. If the tenements did not generate enough income to cover these charges, the costs of Beauchamp's chantry were to be reduced proportionally. If the Dean and Chapter failed in their management duties, then the chaplain or a representative of the earl of Warwick was empowered to take possession of the tenements in order to meet the chantry's costs. The Dean and Chapter agreed that the bishop of London, or one of his officials, should act as arbiters if necessary.

Another strategy to ensure that the tenements were well maintained and produced sufficient income was to assign the entire responsibility for their management to the chantry chaplains. The earliest instance of this procedure dates from the thirteenth century, when the foundation deed of Godfrey de Acra's chantry (1262 × 1268) reveals that the chaplain was responsible for his own

---

[132] Sharpe, vol. 2, pp. 434–6.
[133] GL Ms 25121/732.
[134] GL Ms 25121/1925.

stipend, in addition to an annual charge of one pound of wax to the Dean and Chapter to illuminate major altars at the feast of the commemoration of St Paul and, after the founder's death, provide funding for his obit.[135] He also had to pay the ordinary charges linked to the tenements and, above all, finance all repairs. If the chaplain proved negligent, he was to be rebuked by the Dean and Chapter; if incorrigible, he was to be replaced. Negligence was a serious offence. The chaplain serving the chantry of Reginald de Brandon shouldered responsibilities and duties of this kind. In 1307 de Brandon's executors gave the tenements located in Friday Street to John Russingden, the first priest to occupy this chantry.[136] In return, Russingden was to keep them in good condition. Negligence was to be punished by the Dean and Chapter. The indenture for these ordinances was tripartite: one part was to be kept in the treasury of the cathedral; another by the chaplain and his successors; and the last one in the treasury of the convent of the Holy Trinity, near Aldgate. This, it may be suggested, was another means of supervision. If the chaplains or the Dean and Chapter failed to fulfil their duties, then it was intended that another party could take action against them.

Founders may have assumed that chantry chaplains, because their own sources of income were heavily dependent on the tenements, were well placed to manage them; in consequence they were put in charge of collecting the rents from tenements and overseeing any maintenance work. This form of management was not, however, without its pitfalls. As a result, founders established different kinds of strategies to secure their endowments. In order to minimise the risks of defective administration and possible corruption, founders imposed another layer of supervision by assigning a third party with responsibility for overseeing the chaplains. In 1309 Richard de Newport named the two cardinals as chantry patrons.[137] In addition to their duties in appointing chaplains, they had to inspect the tenements two or three times a year and assess whether repairs were required. Richard Grene/de Gravesend also made elaborate provisions to solve problems arising from bad administration. In his foundation deed (1310), he emphasised the need to put aside money for future work carried out on the tenements, either for new construction or for renovation.[138] He stipulated that the houses and buildings be inspected each year, without however specifying who was to make the inspection. The responsibility probably fell on a cathedral canon, either major or minor. After the inspection, the chaplain was to be informed of work to be done on the tenements, and was given a month in which to carry it out.

---

[135] GL Ms 25121/343.
[136] GL Ms 25121/1920.
[137] GL Ms 25121/741.
[138] GL Ms 25121/1962.

If he exceeded the time limit, the chaplain was to be fined. Finally, he had to give an account of his expenses.

Another means of protection was to specify that chaplains should render their accounts to the Dean and Chapter, or to another party, in addition to their other tasks. For instance, the responsibilities of de Chaddleshunt's chantry chaplain included financing any repairs required by the chantry tenements.[139] Each year two major canons had to visit these tenements to ensure that the chaplain had carried out his work effectively. In addition, the chaplain had to give account to the Dean and Chapter each year within fifteen days after Michaelmas, and if they judged the administration to be defective, then the chaplain could be replaced.

Over the years, founders also became more specific about access to a chantry's 'common chest'. Evidence from chantry regulations indicates that each chantry possessed its own chest, which was placed in its chapel or near the altar where the chantry was celebrated. Controlling access to the chantry chest was another way of safeguarding a chantry's economic security. The chaplains of Holme's College were in possession of a 'common chest', which was to have three keys, two in the hands of the two senior chaplains and the last in the hands of the cathedral chamberlain.[140] Roger Holme ordered that the chest was to be opened and closed in the presence of the three key holders only when the majority of the chaplains agreed to it. Thomas de Eure's foundation deed (1411) stipulated that any spare revenue should be kept in a 'common chest' made of iron, and the keys for this were distributed to the chamberlain, the chantry chaplain and his servant.[141] De Eure's executors expressed their unease about the depreciating value of an endowment by making provisions for money to be kept in the chantry chest that could then be used to compensate for any fall in rents in London.

Although different practices of management, relating to the different kinds of assets with which the chantries were endowed, coexisted at St Paul's Cathedral, a linear development of strategies can be observed from the earliest chantry foundation deeds to those of the mid-fifteenth century. As already discussed, chantry founders entrusted their chaplains with ever-more elaborate administrative duties. This development reached its apogee in the fifteenth century with two chantries instituted as two fully fledged corporations, those of Thomas More (1424) and Walter Sherrington (1447).[142] With incorporated status, chaplains obtained the right to plead in court, and to buy and sell lands and tenements belonging to the chantry. This tendency towards entrusting chaplains

---

[139] GL Ms 25121/860.

[140] GL Ms 25145.

[141] GL Ms 25138.

[142] *CPR, 1413–1416*, p. 365; *CPR, 1422–1429*, pp. 179–80, 269; *CPR, 1441–1446*, pp. 446, 462; Lambeth Palace Ms 2018, fol. 1v.

with an increasing weight of responsibilities came to an end in the sixteenth century. The last three chantries established at St Paul's, those of John Dowman, Richard FitzJames and John Withers, laid no management responsibilities or duties on the chaplains.[143] Moreover, the tasks to be performed by the Dean and Chapter were minimised, for these three chantries were endowed with quit-rents from city companies of London. This initial provision could have been covered by a sum of money or by the devise of tenements. In return, the city companies were obliged to provide annual quit-rents to the Dean and Chapter, who paid the chaplains' stipends from these contributions. The master and wardens were also appointed as chantry patrons. They could be asked to appoint the chaplains and to supervise the chapel in which the chantry was located. For example, the master and wardens of the fraternity of St Katherine of the Haberdashers had to inspect the ornaments and vestments belonging to Dowman's chantry once a year and notify the Dean and Chapter if any repairs were needed.[144] These foundations also included provisions for reversion in case of non-observance of the regulations. The Merchant Tailors could transfer the annual rent of twenty marks, allocated to the Dean and Chapter for FitzJames's chantry and obit, to the bishop of London if they failed to fulfil their obligations.[145] In return for its involvement, a city company could expect the chantry chaplains to participate in its own religious activities. The two chaplains serving Withers's chantry, associated to the craft of the Saddlers, were expected to attend some of the company's ceremonies and festivals, especially funerals.[146] The companies' involvement in the chantry management arose from a desire to ensure effective management of the endowments.

In short, with the passage of time, founders developed different strategies to guarantee the survival of their chantries. They became increasingly precise in their definition of chaplains' tasks and in their elaboration of systems of supervision. But, ultimately, the solution favoured by the last founders was to withdraw managerial responsibility from chaplains altogether and give it to a third party. Although the last three founders were themselves high-ranking clerics in the cathedral, they chose to place their chantry endowments in the care of London merchants. Masters and wardens of city guilds were possibly judged more reliable than chaplains, or indeed even the Dean and Chapter, since they were experienced in managing London properties. This shift is highly significant, for it expresses a new perspective on the part of founders. This change should be understood not so much as the expression of a diminishing trust in

---

[143] GL Ms 25271/73; LMA HC roll 240(28); HC roll 241(18).

[144] GL Ms 25271/73.

[145] LMA HC roll 240(28).

[146] LMA HC roll 241(18).

the chaplains' ability or in the cathedral authorities' competence to supervise, but, rather, as the acceptance of the benefits of division and specialisation of tasks. Presumably these founders believed that their endowments would have more chance of flourishing if administered by experienced business managers, rather than clerics. The spiritual quality of their foundation may, moreover, have profited from this new division of labours, for the chantry chaplains, liberated from all administrative activities, were then free to devote themselves entirely to religious occupations. Although these foundations were undoubtedly innovative, there was a precedent. When Dean John Colet reformed the cathedral grammar school in 1512, he made an endowment, sufficient to cover the costs of education for 150 boys, not to the cathedral authorities but, rather, to the Mercers' Company, to which his father had belonged.[147] Although Colet's relations with his colleagues at the cathedral were cold to the point of hostility throughout his deanship, his foundation arrangement with a city company may have influenced subsequent chantry founders.[148]

Founders all wished that their endowments should meet the various charges involved in running their chantry foundation and, in some cases, the income was also expected to finance additional beneficial provisions, which contributed to the communal, liturgical, charitable or educational life of the cathedral. Chantry endowments had to generate sufficient income to meet the principal expense, namely the chaplains' wages. Although these wages were left at the discretion of the founders, who specified the sum allocated for their chaplains in their ordinances, in practice the salaries had to meet market rates. Not surprisingly, wages were similar from one chantry to another. From the mid-thirteenth to the early fourteenth century the chaplains' income varied from four to nine marks, with an average of six marks.[149] In c.1370 the average had increased to seven marks, the highest stipend being £10 given to the chaplain serving de Acra and de Weseham's chantry.[150] Although in 1378 Archbishop Sudbury had fixed the maximum wages for stipendary priests at seven marks a year, by the end of the fourteenth century wages below ten marks appear not to have been considered sufficient to attract chaplains.[151] As a result, Bishop de Braybroke organised the

---

[147] Sharpe, vol. 2, p. 640.

[148] On John Colet, see Jonathan Arnold, *Dean John Colet of St Paul's: Humanism and Reform in Early Tudor England* (London, 2007). *Idem*, 'John Colet, Preaching and Reform at St Paul's Cathedral, 1505–19', *Historical Research*, 76/194 (2003), pp. 450–68. Christopher Harper-Bill, 'Dean Colet's Convocation Sermon and the Pre-Reformation Church in England', *History*, 73 (1988), pp. 191–210.

[149] GL Ms 25502, fols 100–101; Ms 25504, fols 93–93v., 127v.

[150] GL Ms 25121/1954.

[151] *Sudbury*, vol. 1, pp. 190–93; Hill, '*Chaunterie for Soules*', p. 243.

amalgamations of 1391 and secured an income of between eleven and fifteen marks per annum for most of the united chantries.[152] These wages appear to have related to the cost of living in London, as they remained unchanged until the dissolution. For example, Thomas More's chantry chaplains were allocated twelve marks per annum in 1424, as were Richard FitzJames's chantry chaplains a century later, in 1529.[153] Although these salaries were not exceptional, they were slightly higher than the stipends allocated to chantry chaplains elsewhere.[154] Following the reorganisation of 1438–1439, the chantry chaplains at Exeter were ensured annual wages of £4.[155] The higher wages given at St Paul's presumably related to the higher cost of living in the capital.

Chantry chaplains were not the only ones to benefit from chantry foundation. Occasionally, boy choristers could be beneficiaries. In 1318 Richard de Newport left a tenement in the parish of St Gregory to the almoner to cover the costs of maintaining the chapel of the Virgin and for the maintenance for two years of one or two choristers whose voices had broken, provided they had no other source of income.[156] A range of cathedral officers received monetary compensation for their managerial roles. For example the two cardinals received 13s 4d annually for auditing the accounts of de Gravesend's chantry.[157] More's chantry regulations called for the participation of the cathedral chamberlain in auditing the accounts and inspecting the chantry tenements. His annual wages, initially settled at 13s 4d in 1424, were increased to 13s 8d after the revision in 1432.[158] Monetary compensation certainly appears to have been discretionary, for Roger Holme allocated 10s to his chantry patrons for their contribution towards the management of his college.[159] Although the practice of including cathedral officers in chantry organisation seems primarily to have benefited the minor clergy, in at least one case major canons were to be remunerated. Thomas de Eure provided 12d as a payment to the major canons in return for conducting his annual audit.[160]

---

[152] Simpson, *Registrum Statutorum*, pp. 142–58.

[153] Lambeth Palace Ms 2018, fol. 3; LMA HC roll 240(28).

[154] Robert Swanson suggests that because of the shortage of priests, testators were offering stipends of ten marks or more to priests to pray for their souls by the mid-fifteenth century: *Church and Society in Late Medieval England* (Oxford, 1989), p. 51.

[155] Orme, 'Medieval Chantries: Part 1', p. 320.

[156] Sharpe, vol. 1, p. 281.

[157] GL Ms 25121/1957.

[158] Lambeth Palace Ms 2018, fols 4v., 6v.

[159] GL Ms 25145; Ms 25146.

[160] GL Ms 25138.

Members of the cathedral could regularly obtain remuneration by participating in the anniversaries or obits celebrated at St Paul's. An anniversary, or obit, provided for the commemoration of the funeral of an individual, by the celebration of a mass on a fixed date, either the date of the founder's death or the feast of a saint. It was expected that this celebration would be attended by the clerical community.[161] Anniversaries embodied the principle of a perpetual repetition of masses in very much the same manner as intercessory masses procured by chantry foundations; as such, chantry and obit were often compounded in the same pious foundation.[162] At St Paul's, the earliest association of chantry and anniversary in the same foundation dates from the beginning of the thirteenth century.[163] Until the dissolution of the chantries the association remained a common characteristic of the commemorative foundations of the cathedral.[164]

Although the obit consisted of a single event, beginning on one day with the celebration of the office of the dead and ending on the following morning with the mass of Requiem, its cost was far from insignificant; indeed it represented a considerable proportion of the total expenditure of chantry foundations. For example Fulk Lovel's foundation allocated 100s annually for the chaplain's wages and 50s for the anniversary.[165] In 1314, similarly, Richard Grene/de Gravesend allocated 100s to the chantry chaplains and 40s for his obit.[166] In the fifteenth century, although the chaplains' wages had increased, the cost of the obit remained the same. Of the total income of £9 6s 8d provided each year to the Dean and Chapter for the Thomas Stowe's chantry, £7 6s 8d was allocated to the chaplain, 40s for the obit, and the remainder was meant to cover other charges.[167]

The provisions for John of Gaunt's chantry reveal in detail the solemn aspects of the obit and its financial burden. As part of their obligations, the Dean and Chapter were to pay the costs of the anniversaries of the duke and duchess, held on 4 February and 12 September, respectively. At both anniversaries, a *placebo* and a *dirige*, with nine antiphons, nine psalms and nine lessons, and, on the

---

[161] For an examination of the uses and forms of the anniversary, see Clive Burgess, 'A Service for the Dead: The Form and Function of the Anniversary in Late Medieval Bristol', *Transactions of the Bristol and Gloucestershire Archaeological Society*, 105 (1987), pp. 183–211; David Lepine, '"Their Name Liveth for Evermore"?: Obits at Exeter Cathedral in the Later Middle Ages', in Caroline M. Barron and Clive Burgess (eds), *Memory and Commemoration in Medieval England. Proceedings of the 2008 Harlaxton Symposium* (forthcoming).

[162] Chiffoleau, *La comptabilité de l'Au-delà*, p. 336.

[163] GL Ms 25501, fol. 25.

[164] Kitching, nos 108–13.

[165] GL Ms 25121/605.

[166] GL Ms 25121/1962.

[167] LMA HC roll 152(42/43).

following day, a mass of Requiem at the high altar were to be celebrated with music.[168] All cathedral members were required to attend and to take part in these celebrations. In return they received a stipend, varying according to their status in the cathedral hierarchy. City officials were also paid for attending these two anniversaries. A surviving list of disbursements for the anniversaries of the duke and his consort indicates that the costs of these various charges amounted to £12 per annum.[169] One hundred and eleven obits celebrated annually at the cathedral at the beginning of the fourteenth century generated an income of £183 18s 3½d.[170] These celebrations of obits brought more than financial rewards to cathedral members; the impact of these ceremonies on the overall liturgical life of the cathedral should not be underestimated.[171]

Some chantries ensured that almsgiving was an integral part of their provisions. The major part of such distribution normally took place during the anniversaries or on feast days. The Dean and Chapter were asked to distribute half a mark to the poor at the anniversary of Dean William de Sanctae Mariae Ecclesia, on St Gregory's day (12 March).[172] The chaplain serving de Roos's chantry was to give thirty pence to thirty poor people every Good Friday.[173] De Eure's obit also included a provision for distributing 2s to the poor.[174] As patrons of de Waltham's chantry, the almoner and the cardinal were required to distribute one hundred pence to one hundred poor people at ten religious feasts.[175] The intrusion of such charitable provision within the frame of chantry foundation was a practical result of the belief in the beneficial aspects of prayers for the salvation of souls resting in purgatory.[176] Engaged in a system of reciprocity, the poor, as beneficiaries of alms, were instructed and expected to pray for the benefactor's soul. In this sense, charitable donations constituted an addition to the intercessory prayers that founders were providing for their souls. The ordinances of Holme's collegiate chantry also married pious obligation with regular acts of charity. The chaplains were required to distribute money to the

---

[168] GL Ms 25154.

[169] GL Ms 25121/1942.

[170] Simpson, *S.Paul's Cathedral and Old City Life*, p. 98.

[171] Burgess, 'A Service', pp. 204–6.

[172] GL Ms 25121/1947.

[173] Dugdale, pp. 354–7.

[174] GL Ms 25138.

[175] GL Ms 25121/1650.

[176] Burgess, 'London Parishes', p. 155; J.A.F. Thomson, 'Piety and Charity in Late Medieval London', *Journal of Ecclesiastical History*, 16 (1965), pp. 178–95, esp. p. 194; Goodall, *God's House*, p. 6.

poor on a weekly basis.[177] The chaplain who was designated to celebrate the mass of the Holy Cross with music was expected, after his mass, to go through the city and distribute forty pence to forty poor people of London or the suburbs, in exchange for prayers for all who had contributed to the foundation and maintenance of the chantry. The chaplain was to inform the next designated chaplain of where he had begun and ended his distribution, so that the money was distributed in different parts of the city each week.

The chantry regulations of St Paul's Cathedral also shed light on the question of chantry contribution to education. The first observation to be made is that none of the chaplains was required by their statutes to teach.[178] From the twelfth century onwards, the cathedral hosted a grammar school and a song-school directed by the almoner.[179] As a result there was no vacuum to fill, so it is hardly surprising that no chantry provided for teaching. Chantry provision for education was less common than poor relief.[180] Chantry priests, however, may have played an educational role on an informal basis.[181] Providing a teacher to teach local children their alphabet was not the only means by which chantries could contribute to education. They may also have provided financial support for higher study. Four chantry foundations in St Paul's Cathedral contain provisions for sending boy choristers to university. The earliest reference dates from 1320, when the chaplains of de Baldock's chantry had to contribute 30s each year for the exhibition at the university of boys chosen from among the

---

[177] GL Ms 25145.

[178] In her article Kate Heard convincingly demonstrates how the chaplain of Wilcote chantry schooled children, although no reference to that activity was prescribed in the chantry regulation, 'Death and Representation in the Fifteenth Century: The Wilcote Chantry Chapel at North Leigh', *Journal of British Archaeological Association*, 154 (2001), pp. 134–49.

[179] On the schools of St Paul's, see A.F. Leach, 'St Paul's School before Colet', *Archaeologia*, 62 (1910), pp. 191–238; Caroline M. Barron, 'The Expansion of Education in Fifteenth-Century London', in J. Blair and B. Golding (eds), *The Cloister and the World* (Oxford, 1996), pp. 219–45; and Hannes Kleineke, 'The Schoolboy's Tale: A Fifteenth-Century Voice from St Paul's School', in Davies and Prescott, *London and The Kingdom*, pp. 146–59.

[180] Nicholas Orme, 'The Dissolution of the Chantries in Devon', *Report and Transactions of the Devonshire Association*, 111 (1979), pp. 75–123, esp. p. 88. Contradictory views on the subject can be found in Kathleen E. Kennedy, 'A, B, C is for Chantry? Fifteenth-Century Provincial Merchant Education', *Medieval Perspectives*, 14 (1999), pp. 125–39, esp. p. 132.

[181] See Chapter 4, p. 100 and Chapter 5, p. 119. Nicholas Orme presents some examples of chantry priests acting as schoolmasters, but insists on their limited number, in 'Schoolmasters, 1307–1509', in Cecil Clough (ed.), *Profession, Vocation and Culture in Later Medieval England. Essays dedicated to the Memory of A.R. Myers* (Liverpool, 1982), pp. 218–41.

choristers who had been in the cathedral at least two years.[182] They were allowed
to attend either Oxford or Cambridge and undertake the study of their choice.
A surviving account proves that de Baldock's wishes were respected, for in
1410–1418 the sum of 30s was paid to boys studying in Oxford.[183] Similarly,
the provision for de Eure's chantry (1411) stipulates that the chaplain and his
servant should fund the education of poor boys who had no other means of
support, to be elected from among choristers who had been at the cathedral at
least three years.[184] The foundation of Thomas Kempe (d.1489) also contains a
clause providing a scholarship grant.[185] The income from the church of Chigwell,
appropriated to cover the foundation's costs, was to be divided into four parts,
one to pay chantry expenses, one to cover the church expenses, one to be given
to the College of Wye, Kent, for sending two scholars from grammar schools
to the university of Oxford to study law or sciences, and the final part went to
the bishop's nephew to use in charitable deeds. The instructions for Dowman's
chantry included the clause that if some of the minor clergy were absent from
his anniversary, they were excluded from payment: money saved in this way was
to go to the almoner to provide for the expenses of cathedral choristers who
'herafter shall fortune to go to lernyng to any of the universities of Cambridge or
Oxford'.[186] These examples correspond to the findings of other historians. Rather
than developing schooling facilities in York Minster, canons maintained poor
scholars at Oxford and Cambridge, while most educational benefaction made
by Lancastrian bishops consisted of sending boys of their diocese or cathedral
chapters to universities.[187]

One chantry of St Paul's included the foundation of a library. At their
induction, the chaplains of Sherrington's chantry also became librarians.[188] Hence
their daily routine also involved obligations related to the library, such as caring
for the books and opening the library. The chaplains could lend books, but only
for a certain time and with the authorisation of the Dean and Chapter. Another

---

[182] GL Ms 25501, fol. 96.

[183] GL Ms 25137/3.

[184] GL Ms 25138.

[185] TNA PROB 11/8, fols 226v.–228v.

[186] GL Ms 25271/73.

[187] R.B. Dobson, *Church and Society in the Medieval North of England* (London, 1996),
p. 210; Joel T. Rosenthal, 'Lancastrian Bishops and Educational Benefaction', in Caroline M.
Barron and Christopher Harper-Bill (eds), *The Church in Pre-Reformation Society: Essays in
Honour of F.R.H. Du Boulay* (London, 1985), pp. 199–211, esp. p. 206.

[188] Hearne, *History and Antiquities*, pp. 193–4. For more information on the library, see
Nigel Ramsay, 'The Library and Archives to 1897', in Keene, Burns and Saint, *St Paul's. The
Cathedral Church of London*, pp. 413–25, esp. pp. 415–17.

additional duty assigned to chantry chaplains consisted of preaching: the three chaplains of Thomas More's chantry, founded in 1424, had to preach at the gate of St Mary Bishopsgate hospital in Holy Week, and to encourage Londoners to pray for the soul of the founder, Thomas More.[189] In the chantry certificate of 1548, the sum of 5s 3d was allocated to the 'preachers at St Mary's Spittal'.[190]

Chantry founders took the opportunity granted to them to shape their foundations according to their own preferences. They left personalised instructions regarding the selection of priests, the religious, administrative and charitable duties assigned to them, and mechanisms devised to ensure the financial stability of their pious enterprises. Most importantly, they involved actors of their choice to participate in their projects. Chantry patrons were selected among the cathedral personnel, city officials and city companies. Founders relied on their integrity and expertise to supervise the priests assigned to their chantries and to oversee the management of their endowments.[191] The survival rate of chantry foundations at St Paul's is a testimony to their dedication. These patrons and the cathedral authorities maintained these chantries long after the founders passed away because they considered them to be worthy projects, which profited the multitude rather than the few. Chantries contributed to the multiplication of religious services that aimed to benefit the living and the dead. They also incorporated a variety of ancillary functions, ranging from almsgiving, educational sponsorship, preaching and even library keeping. These provisions were motivated by the desire to attract more prayers for the benefits of the founders' souls and to contribute to the greater good. The social benefits of the chantry foundations were manifold: money was distributed to the poor; boys sent to universities; sermons preached in London; and religious services celebrated. Both the immediate community formed by the cathedral and the surrounding community within the walls of the city of London benefited from these additional activities undertaken by the chantry chaplains of St Paul's Cathedral.

---

[189] Lambeth Palace Ms 2018, fol. 10.

[190] Kitching, no. 111.

[191] Their involvement is discussed in Chapter 4.

Chapter 3
Housing Chantries

The arrival *en masse* of chantry chaplains had many repercussions on life in the cathedral. Not only did the chaplains considerably increase the number of lesser clergy placed under the jurisdiction of the Dean and Chapter, but they also modified the physical environment of the cathedral significantly. Chantry foundation lay behind the erection of many altars and chapels, both within the cathedral church and in the precinct. Chantries also spurred the construction of colleges where, after 1391, the chaplains were obliged to reside.

Places of Worship

Chantry founders and cathedral officials employed the term *cantaria* to designate an institution, as opposed to a place, chapel or altar. Created by an endowment of soul-masses, this institution generated an activity, the celebration of religious services, that delineated the space in which it was performed.[1] As a result, although the material and physical aspects of chantries remained secondary to their foundations, the formation of such spaces was implicit in their foundations. Such chantry 'space' surrounded the altars at which the liturgical ceremonies were performed, and often integrated the tombs of chantry founders.

Spatial arrangements concerning chantries within the cathedral boundaries varied according to the founders. In their chantry ordinances, founders almost invariably left instructions designating a specific altar or chapel where the chaplains should celebrate.[2] For only three chantry foundations at St Paul's was the responsibility for assigning an altar given to the cathedral authorities.[3] What prompted the selection of a specific altar? Several factors were at work, such as availability, costs, devotion to patron saints, and attachment to a particular place within the cathedral. These factors affected different chantries in various ways,

---

[1]   Stacey Boldrick argues that the term 'space' is more appropriate than 'chapel': 'The Rise of Chantry Space in England from c.1260 to c.1400' (PhD thesis, University of Manchester, 1997), pp. 12–14.

[2]   See the Appendix for details of the location of chantries.

[3]   Geoffrey de Lucy (d.1241), Richard of St Alban (d.1240–41), Richard Grene/de Gravesend (1310).

and can only be isolated from each other with difficulty, and with a degree of caution. For example, although the selection of an existing altar may be seen as a reflection of personal devotion on the founder's part to the saint to whom the altar was dedicated, generalisations of this kind are hazardous. When chantry foundation became a popular form of pious practice from the late twelfth century onwards, many altars at St Paul's, as elsewhere, would already have been in place for some time.[4] Furthermore, in some cases there was a discrepancy between the dedication of the chantry and the dedication of the altar. Richard de Newport dedicated his chantry to God, the Virgin Mary, SS Peter and Paul, but by c.1320 his chaplains were celebrating at the altar dedicated to another saint, St Radegund.[5] On the other hand, Withers's chantry (1535) was dedicated to 'our saviour Jesus Christ his glorious mother and virgin Marie and blessed apostells and sayntes Peter and Paul', as customary, but also to 'Saint Mary Madelyn and Saint Andrew', and was established at the altars of SS Mary Magdalene and Andrew in the Long Chapel, revealing a particular devotion to these two saints.[6]

Founders' devotions to particular altars as places of worship were in many cases supplemented by placing their tombs near these altars. In this context, chantry foundation at St Paul's became the final accomplishment of their burial. These chantry founders contributed to the proliferation of funeral monuments within the cathedral, which 'secured a continuous flow of prayers on behalf of the deceased'.[7] Although bishops of London formed an important contingent among these founders, they were accompanied by cathedral dignitaries and several lay founders, including the Duke of Lancaster, John of Gaunt, and his wife Blanche, whose double tomb was situated in the cathedral chancel.[8] The

---

4   Julia Barrow, 'Vicars Choral and Chaplains in Northern European Cathedrals 1100–1250', in W.S. Sheils and Diana Wood (eds), *The Ministry: Clerical and Lay. Papers read at the 1988 Summer Meeting and the 1989 Winter Meeting of the Ecclesiastical History Society*, Studies in Church History, 26 (Oxford/Cambridge, Mass., 1990), pp. 87–97, esp. p. 93.

5   GL Ms 25121/741; Ms 25502, fols 100–101.

6   LMA HC roll 241(18).

7   Malcolm Norris, 'Later Medieval Monumental Brasses: an Urban Funerary Industry and its Representation of Death', in Steven Bassett (ed.), *Death in Towns. Urban Responses to the Dying and the Dead, 100–1600* (Leicester/London/New York, 1992), p. 184.

8   For a survey of founders' tombs, see the Appendix; and of tombs in general at St Paul's, see Carol Davidson Cragoe, 'Fabric, Tombs and Precinct 1087–1540', in Keene, Burns and Saint, *St Paul's. The Cathedral Church of London*, pp. 127–42, esp. p. 128; and Christian Steer, 'The Canons of St Paul's and their Brasses', *Transactions of the Monumental Brass Society* (forthcoming). For a discussion of the political discourse of chantry chapels and tombs, see John Goodall and Linda Monckton, 'The Chantry of Humphrey, Duke of Gloucester', in Martin Henig and Phillip G. Lindley (eds), *Alban and St Albans: Roman and*

combination of chantry and tomb appears to have been seen as a customary as well as an intrinsic association, possibly supported by church authorities. In the late thirteenth century, the archdeacon of London arbitrated in a dispute between the church of All Hallows Honey Lane and St Paul's charnel house regarding Henry de Edelmeton's chantry.[9] The dispute arose following the executors' decision to establish the chantry where de Edelmeton had expressly wished to be buried, namely in St Paul's charnel house, although he had also made provision to found a chantry in the parish church of All Hallows.[10] The ruling in favour of the charnel house suggested that an association of chantry and burial place was considered beneficial for the salvation of a founder's soul. This dispute also illustrates, however, that the association, although usual, was not automatic. For various reasons some founders may have preferred to have their chantries separated from their tombs.

The proliferation of chantries at St Paul's Cathedral clearly had repercussions on the number and availability of altars. As a response to the acute demand generated by chantry foundation, new altars were consecrated, either by the cathedral authorities or by the chantry founders themselves. At the end of the twelfth century the altar of St Radegund and the altars of SS Thomas the Martyr and Denis, to be used by Chesthunt's chantry, were set up by Bishop Fitz Neal.[11] In the 1240s, Alexander de Swereford paid for the construction of the altar of St Chad, which stood in the nave, and John Lovel built an altar near the north door of the cathedral dedicated to St Andrew.[12] Similarly, John Pulteney subsidised the construction of a new chapel in the north transept, dedicated to St John the Baptist, which the Merchant Tailors later used.[13] The lists of chantries drawn up by the cathedral authorities reflected this increase in the number of side altars, which had been established as a result of chantry foundation. In c.1253 the chantry chaplains were celebrating at nine altars and at the chapel in the bishop's palace.[14] They were serving at fifteen altars in 1271, seventeen in c.1295 and twenty-two in c.1320.[15] Furthermore, these lists reveal that it

---

Medieval Architecture, Art and Archaeology, British Archaeological Association, Conference Transactions, 24 (Leeds, 2001), pp. 231–55; Andrew Martindale, 'Patrons and Minders: The Intrusion of the Secular into Sacred Spaces in the Later Middle Ages', in Diana Wood (ed.), *The Church and the Arts* (Oxford, 1992), pp. 143–78, esp. pp. 153–4.

[9]   GL Ms 25271/79; Ms 25501, fol. 68.
[10]   Sharpe, vol. 1, p. 10.
[11]   See Chapter 1, pp. 11–12.
[12]   GL Ms 25501, fol. 44; Ms 25502, fols 100–101.
[13]   GL Ms 25271/35.
[14]   GL Ms 25504, fols 93–3v.
[15]   GL Ms 25502, fols 100–101; Ms 25504, fols 93–93v., 127v.; Ms 25505, fols 65v.–66.

was not uncommon to find two or three chantries at the same altar. Sharing an altar became common at the cathedral and prompted chantry founders to make special arrangements. While Roger Holme required his seven chaplains to celebrate masses one after the other at the altars dedicated to SS Andrew and Mary Magdalene in the chapel of the Holy Ghost in the north transept, he authorised chaplains from other chantries to use the altar of SS James and Laurence in the same chapel.[16] Respect for founders' intentions is a striking aspect of these chantry foundations: with few exceptions, the chantries remained at the same altars. The very few chantries that were moved from one altar to another were those that experienced financial difficulties at an early stage. For example, the chantry of Hugh of London successively occupied the altars of St John the Evangelist (c.1253), of the Apostles (1271), of St Hippolitus (c.1295), and of Sylvester in c.1320.[17] It seems likely, however, that the amalgamations of 1391 were accompanied by a relocation of several chantries. See Figure 3.1 for a map of St Paul's precinct.

As observed in other great churches, particular sites within the cathedral church and precinct were especially popular among chantry founders.[18] At York the majority of chantries were located in the east end and in the crossing near the burial place of St William, while the two transepts and the nave were relatively neglected.[19] Chantries were established 'along public pathways at Rochester, in the Lady Chapel at Hereford, in the west end of Exeter cathedral and in the nave at Winchester'.[20] At St Paul's Cathedral the location of chantries appears to be less concentrated at one site, but rather scattered in different parts of the church. The New Work, construction of which began in 1259, attracted a fair number of chantries.[21] It housed chantry altars dedicated to SS Dunstan, Erkenwald, George, John the Baptist, Michael and Thomas the Martyr.[22] Roger de Waltham

---

[16]   Later known as Holme's Chapel and as Long Chapel, GL Ms 25145; GL Ms 25526, fol. 6.

[17]   GL Ms 25502, fols 100–101; Ms 25504, fols 93–93v., 127v.; Ms 25505, fols 65v.–66.

[18]   Peter B.G. Binnal, 'Notes on the Medieval Altars and Chapels in Lincoln Cathedral', *The Antiquaries Journal*, 42 (1962), pp. 68–80; Eric Gee, 'The Topography of Altars, Chantries and Shrines in York Minster', *The Antiquaries Journal*, 64 (1984), pp. 337–50.

[19]   Gee, 'Topography', p. 337.

[20]   Boldrick, 'The Rise of Chantry Space', p. 217.

[21]   On the New Work, see Richard K. Morris, 'The New Work at Old St Paul's Cathedral and its Place in English Thirteenth-Century Architecture', in Linda Grant (ed.), *Medieval Art, Architecture and Archaeology in London* (London, 1990), pp. 74–100.

[22]   E. Gorton Whatley (ed.), *The Saint of London. The Life and Miracles of St Erkenwald* (Text and Translation) (Binghamton, New York, 1989); Benjamin Nilson, *Cathedral Shrines of Medieval England* (Woodbridge, 1998), p. 66.

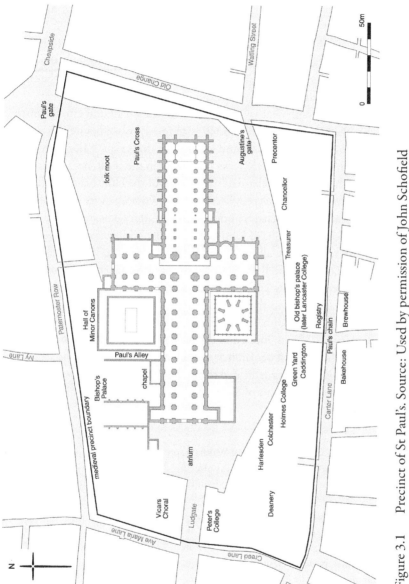

Figure 3.1　Precinct of St Paul's. Source: Used by permission of John Schofield

erected the altar of St Laurence in the south part of the choir.[23] At the beginning of the fourteenth century, altars were erected near the much venerated rood of the north door in the north transept. When Adam de Bury left instructions that he was to be buried in the chapel of the Holy Ghost, he indicated that the chapel stood near the rood.[24] The north transept also contained the chapel of St John the Baptist, granted to the Merchant Tailors by Simon Sudbury in the late fourteenth century. The south transept appears to have been less crowded, for only the chapel of St Katherine, with the altar of SS Martha and Mary Magdalene, and the chapel of St John the Evangelist, can be located there with certainty.[25]

By the mid-fourteenth century the crypt also housed a number of chantries. The tomb of William de Everdon (d.1349) occupied a place before the recently built altar in the chapel of St Radegund in the cathedral crypt.[26] The chaplains of Alan de Hotham's chantry (d.1352) also celebrated in the crypt, near the tomb of the founder, at the altar of St Sebastian.[27] The guild of the Holy Name in the Jesus Chapel was founded in the crypt.[28] The nave also contained its share of altars. Near the door leading to the chapter house stood an altar dedicated to the Virgin, where, in c.1295, the chaplains of John de Chishull's, John de Sancta Maria's and Ralph de Dunion's chantries all celebrated.[29] An image of the Virgin was located near the altar; Hamo Chigwell (d.1333) asked that his chantry be located at the altar of the image of the Blessed Mary in the Old Work.[30] Sir John Beauchamp's tomb (d.1360) was placed nearby.[31] In 1423, when leaving instructions in his will for Dean Stowe's chantry, John Westyerd requested that the chaplain celebrate at the altar of Mary the Virgin, located in the nave near Beauchamp's tomb.[32] Near that altar stood the altars of SS Thomas and Denis, in a gallery of the nave. The nave also contained the altars dedicated to St Chad and to the Apostles. Although the precise location of the altars of SS Stephen, Sylvester and Hippolitus remains

---

[23]   Sandler, 'The Chantry of Roger of Waltham', pp. 168–90.

[24]   GL Ms 25145. The north door was also the site for a temporary chantry: TNA PROB 11/9, fol. 166–167v. I am grateful to Jennifer Ledfords for this reference.

[25]   GL Ms 25271/73; Dugdale, p. 334.

[26]   GL Ms 25121/1940.

[27]   GL Ms 25264. Founder William Say (d.1468) was also buried in the crypt, near the altar of the Blessed Virgin Mary that he had renovated: TNA PROB 11/5, fols 199v.–200v.

[28]   Elizabeth A. New, 'The Jesus Chapel in St Paul's Cathedral, London: A Reconstruction of its Appearance before the Reformation', *The Antiquaries Journal*, 85 (2005), pp. 103–24.

[29]   GL Ms 25505, fols 65v.–66.

[30]   Sharpe, vol. 1, pp. 382–3.

[31]   GL Ms 25121/1925.

[32]   Sharpe, vol. 2, pp. 434–6.

uncertain, the order in which they appear in the various chantry lists suggests that they were also erected in the cathedral nave.[33]

Two stone-cage chantry chapels (free-standing chapels enclosed with screens made of stone and probably some timber) also stood in the nave. The chapel of Thomas Kempe (d.1489), dedicated to the Holy Trinity, occupied the space between the second and third piers of the nave north arcade from the crossing, while the two-storey chapel of Richard FitzJames (d.1522) presumably also stood in the nave.[34] These architectural compositions were peculiar to England, for in continental Europe the construction of chapels incorporated pre-existing structures: for example, at Notre-Dame in Paris the spaces between the buttresses provided for thirty-five chantries.[35] In addition to the use of these pre-existing structures, in England a more *ad hoc* approach enabled the development of stone-cage chantry chapels.[36] Art historians have considered these architectural structures as a characteristic of the appropriation of public space for exclusively private uses, since they were 'inherently anti-communal'.[37] Recent research, however, highlights the public use made of chantry chapels.[38] For example, the devotional programmes represented in the screens, inside and outside, of these chapels may have been used by the congregation for their own pious ends.[39] Furthermore, enclosed chapels may have provided oases of calm and spiritual focus in a very crowded establishment, where secular activity, including business negotiations, was customary.[40]

Chantry foundations not only reshaped the interior of the cathedral church with the erection of numerous altars and chapels; they also modified the cathedral precinct. A number of additional chapels, built to accommodate chantries, were located mainly on the north side of the precinct. The earliest extra-mural foundation (1199) was established in the old bishop's palace, south of the precinct, but by the 1230s, the chantry of Bishop William of Ste-Mère-

---

[33]   GL Ms 25502, fols 100–101; Ms 25505, fols 65v.–66.

[34]   John Stow, *A Survey of London*. Reprinted from the text of 1603, introduction and edition by Charles L. Kingsford (Oxford, 1908), vol. 1, p. 337.

[35]   Howard Colvin, *Architecture and the After-Life* (New Haven/London, 1991), p. 155.

[36]   Paul Binski, *Medieval Death, Ritual and Representation* (London, 1996), p. 118.

[37]   *Ibid.*, p. 120.

[38]   Simon Roffey, *The Medieval Chantry Chapel. An Archaeology* (Woodbridge, 2007), Chapter 6.

[39]   For an example of specific devotions illustrated by the decoration of a chapel, see Nicholas Orme, 'Sir John Speke and His Chapel in Exeter Cathedral', *Report and Transactions of the Devonshire Association*, 118 (1986), pp. 25–41.

[40]   Keene, 'From Conquest to Capital', pp. 27–9; Barron and Rousseau, 'Cathedral, City and State', pp. 38–9.

Eglise was relocated in the new palace, which lay north of the cathedral nave, bounded on the east by Paul's Alley and on the west by Ave Maria Lane. The palace comprised a great hall, apartments and a walled garden, and the chapel dedicated to the Virgin Mary which housed the chantry.[41] Also lying to the north of the cathedral, adjacent to the north transept, was the Pardon Churchyard. While Thomas More was dean (1406–1421) the cloister surrounding the Pardon Churchyard was rebuilt and a chapel, dedicated to SS Anne and Thomas the Martyr, erected in its centre. Dean More set up his chantry of three priests within this chapel.[42] Soon after, John Carpenter, the city's common clerk, subsidised the painting of the Dance of Death on thirty-six boards, each one portraying a skeleton leading by the hand a character representative of a level of medieval society, to be hung on the four cloister walls.[43] The Dance of Death paintings were accompanied by a dialogue in poetic form, between the skeletons and the respective characters. Stow reported that John Lydgate, a monk of Bury St Edmund's, had translated these verses from French into English based on those accompanying the *Danse Macabre* painted at the cemetery of the Holy Innocents of Paris, which he had visited during his stay in the French capital in the mid-1420s.[44] In the mid-fifteenth century another chapel was built in the Pardon Churchyard cloister to house a chantry: Sherrington's chapel dedicated to the Virgin and St Nicholas stood near the door of the north transept. Walter Sherrington also constructed a library, which was located on the second storey of the east wing of the Pardon Churchyard cloister.[45]

The charnel house owes its foundation to the major construction work undertaken on the site of the cathedral in the twelfth century. The excavations made for the crypt of the New Work uncovered graves and bones from the cathedral cemetery, which required a new shelter. This repository for the bones was located on the north side of the cathedral precinct, beyond the Canons Alley, and formed a vaulted structure.[46] In the 1270s a chapel dedicated to the

---

[41] G.H. Cook, *Old St Paul's Cathedral. A Lost Glory of Medieval London* (London, 1955), p. 65.

[42] Lambeth Palace Ms 2018, fol. 1.

[43] Amy Appleford, 'The Dance of Death in London: John Carpenter, John Lydgate, and the Daunce of Poulys', *Journal of Medieval and Early Modern Studies*, 38 (2008), pp. 285–314; Sophie Oosterwijk, 'Of Corpes, Constables and Kings: The Danse Macabre in Late Medieval and Renaissance Culture', *The Journal of the British Archaeological Association*, 157 (2004), pp. 61–90; J.M. Clark, *The Dance of Death in the Middle Ages and Renaissance* (Glasgow, 1950).

[44] Stow, *Survey of London*, vol. 1, p. 327.

[45] See Chapter 2, p. 64.

[46] Cook, *Old St Paul's Cathedral*, pp. 67–8.

Virgin Mary was added to this charnel house. The charnel house and its chapel aroused the interest of Londoners, who expressed a desire to be buried there and in some cases to have chaplains praying expressly for their souls. Within a few years of its construction, the chapel housed the chantries of Roger Beyvin (1278), Henry de Edelmeton (1281) and Aveline of St Olave (1282–83).[47] The chapel seems to have been a combined project, in which both the cathedral authorities and the city government participated. In 1282 the mayor Henry le Waleys and the commonalty of Londoners agreed to contribute ten marks per year towards the cost of the new chapel and a further five marks to maintain a chaplain there.[48] This 'communal chantry' offered perpetual intercessory prayers for the welfare of the bishop, the Dean and Chapter, the mayor and Londoners, and all the faithful departed. The right of appointment was granted to the mayor, as was the case for Roger Beyvin's chantry. When the chaplain Hugh de Sturmere received custody of the chapel in 1302, he was required to open the doors to pilgrims, who were to have access to the charnel house every Friday and on certain days, such the Feast of the Dedication of the cathedral, three days after Whitsun, and the feast of the Relics.[49] The chaplain had to meet the costs of any repairs to the house and provide candles for the chapel. He also collected the doles offered by the pilgrims and kept custody of the funds. It appears that the 'communal chantry' and the chantry of Roger Beyvin were amalgamated at an early stage. This suggestion is based on the fact that although the mayor of London inherited the right of appointment for the 'communal chantry', no records of such an appointment were ever registered in the city archives, while a number of civic appointments were made to Beyvin's chantry.[50] The chaplain of this double foundation also acted as warden of the charnel house. It was in this capacity that in 1447 Walter Hammes appeared before the Dean and Chapter to defend his title to the donations made in the charnel house.[51] Richard Hayman, rector of St Faith's parish church, had asserted that because the charnel house lay within the boundaries of his parish, he was entitled to claim tithes on the

---

[47] Sharpe, vol. 1, pp. 29–30; GL Ms 25121/1955; Ms 25271/79; Ms 25501, fol. 68. In 1278 Walter de Vaus left 12d for the fabric of the chapel, and between 1277 and 1283 Dyonisia de Montchesney left a quarter of wheat for the maintenance of the chapel and the sustenance of the chaplains celebrating there; GL Ms 25271/6; Ms 25122/464. Another donation was made in 1279 by Hamo de Wrokeshelle; Sharpe, vol. 1, p. 42.

[48] GL Ms 25501, fol. 103.

[49] GL Ms 25121/1956.

[50] For specific appointments, see Marie-Hélène Rousseau, 'Chantry Chaplains at St Paul's Cathedral, London c. 1200–1548', *Medieval Prosopography*, 26 (2005), Table 1.

[51] GL Ms 25513, fol. 259v.

offerings there. The claim was overruled, and the warden of the charnel house retained his financial privileges.

Londoners took the fate of the charnel house seriously. When in 1379 the charnel house was in decay, they responded to the call for help sent by Simon Sudbury, archbishop of Canterbury, who promised a 'great pardon' to all who contributed towards its restoration. As a result, the fraternity of All Souls was formed to repair and maintain the chapel.[52] Nevertheless, the chantry of Henry de Edelmeton located there was last referred to in c.1370, while the chantry of Aveline of St Olave was amalgamated with Walter de Thorp's chantry in 1391 and relocated in the cathedral church.[53] The need for supplementary financial assistance presumably prompted John Carpenter, the city's common clerk, to augment the original endowment of Beyvin's chantry in the 1430s. In his role as executor of Richard Whittington's will, he allocated funds to produce an annual stipend of eight marks to support the chaplain of the charnel house, whose duties included prayers for the original founder, Roger Beyvin, as well as for Whittington and Carpenter himself.[54] This additional augmentation to the original chantry foundation strengthened the ties between the charnel house and the city of London, ties that were already strong. In 1418 John Bryggewater, who served Beyvin's chantry, had received an annual civic livery from the mayor of London in 'recognition of his great services'.[55] Furthermore, Henry Barton (d.1435), skinner and twice mayor of London, requested that the mayor, aldermen and most of the city's leading citizens attend his obit to be celebrated at the charnel house on All Saints' Day and All Souls' Day.[56] It appears that Barton's commemorative plans also included a chantry. In 1439 Robert Candeler alias Heyward was appointed to serve the chantry for Henry Barton and John Barry in the charnel house, but this appointment remains the only reference to any such chantry.[57] Not surprisingly, Barton also asked to be buried in the charnel house. Stow recorded his tomb and an effigy in the charnel house, together with the tombs of two other skinners.[58] At St Paul's, the choice of the charnel house as a burial site by skinners appears to have been individualised

---

[52] Westlake, *Parish Gilds*, p. 28.

[53] GL Ms 25121/1953, 1954.

[54] GL Ms 25513, fols 156–159.

[55] *Letter-Book I*, p. 194; also LMA, Journal 1, fol. 14.

[56] Barton's will is translated in J.E. Price, *A Descriptive Account of the Guildhall of the City of London* (London, 1886), pp. 123–5.

[57] GL Ms 25513, fol. 177v. It was presumably a temporary chantry. Therefore it was not included in the Appendix.

[58] Stow, *Survey*, vol. 1, pp. 329–30.

rather than institutionalised as at Exeter, where the company of skinners had adopted the charnel house as burial sites.[59]

In short, the charnel house formed a bridge between the city government and the cathedral community until the Reformation. The chamberlain of London was responsible for supervising the upkeep of the fabric, and each time a vacancy occurred at the charnel house, the mayor of London presented the Dean and Chapter with a chaplain who joined the lesser clergy of the cathedral.[60] These appointments may have made a significant impression on the cathedral community; for example the last chaplain, Edmund Brograve, held the post for over forty years before being dismissed in 1548.[61] In the same year the charnel house was demolished and the bones hitherto sheltered were removed to Finsbury Field.[62]

Places of Residence

Chantry foundations modified the physical environment in which they were established not simply by requiring a site for celebration, but also by creating a need for their celebrants' accommodation. *Ad hoc* solutions were found for chantries established in parishes; as a result, chantry chaplains often lodged with parish incumbents. In some cases founders provided houses for their chaplains.[63] At St Paul's, it seems that only in the early fourteenth century was a specific area provided for housing chantry chaplains. Earlier than this it is possible that some chaplains rented chambers in one of the many buildings situated within the close, while others found their own accommodation in the city of London. Only rarely were specific lodgings provided when chaplains were appointed to chantries. In 1275, John de Braynford's house on Do Little Lane in the parish of St Mary Magdalene Old Fish Street was given to his first chaplain, John de Camera, as his residence.[64] The chaplain was to keep the house in good condition at his own

---

[59] Nicholas Orme, 'The Charnel House of Exeter Cathedral', in Francis Kelly (ed.), *Medieval Art and Architecture at Exeter Cathedral* (Oxford, 1991), pp. 162–71, esp. p. 166.

[60] LMA, Repertories vol. 2, fol. 98. In 1510 the chamberlain undertook reparations at the charnel house.

[61] LMA, Journal 10, fol. 313v.; Repertories vol. 12, fol. 29.

[62] See Chapter 6, p. 159.

[63] W.A. Pantin, 'Chantry Priests' Houses and Other Medieval Lodgings', *Medieval Archaeology*, 111 (1959), pp. 216–58, esp. p. 217; and C.J. Godfrey, 'The Chantries of Mere and Their Priests', *The Wiltshire Archaeological and Natural History Magazine*, 55 (1953), pp. 153–60.

[64] GL Ms 25121/1934.

expense and transfer it to his successor. In 1307, Walter de Blockele bequeathed a house on Ivy Lane in the parish of St Nicholas to his chantry chaplain.[65] The house was of two parts: one had belonged to de Blockele himself; the other had been allocated to him by the Dean and Chapter, as he had been the chaplain of Roger de La Legh's chantry. This particular example would seem to suggest that the Dean and Chapter provided the chantry chaplains, or at least some of them, with lodging in London: there is no evidence that Roger de La Legh provided a house for his chantry chaplain. At his death, Walter de Blockele transferred the house both to the chaplain who would serve his chantry and to the chaplain of Roger de La Legh's chantry. They were to share the house, but if they did not want to live together, de Blockele left instructions that the house was to go to one of them. In exchange for the house, he, or both of them if they lived in it together, had to pay each year at de Blockele's obit one penny to every one present at the service.

The early fourteenth-century boom in chantry foundation considerably increased both the number of chaplains celebrating private masses in the cathedral and the number who participated in choir services. Such an increase had a direct impact on the availability of lodgings, since chaplains needed to be lodged within a reasonable distance of the cathedral precinct to fulfil their choir obligations. Housing must have become an acute problem during these years, and the understandable shortage of proper lodgings in London may have influenced the Dean and Chapter to allocate land within the cathedral close to chantry chaplains. The resulting accommodation would have relieved chaplains of the need to wander in the city at night. In 1315 Nicholas Husband, minor canon, petitioned the Dean and Chapter for a piece of land within the cathedral precinct, because he was concerned about the journey home along the dimly lit streets of London by night.[66] He feared the crowd of thieves, criminals and 'loose women' who then took possession of the city. The Dean and Chapter took the complaint seriously: Husband was granted a piece of land within the precinct boundaries near Sermon Lane.[67]

The first mention of a house for chaplains is in 1320, when the chaplains serving the newly founded chantry of Ralph de Baldock were given a house built at the founder's expense. The house was said to be located near the *mans[ionem](?) aliorum capellanorum*, revealing that there was already a lodging

---

[65]   Sharpe, vol. 1, pp. 184–5.

[66]   GL Ms 25121/621.

[67]   Brooke, 'Early Times', p. 74. In a later petition Husband requested the right to have access to the cathedral from his house through the cloister by day and by night: GL Ms 25121/1855 and translation in H.C. Maxwell Lyte, *Ninth Report of the Royal Commission on Historical Manuscripts* (London, 1883), p. 105.

for chaplains within the cathedral boundaries.[68] In 1328 Roger de Waltham also provided chambers for his two chantry chaplains within the 'close of the chaplains', the *area clausi capellanorum*.[69] His charter also refers to a chamber for de Mondene's chantry chaplain. In another document (dated 1330), Robert de Mondene granted to chaplain John de Henle the chamber belonging to his brother's chantry, described as *de novo edificatam*.[70] This would suggest that the close of the chaplains was being built throughout the 1320s. At first the *clausum capellanorum* seems to have referred only to a specific area within the precinct walls, as opposed to a definite structure. The building seems to have been composed of separate units. According to Roger de Waltham's chantry ordinances of 1328, the site for building rooms for his chantry priest assigned to Roger by the Dean and Chapter was next to the chamber of de Mondene's chantry chaplain.[71] The actual size was left to Roger de Waltham's discretion, provided that it did not exceed forty feet in length. The fact that the document designates his rooms as *domos* instead of *camere*, as had been the case for the room of de Mondene's chantry chaplain, may suggest that de Waltham's rooms were to be of an unusual size. Over the years, as more rooms were constructed, the chaplains' close seems to have been transformed into a more complex establishment, a building with communal elements. In 1366, the chaplain assigned to Gilbert de Bruera's chantry received the east room within the gate of the close of the chaplains, built over the cellar of the said chaplains.[72] The room was enhanced on the west side with a chimney [*camino*] and wardrobe [*garderobe*]. The chaplain was to have the free access to this room, which de Bruera had built at his own expense.

These chambers became part of the chantry endowments and were allocated to the chaplains at their induction. The Dean and Chapter presumably financed the construction of chambers for individual chantries that did not have specific lodgings. Furthermore, when founders did provide accommodation, the Dean and Chapter took some responsibilities for the premises. The 1328 ordinances for Roger de Waltham's chantry clearly stipulated that the chaplains were to be evicted by the Dean and Chapter from their chambers if they did not themselves live there.[73] On no occasion were they allowed to sublet their rooms to other chaplains. The chaplains were also to be expelled from their chambers should

---

[68] GL Ms 25501, fol. 96.

[69] GL Ms 25121/1938.

[70] GL Ms 25121/1918.

[71] GL Ms 25121/1938. The location the chamber of John de Mondene is said to be *ultra portam dicti clausi capellanorum*.

[72] GL Ms 25121/732.

[73] GL Ms 25121/1938.

they fail to fulfil their choir duties, or if they failed to keep them in good condition at their own expense.[74]

When did the 'close of the chaplains' cease to be a collection of individual lodgings and take the form of a common house? In 1366 the building was still referred to as the *clausum capellanorum*.[75] But by 1391 it was known as the *Presteshous*, when Bishop de Braybroke required all the chaplains serving the united chantries, and members of the cathedral choir, to reside there if they were not already members of another college.[76] The chaplains who, as a result of de Braybroke's amalgamations, had a claim on two chambers had to choose one of them, and the Dean and Chapter would then assign the spare chambers to those chaplains who had none. In this way residence at the *Presteshous* appears to have become the norm for St Paul's chantry chaplains. In 1424 thirty-five chaplains lived there.[77] At the beginning of the sixteenth century, when Dean Colet reiterated the obligation of the chaplains, who were members of the cathedral choir, to reside in the chaplains' house, he referred to the house as St Peter's College.[78] The old name did not, however, totally disappear. In expressing his desire for John Withers's chantry chaplains to dwell there in 1535, Robert Brokel explicitly referred to 'St Peter's College otherwise called Prestes house'.[79]

This communal house was located on the west side of the cathedral precinct.[80] The 1424 document refers to common stairs, which suggests that the *Presteshous* had at least two storeys.[81] The three chaplains of Thomas More's chantry were given the right of access through the common door and use of the common stairs to reach their own chambers. The stairs were situated in the room of John Gloucester serving Hiltoft's chantry, and it appears that some of the chaplains had more than one room. In 1541, John Harryson referred to his high and low chambers.[82] Furthermore, the house also contained communal areas, such as a

---

[74]　GL Ms 25121/1650.

[75]　GL Ms 25121/732.

[76]　Simpson, *Registrum Statutorum*, p. 149.

[77]　GL Ms 25121/1960.

[78]　Simpson, *S.Paul's Cathedral and Old City Life*, Chapter 5; Jonathan Arnold, 'John Colet and A Lost Manuscript of 1506', *History* 89 (2004), pp. 174–92.

[79]　LMA HC roll 241(18). Roderick MacLeod mistakenly referred to the *Presteshous* and St Peter's College as two distinct buildings, in 'The Topography of St Paul's Precinct, 1200–1500', *London Topographical Society*, 26 (1990), pp. 1–14.

[80]　Stow, *Survey*, vol. 2, p. 21.

[81]　GL Ms 25121/1960.

[82]　GL Ms 25626/1, fol. 25.

chapel and a room where chaplains gathered for meals.[83] The *Presteshous* never obtained an incorporated status.[84] The 1424 agreement concluded between its chaplains and the chaplains of More's chantry was witnessed by all the residents named individually.[85] The Dean and Chapter took responsibility for the regulation and maintenance of the *Presteshous*, and held the property for the chaplains' use. The chaplains were all individually responsible for their own chambers. When, in 1422, Thomas Markand received an empty and ruinous chamber in the *Presteshous*, he promised the Dean and Chapter that he would undertake the work necessary to renovate it.[86] Even when, in 1431, three chaplains obtained the right to build new chambers in the vacant space allocated to them, they were to cover the charges separately, and their successors were to pay rent individually.[87] Bishop William Gray granted a piece of vacant ground to these three chaplains, forty feet in length, with the chamber of de Brandon and de Newport's chantry to the west and the house of Thomas More's chantry to the east. The plot was eight feet wide with the decayed chamber of Hiltoft's chantry to the south and the walls (of the *Presteshous*) to the north. The three chaplains were given the right to demolish the old chamber of Hiltoft's chantry and to use the land to build three new chambers. Only in the case of Thomas More's chantry, where the chaplains formed a corporate identity, were they communally responsible for their annual rent of 20s.[88] In the course of fifteenth century, however, official positions – two proctors and a pittancer – emerged within the *Presteshous* and these offices were held by chantry chaplains. In 1442 the Dean and Chapter put them in charge of locking the common door at night, at eight o'clock in winter, and at nine o'clock in summer.[89] Each was in turn to be responsible for the door key for a week at a time. The two proctors must have been representatives of the chaplains living at the *Presteshous*, although there is no information about their mode of election or nomination. The allusion to a *pitanciarius* suggests that someone was in charge of the distribution of food. In addition to these elective positions, paid staff kept the place in good shape. In their wills, chaplains referred to room keepers, servants and launders.[90] When Dean Colet compiled his statutes regulating the chantry chaplains at St Paul's, he required that a copy should be placed in the hall of

---

[83] The chapel is referred to in the will of Thomas Surdevall (d.1522): TNA PROB 11/20, fol. 228. For the meals, see Chapter 4, p. 104.

[84] Edwards, *English Secular Cathedrals*, p. 300.

[85] GL Ms 25121/1960.

[86] GL Ms 25121/1922.

[87] GL Ms 25121/1950.

[88] GL Ms 25121/1960; Lambeth Palace Ms 2018, fol. 3.

[89] GL Ms 25513, fol. 206.

[90] GL Ms 25626/1, fols 24, 31–31v.

St Peter's College, thus emphasising the importance of the college in the lives of the chantry chaplains.[91] Apart from those chantries where the chaplains were chosen from among the minor canons, and the chantry colleges such as Holme's College and Lancaster College, all chantry chaplains were residents of St Peter's College.[92]

Did the chantry priests keep the same chamber, or was there a rotation of chambers as there was a rotation of chantries? The chaplain John Gloucester was in the same room in 1424 and in 1431, but since he was serving the same chantry, this is not surprising.[93] When Simon Deken resigned from de Eyton's chantry on 3 October 1418 in order to accept the combined chantry of de Brandon and de Newport, he had to vacate his room at the *Presteshous*.[94] At his new admission, he had to swear a new oath of residence, and the Dean and Chapter then allocated him a different room. His former chamber was then assigned not to de Eyton's new chaplain, but to Thomas Rothel, chaplain of de Everdon and de Dunion's chantry.[95] Since Thomas Rothel had already, at his admission on 30 March 1418, sworn an oath of residence, it may be assumed that he had lived in another room during these few months before being transferred to this new room.[96] This suggests some kind of chamber rotation within the *Presteshous*. An entry in the Chapter Act Book suggests that the chaplains could sometimes choose their room. On 31 July 1424, when Edmund Baldwyn was admitted at the chantry of de Northburgh and de Idesworth, he was asked to select one of two chambers in the *Presteshous* offered to him by the Dean and Chapter.[97]

As already discussed, the establishment of the *Presteshous* appears to have been the result of *ad hoc* interventions by chantry founders and the cathedral authorities. St Paul's Cathedral was the first secular cathedral to have such an institution, and the *Presteshous* was clearly created in response to the chantry foundation boom experienced by St Paul's in the late thirteenth and early fourteenth centuries, which precipitated a shortage of chaplains' housing.[98] The *Presteshous* preceded similar establishments in other English secular cathedrals. Colleges for chantry priests were set up at Wells in 1401, while Lichfield established a house for its

[91]   Simpson, *S.Paul's Cathedral and Old City Life*, p. 112.

[92]   There were two other exceptions: the chaplains serving the chantries of Bishop William of Ste-Mère-Eglise and of Roger Beyvin.

[93]   GL Ms 25121/1960; Ms 25121/1950.

[94]   GL Ms 25513, fol. 61v.

[95]   GL Ms 25513, fols 61–62.

[96]   GL Ms 25513, fol. 59v.

[97]   GL Ms 25513, fol. 99.

[98]   Edwards, *English Secular Cathedrals*, p. 300.

chantry chaplains in 1415.[99] As with the *Presteshous*, these common halls of residence were put under the jurisdiction of the Dean and Chapter and lacked a corporate status. St William's College, established at York Minster in 1461, was an exception.[100] In this case, the chantry priests formed a corporate body, obtained a common seal, and had the right to purchase and hold lands in common. The later date of foundation may explain its exceptional nature.

At about the same time that Bishop de Braybroke compelled all chantry chaplains to live together as a community, Roger Holme, major canon, lavishly augmented the recently founded chantry for Adam de Bury. Not only did Holme increase the number of chaplains from three to seven, but he also provided them with a place to live and rules to follow. Like Bishop de Braybroke, Canon Roger Holme was convinced of the advantages of a communal life. In the ordinances for his college, he explained his motives by citing a passage from the Gospels which stated that when a few disciples came together in Christ's name, then Christ would be among them:

> Et congregacionem instituere dignebat(ur) cum disciplos elegit et in unum p(ar)it(er) congregavit dicens illis ubi duo vel tres congregati fu(er)int in nomine meo in medio eorum sum.[101]

London witnessed the foundation of a number of colleges between c.1340 and c.1450. The College of St Laurence Pountney (1344) was served by thirteen chaplains, Walworth's College in St Michael Crooked Lane (1381) by ten chaplains, while the College in the Guildhall Chapel (1368) and Whittington's College (1424) both had five chaplains. Only the College in All Hallows Barking (1442) was served by two chaplains.[102] In founding colleges, the benefactors could draw up their own rules to be observed by the chaplains, and the exercise of this degree of control over their chaplains' lives may have appealed to founders.[103]

---

[99]   It appears that the attempt to unite all chantry chaplains in one communal establishment at Exeter in 1410 did not succeed. It was only in the late 1520s that they obtained a common residence. See Orme, 'Medieval Clergy: 1. Vicars and Annuellars', p. 98.

[100]   J.A. Thomson, *The Early Tudor Church and Society, 1485–1529* (London/New York, 1993), p. 185; see P.R. Newman, *The History of St William's College* (York, 1994).

[101]   GL Ms 25146; Matthew 18:20.

[102]   M. Reddan, 'Religious Houses', in William Page (ed.), *Victoria History of the Counties of England*, vol. 1: *A History of London*, (London, 1908), pp. 574–80; repr. in Barron and Davies, *Religious Houses*, pp. 196–226; Caroline M. Barron, *The Medieval Guildhall of London* (London, 1974), pp. 35–9; S.J. O'Connor (ed.), *A Calendar of the Cartularies of John Pyel and Adam Fraunceys*, Camden, 5th series, 2 (London, 1993).

[103]   For examples of set rules for chantry college, see E.K. Bennett, 'Notes on the Original Statutes of the College of St John Evangelist of Rushworth, co. Norfolk; founded by Edmund

Canon Roger Holme required his chaplains to live together, and he built a house for this purpose in the cathedral close, between the southern wall and the east gate of Saint Augustine.[104] The dimensions of the house were not recorded, but it was of sufficient size to lodge seven chaplains, and included a kitchen and a dinner room.[105] Holme left his chaplains detailed ordinances, which were drawn up to ensure harmonious relations between them, but also to develop a sense of community and of belonging to the college by exclusivity, secrecy and oaths. At their admission to the college, the chaplains had to swear publicly to keep confidential all secrets of the house and to observe all the rules, which were to be read four times a year before the whole community. It was the chaplains' responsibility to be present at these readings, so that afterwards they could not pretend ignorance.[106] The chaplains had to contribute to the common housing by paying entry fees of 10s. In order to ensure order and control, Roger Holme established a self-regulating system of surveillance by the chaplains based on a rota. Each year two different proctors were chosen from among the seven chaplains to supervise and provide for the good harmony of the group, in addition to their administrative role in supervising the college endowment.[107] They were to be responsible for punishing disobedient chaplains and giving them the appropriate penalties, according to the table of graded offences and fines established by Holme himself. The proctors had then to redistribute the money collected in fines to the chaplains in the form of pittances. Holme may have established this system because it discouraged chaplains from disobeying the rules for fear of the financial penalties, and also because it encouraged the chaplains to report faults. The community gained directly from correcting the errors of others. Instead of causing conflicts within the group, this self-regulating system may have increased the sense of community by eliminating as far as possible external interference in the internal management of the college.

Another way of ensuring the chaplains' concern for the welfare of the college was to give them the regular responsibility for its daily management. Each week, in turn, beginning with the senior member, a chaplain was to be designated as the steward. At the beginning of his term of office, that is, on Friday or on Saturday

---

Gonville AD 1342', *Norfolk Archaeology*, X (1888), pp. 50–64; A. Hamilton Thompson, 'The Early History of the College of Irthlingborough', *Northampton and Oakham Architectural Society*, 35 (1920), pp. 267–85.

[104] GL Ms 25121/1737.

[105] GL Ms 25146; Ms 25626/1, fols 49–49v.

[106] The same instructions were given to Whittington's College; see Jean Imray, *The Charity of Richard Whittington. A History of the Trust administred by the Mercers' Company, 1424–1966* (London, 1968), p. 36.

[107] GL Ms 25146.

after the midday meal, he would receive all common goods [*communas*] and the accounts of the past week's expenses. If the accounts were not handed over within two days, the previous steward was to be fined 6d. Each steward was to be paid 12d for his labour, and he was expected to spend the college money wisely for the common good. At all times he was to carry on him the key for the food cupboard and to supervise the provision of bread, beer, meat and other condiments, and he was in charge of all purchases and the distributions of all allowances. At the end of the week, the steward had to be able to give a detailed account of all transactions. Undoubtedly, involving each chaplain in turn in college management was aimed at curtailing any excess in spending or carelessness in accounting.

The college ordinances mention various fees charged to the chaplains. A chaplain who stayed more than five days was considered a full commoner [*integer communarius*] and one who stayed less than three days a half commoner [*dimidius communarius*]. This distinction between half and full commoners may suggest that the college provided temporary boarding for visiting chaplains who came to the cathedral only for short periods of time. On the other hand, it was likely that the chaplains of Holme's College would be expected to take on administrative duties in the cathedral, which might involve occasional absence from the college. The second hypothesis appears more likely, for chantry chaplains were often chosen to undertake administrative work for the cathedral.[108] Guests were, however, welcomed at the college, probably the friends or relations of the chaplains, and they paid 4d for their daily expenses to the steward, that is 3d for the midday meal and 1d for the evening meal. If the guest was a priest he had to pay only 2d. Chantry benefactors were exempted from payment.[109] In the same way, these benefactors were the only ones who enjoyed the privilege of being admitted to the college meetings. The rules concerning women were also very strict. Women whose reputations were doubtful were not allowed inside the house, and fines for any offence were as high as 40d; however, women who were considered to be virtuous could enter the house, but only in certain circumstances in order to prevent scandal.[110] Any physical violence between chaplains was punished by a substantial fine.

Roger Holme also insisted on communal meals. Attendance at the midday and evening meals was compulsory throughout the year. Each chaplain was

---

[108] See Chapter 5, p. 128.

[109] Roger Holme drew up a long list of the chantry patrons and benefactors of his chantry, see Chapter 2, p. 45.

[110] The special circumstances are not specified. However, in the rules of the College in the Guildhall Chapel laid down by Bishop Bonner in 1542, no woman was allowed within the college except in case of illness. See Reddan, 'Religious Houses', pp. 576–7.

allowed to have one drink (possibly a tankard of beer) after grace at midday, and two after grace at the evening meal, and during fast days they could have two drinks at dinner, but apparently none at midday. At the midday meal, the chaplain who had been steward the previous week would read every day from the legends of the saints [*lectionem de legenda sanctorum*] or from any noteworthy reading [*de aliqua notabi lectura*] to all the chaplains. He would also say grace during the week. After the meal each chaplain would spend time in reading, prayers or other appropriate occupation in his chamber, or elsewhere, as he thought best. Meals therefore seem to have been the main focus during the day when the chaplains gathered together and enjoyed a communal life, and even if there was reading during the meals, silence was not imposed. We may imagine that the chaplains took advantage of this time for discussion or to settle affairs between themselves. The fact that meals were accompanied by public reading, and that private reading was also one of the after-meal activities proposed for the chaplains, suggests that Roger Holme may have provided his college with some books to be kept within the college and put at the disposal of all the chaplains. There are, however, no references to specific books. Other events that must have shaped the college's sense of community were the weekly religious celebrations, which were performed by the chaplains over and above their specific chantry duties in their college. Each Saturday the chaplains had to sing various antiphons of the Holy Ghost: *Veni sancte*; *Emitte spiritum tuum*; *Deus qui caritate dona p(er) gratiam sancti spiritu*, and to pray especially for the founders and friends of Holme's College, and to recite *De profundis*. When they had performed their religious and commemorative duties, the chaplains had the chance to socialise, for Roger Holme allowed them to drink together if they wished.

The statutes of the Holme's College do not vary much from the statutes for common living found in other colleges established in London in the fourteenth and fifteenth centuries. The rules of the College of St Laurence Pountney, laid down in 1347, prescribed the communal residence, attendance at meals, the obligation to acquire leave of absence from the master and the attendance at religious services.[111] The founders of the College in the Guildhall Chapel did not leave any ordinances for communal living at the time of the foundation in 1368. It is only in 1542 that Bishop Bonner laid down rules for the life and conduct of the chaplains, similar to those of Holme's College: each year two proctors were to be appointed and each week a steward was nominated. Presence at meals was compulsory and late arrival was punished. Physical violence between the commoners was punished severely and no women were allowed except in case of illness.[112]

---

[111] See article in Barron and Davies, *Religious Houses*, pp. 218–19.
[112] *Ibid.*, pp. 221–2.

The atmosphere of the other chantry college of St Paul's Cathedral must have been somewhat different because of its smaller size. In 1403 the two chaplains serving John of Gaunt's chantry were compelled by the Dean and Chapter to lodge and take their meals together in the house called 'Lancaster College'.[113] This house was built on a piece of land granted by Bishop de Braybroke, which had been part of the bishop's old palace. The chaplains together paid an annual rent of 10s for the house to the bishop.[114] Except for the obligation to live in the house and to share their meals, there are no other statutes regarding the common residence of the two chaplains. Perhaps it did not seem necessary to lay down specific rules since there were only two chaplains living there. The chantry founders clearly expected them to settle their own problems. When a compromise could not be reached, however, the Dean and Chapter would have intervened, for they adjudicated on all matters of discipline within the cathedral close. There may have been other residents in the college, for the Chapter Act Book referred to the college's *commensales*.[115]

Two chantries, however, never made provision for their chaplains to be residents of the *Presteshous*, nor were they attached to the private chantry colleges. These chaplains had their own residence within the close, provided at their place of work. The chaplain who served the chantry of Bishop William of Ste-Mère-Eglise in the chapel of the bishop's palace was expected to reside in the palace.[116] Apparently he fulfilled this requirement.[117] In 1404, an additional chantry was established at the altar of St Mary within the bishop's palace by Gerard de Braybroke, Edmund Hampden, John Boys,and Roger Albrygton. Not long after, this new chantry was united to the older chantry of Bishop of Ste-Mère-Eglise by Bishop Richard Clifford.[118] It can be assumed that the chaplain serving this new amalgamated chantry continued to occupy a chamber within the bishop's palace. The chaplain serving the charnel house was also exempted from residing in the *Presteshous*.[119] Since he was praying in the chapel above the charnel house, it may be assumed that he was also provided with a lodging there, but this remains only a supposition. When John Carpenter augmented this chantry in 1436, he made

---

[113] For more information about John of Gaunt, see Post, 'Obsequies of John of Gaunt', pp. 1–12.

[114] GL Ms 25121/1941.

[115] GL Ms 25513, fol. 143v.

[116] GL Ms 9531/12, fols 54v.–55; see above, pp. 73–4.

[117] The chaplain was not included in the list of chaplains dwelling in the *Presteshous*, GL Ms 25121/1960.

[118] *CPR, 1401–1405*, p. 239.

[119] In the Chapter Act Book there is no reference to him living in the *Presteshous*.

no reference to the chaplain's lodging.[120] It appears, however, that the chaplain serving Barton and Barry's chantry in the charnel house in 1439 became resident of the *Presteshous* at his induction, suggesting either that, if there were a lodging at the charnel house it was too small to contain two chaplains, or that the new founders considered *Presteshous* to be a more suitable residence.[121]

The minor canons who also acted as chantry chaplains were exempted from living in the *Presteshous* or other chantry colleges, since they had their own communal house known as the college of minor canons.[122] The organisation of the minor canons into a group of clerics, bound by the obligation of communal living, dates from the mid-fourteenth century. Their relatively independent status may be suggested as an explanation for the late date of these communal regulations. Whereas the vicars choral were bound to reside in a common hall by 1273, the minor canons were provided with individual accommodation within or without the cathedral precincts. In the course of the fourteenth century, however, the same ideal of communal living that spread among the vicars choral of other English secular cathedrals influenced St Paul's minor canons to seek communal lodging.[123] In 1353 Dean Gilbert de Bruera and the Chapter approved the erection of a new hall for minor canons on a piece of land located on the north side of the precinct. Negotiations must have preceded this decision for a number of years, for in 1351 Adam de Hotham, major canon, had bequeathed the minor canons twenty pounds towards the building of a new common hall for the priests, and a mazer cup for use in the hall.[124] Although de Hotham did not especially request in his will that the chaplains serving his chantry should be selected from among the minor canons, they often were, probably because he gave the right of

---

[120] GL Ms 25513, fols 156–159.

[121] GL Ms 25513, fol. 177v.

[122] William Sparrow Simpson, 'Charter and Statutes of the College of the Minor Canons in St. Paul's Cathedral', *Archaeologia*, 43 (1871), pp. 165–200. Repr. in *idem*, *Gleanings from Old St. Paul's* (London, 1889), pp. 1–31; Maurice Frederic Foxell, 'An Account of the College of Minor Canons of St Paul's Cathedral', *Transactions of the St Paul's Ecclesiological Society*, 10 (1931), pp. 7–10. See also A.R.B. Fuller, 'The Minor Corporations of the Secular Cathedrals of the Province of Canterbury Excluding the Welsh Sees between the Thirteenth Century and 1585 with Special Reference to the Minor Canons of St Paul's Cathedral from their Origins in the Fourteenth Century to the Visitations of Bishop Gibson in 1724' (MA dissertation, University of London, 1947), which includes facsimiles of the official documents relating to the minor canons.

[123] Edwards, *English Secular Cathedrals*, pp. 277–8; T.N. Cooper, 'Oligarchy and Conflict: Lichfield Cathedral Clergy in the Early Sixteenth Century', *Midland History*, 19 (1994), pp. 40–57, esp. p. 48.

[124] Sharpe, vol. 1, pp. 660–1.

appointment to the cardinals.[125] This gift towards housing for minor canons was in some way part of the endowment for his chantry. The construction of the new hall in 1353 was, however, primarily the result of initiatives taken by the minor canons themselves. In that year Robert de Kyngeston, cardinal, gave his house near the Pardon Churchyard for the construction of the new hall.[126] In 1359 John de Ware, William Crullyng and Robert de Keteringham, acting in their capacity as executors of three fellow minor canons, granted rents in the parish of St Martin Ludgate for the use of minor canons.[127] In turn, in 1361 John de Ware bequeathed houses for the use of minor canons, and in 1366 a mortmain licence was granted to three minor canons, John de Ware, Robert de Keteringham and Martin Elys, for the endowment of rents and tenements, valued at £6 13s 4d yearly, in the city of London, toward the maintenance of the common hall of minor canons.[128] This *ad hoc* construction of the college by individual donations follows a long tradition of bequests by minor canons to their successors, revealing a strong *esprit de corps* among them; in 1298 Robert le Seneschal had also left houses that he had inhabited for the use of minor canons.[129] In 1394, Richard II granted incorporation of the minor canons, who received a common seal, and two years later they drew up the statutes relating to the communal dwelling, which were approved by Bishop de Braybroke.[130] Minor canons prefaced their statutes with the same biblical quotation used by Roger Holme: '*Ubi sunt duo vel tres congregati in nomine meo, dicit Dominus, ibi sum in medio eorum.*' This is only one of the many similarities between the statutes of the two colleges. The college also functioned according to a system of honour, obedience and silence. Before admission, minor canons had to take an oath promising to obey the college warden, respect the statutes, and keep the secrets of the house. They also had to pay entrance fees. The task of governing the college was given to one of them, who was elected annually by the community to serve as warden, with another, the pittancer, as his assistant. The warden was in charge of ensuring that all rules were observed and fees collected when necessary. As with Holme's College, the daily government of the college also required the services of a steward, responsible for providing food and for weekly accounting. In 1445, the Dean and Chapter decided that the warden and the pittancer should, at least once a year, inspect the houses and accommodation of each minor canon

---

[125] His chantry became associated with a minor canonry in the sixteenth century; see Chapter 5, p. 127.

[126] Simpson, *Registrum Statutorum*, pp. 321–2.

[127] GL Ms 25121/1774.

[128] GL Ms 25271/45; *CPR, 1364–1367*, pp. 309–10.

[129] GL Ms 25271/10.

[130] Simpson, 'Charter and Statutes', pp. 185–200.

and supervise any repair work deemed necessary.[131] Evidence from wills reveals that the maintenance of communal living relied on communal staff. In 1509, John Church remembered each college servant with money, and in 1531 John Palmer left small monetary gifts to the butler, the master cook and other servants of the minor canons.[132] In a similar manner to the other communal lodgings within the cathedral precinct, the college of minor canons was arranged with communal areas and private space, formed by the minor canons' individual houses. The distribution of houses appears in some ways related to the allocation of minor canonries, but not on an automatic basis. In 1442, following the death of John Cook, William West received his minor canonry, but his house went to John Seton.[133] In general, however, a particular minor canonry and a specific house went together, and these successive allocations of houses to the minor canons were systematically recorded in the Chapter Act Book by the Dean and Chapter.[134]

Not surprisingly, the rules for communal living for the college of minor canons contained strict regulations concerning meals. The minor canons were to gather at midday and in the evening. As in the case of Holme's College, it seems that meals were considered to be the principal occasion for gathering and socialising, which explains why the presence of each minor canon was compulsory. The meals were also accompanied by reading, for at the midday meal a lesson from the Bible was to be read. The college was provided with a library from which the minor canons had the right to borrow any book as long as they notified the warden by sealing a bill with their own seal. The house also had a common seal, which was kept in a box within the treasury, a chamber at the west end of the college house, and the warden had the key to this room where the common chest was also kept. The college rules were intended to ensure the respectability of the minor canons: above all, relations with women were curtailed and in no circumstances were women of suspicious reputation allowed to associate with the canons. Similar punishments were meted out to those who frequented taverns or who attended dishonest plays, and any violence between brothers was also severely punished.

In essence, the rules for the college of minor canons resembled those for Holme's College. In both colleges, the harmony and the solidarity of the group of clerks were based on concepts of obedience, exclusivity and secrecy. Sharing meals reinforced the sense of community and was thus compulsory in both colleges, where regulations were imposed to ensure the respectability of members. But whereas Roger Holme, as founder, dictated his wishes for the communal life

---

[131] GL Ms 25513, fol. 233v.
[132] TNA PROB 11/16, fol. 213; PROB 11/24, fols 92v.–93.
[133] GL Ms 25513, fol. 203v.
[134] GL Ms 25513, fols 131v., 154, 212, 217.

of the seven chaplains serving his chantry, the minor canons gathered together to draw up their own rules. The fact that they took part in the construction of the statutes may have increased their sense of belonging to the college and their pride in that sense of belonging. It seems clear, however, that the chantry chaplains working at St Paul's also developed a strong sense of camaraderie, possibly as a result of the ideal of communal living that they were required to observe.[135] By overseeing good order and discipline in the various priests' houses, the Dean and Chapter presumably contributed to the development of these sentiments and they contributed to the chantries' general welfare by intervening in the management of the endowments and by supervising the liturgical services undertaken by the chaplains. The next chapter will explore the ways in which the Dean and Chapter attempted to regulate the activities of the chantry chaplains.

---

[135] See Chapter 5, pp. 137–9.

Chapter 4
Monitoring Chantries

The success of chantries owed much to the clerical institution in which they were founded. In addition to providing the physical space and liturgical setting, St Paul's Cathedral offered the resources of a well-established clerical community on which the chantry founders could rely for the success of their pious enterprises. The Dean and Chapter not only acted as chantry patrons for some of these foundations, but also intervened in their capacity as leaders of the cathedral's clergy to ensure that the chaplains were fulfilling their duties, that the chantry endowments were well maintained, and that they generated sufficient income to cover the recurrent costs of the chantries. Other actors also contributed to the chantries' prosperity: as chantry patrons and supervisors, the bishops of London and some city officials, such as the mayor and the chamberlain, interceded to defend the interests of the chantries entrusted to them to ensure that the founders' desires were respected.

Supervision and Oversight Responsibilities

The cathedral authorities' involvement began with the appointments of the chaplains, because once inducted to a chantry position, the chantry priests became integral members of the cathedral clerical community. The Dean and Chapter conscientiously registered the successive appointments of chantry chaplains in the Chapter Act Books, of which, unfortunately, only that covering the years 1411 to 1448 survives.[1] In the early sixteenth century, appointments were recorded in the dean's register.[2] The bishops and the London mayors also recorded appointments for the chantries for which they owned the right of nomination.[3] It is clear that these rights of appointment were taken seriously and were well guarded by chantry patrons and St Paul's authorities. In fulfilling vacancies, chantry patrons could and did reward old servants or promote young protégés.[4] When the rights were questioned, chantry patrons referred

---

[1] GL Ms 25513.
[2] GL Ms 25630/1.
[3] *Letter-Books* and bishops' registers.
[4] See Chapter 5, pp. 132–3.

to the chantry's original foundation deeds as proofs of their privileges. At the beginning of the fourteenth century, the executors of Walter de Blockele challenged the induction of a chaplain made by Robert de Baldock, archdeacon of Middlesex, and claimed their own right of appointment by producing de Blockele's will.[5] When necessary, the Dean and Chapter also relied on the testimonies of older chaplains, or other cathedral staff, to confirm or legitimate the right of appointment.[6] In 1424 two chaplains were presented to the chantry of Nicholas Wokyndon, one appointed by the bishop of Winchester, claiming the right of presentation by his possession of the manor of Wokyndon, and the second by Nicholas Rekhull and his wife Isabel, who was the fourth-generation heir of Nicholas Wokyndon. To settle the disagreement, the Dean and Chapter organised a commission and questioned three minor canons, the sacristan, a chaplain and the rector of St Faith's, who unanimously confirmed Nicholas and Isabel's right.[7] In 1435, probably following a dispute about the appointment to the united chantry for Basset's and St Roger's parents, a decision was taken to allocate the right of nomination to the Dean and Chapter.[8] Furthermore, when in 1391 de Meleford's chantry, where the right of appointment belonged to the archdeacon of Colchester, was united to one of Pulteney's chantries, where patronage lay in the hands of the mayor of London, the patrons had to reach a compromise regarding the right of nomination.[9] First, it appears that they shared the patronage by appointing the chaplains jointly, but in 1514 they agreed to take it in turns to nominate priests to the united chantry.[10]

Where the patronage of chantries belonged to the Dean and Chapter, the right of appointment was assigned to the dean and the resident major canons on the basis of a rota. The evidence of the Chapter Act Book suggests that this right was considered an important matter for the major canons and a privilege worth protecting. Any change to the rota was registered if, for whatever reason, it had to be altered, and in case of a prolonged vacancy, the right of appointment was transferred to the next patron on the list.[11] In January 1433, although Dean

---

[5]   GL Ms 25271/48.

[6]   Rachel Ward came across testimonies to verify the terms of various foundations; see 'Chantry Certificates of Norfolk: Towards a Partial Reconstruction', *Norfolk Archaeology*, 43 (1999), pp. 287–306, esp. p. 290; B. Cozens-Hardy, 'Chantries in the Duchy of Lancaster in Norfolk, 1548', *Norfolk Archaeology*, 29 (1946), pp. 201–10.

[7]   GL Ms 25121/1927; Ms 25513, fols 97v.–98.

[8]   GL Ms 25513, fol. 153v.

[9]   GL Ms 25121/1953. Simpson, *Registrum Statutorum*, pp. 142–58.

[10]   GL Ms 25121/1964. Agreement confirmed in 1516 by William Boteler, Mayor of London, in LMA, Journal 11, fol. 279.

[11]   GL Ms 25513, fol. 245.

Reginald Kentwood was third on the rota, he appointed William Marsham to Fulk Lovel and Braynford's chantry because Thomas Damett and John Bernyngham, who had been first and second in the rota, failed to fill the position within the allocated time.[12] The bishops of London also showed no hesitation in using his privilege of appointment if the Dean and Chapter failed to supply a chaplain as required. Bishop Thomas Kempe presented Thomas Swalow to de Bruera's chantry in 1451, because *decanus et capitulum non providebant infra tempus eis in eadem fundacionem assignatur*.[13] Kempe intervened on three other occasions during his episcopate as a result of overly prolonged vacancies.[14] If chantry patrons were too slow in filling the positions, then chantry supervisors were eager to intervene. In 1522, Bishop Cuthbert Tunstall copied out in his register a list of all the chantries in St Paul's for which he was supervisor, and carefully noted the time after which he might present a candidate.[15] Prolonged vacancies were also reproved by officials who did not have any responsibilities for the appointment. In 1345, the mayor of London complained to the Dean and Chapter because a number of chantries were vacant.[16] Such vacancies were not, however, always the result of negligence. It was sometimes difficult for chantry patrons to find chaplains who were willing to accept available positions. The chantry list of c.1370 that recorded a number of vacancies also indicated that the chantries in question did not generate sufficient revenues to support the priests' wages and related costs.[17] As a result, the cathedral authorities tried to remedy the financial weaknesses of some foundations by amalgamating those in need and ensuring that the new united foundations were sufficiently well endowed to support their incumbents. The major amalgamation of chantries at St Paul's took place in 1391, and was the result of an episcopal visitation of the cathedral.[18]

Financial hardship was not a fate unique to St Paul's Cathedral. The Dean and Chapter of Exeter Cathedral undertook successive reorganisations of the chantry endowments.[19] The unions and divisions of the endowments varied from decade to decade, and the fifteenth century witnessed a major reorganisation in 1438–39 in order to ensure a stipend of £4 for each chantry chaplain of the cathedral. At Avignon it appears that there was a similar reorganisation in

---

[12] GL Ms 25513, fol. 142v.
[13] GL Ms 9531/7, fol. 11.
[14] GL Ms 9531/7, fols 56v., 113v., 149v.
[15] GL Ms 9531/10, fol. 3v.
[16] Riley, *Memorials of London*, pp. 224–5.
[17] GL Ms 25121/1954.
[18] See Chapter 1, p. 17.
[19] Orme, 'Medieval Chantries: Part 1', p. 320.

the mid-fifteenth century. Of the forty-nine chantries mentioned in 1433, only twenty-four were listed in an inventory drawn up twenty years later.[20] At St Paul's, Bishop Clifford organised further series of amalgamations following those in 1391. In 1408 he united the chantry of Bishop William of Ste-Mère-Eglise, which had been omitted from the amalgamations of 1391, with the newly founded chantry of Albrygton, Boyes, Hampden and de Braybroke.[21] Both chantries were located in the chapel of the bishop's palace in the cathedral precinct. The Chapter Act Book (1411–1448) provides information about other strategies devised by the Dean and Chapter to remedy the financial difficulties experienced by chantries. They intervened to ensure the payment of chaplains' stipends or the settlement of arrears. In 1439 they petitioned the king in Parliament to obtain the right to distrain the lands and tenements from chantry endowments for payments that were in arrears.[22] In the early sixteenth century, they petitioned the Lord Chancellor about the abbot of Chertsey's misuse of chantry money, claiming that he had converted money given to him to his own use rather than spend it on the repair of a house that was part of a chantry endowment.[23] Chaplains also went to court to defend the interests of the chantries they served.[24] In the early 1530s the chaplains serving Dean de Eure's chantry tried to reach an agreement with the mayor, aldermen and sheriffs of London about a debt they incurred in rebuilding chantry tenements destroyed by fire.[25]

When the chantry tenements were in a poor condition, another option open to the Dean and Chapter was to leave the chantry vacant, and invest the chaplains' wages in the repair and renovation of the tenements. In 1445 they took the drastic decision not to appoint a chaplain to the united chantry of de Thorp and St Olave for three successive years, in order to improve its tenements.[26] In 1532, as a result of the deterioration and ruinous state of the tenements belonging to de Waltham and Basset's united chantry, the Dean and Chapter took possession of the endowments and allocated them to two clerks, thus depriving the chaplain, John Powle, of his right to collect the rents under threat of losing his chantry, and allocated him instead a fixed stipend of £7.[27]

---

[20]   Chiffoleau, *La comptabilité de l'Au-delà*, p. 334.

[21]   GL Ms 9531/4, fol. 111.

[22]   *Letter-Book K*, p. 239.

[23]   TNA C1/567/15.

[24]   TNA C1/433/4; C1/717/39; C1/757/46; C1/1147/75–77.

[25]   TNA C1/642/50.

[26]   GL Ms 25513, fol. 230. This excessive solution was applied to other chantries in financial difficulties. Two examples are reported by Thomson, *Early Tudor Church*, p. 178.

[27]   GL Ms 25630/1, fol. 31.

Powle later recovered the administration of the chantry endowments, for in 1540 he is found agreeing a lease with Henry Lerrand, a London citizen.[28]

The Dean and Chapter were not the only ones who showed diligence in ensuring that the chantry tenements were well maintained and issued sufficient incomes to sustain the chantries. The chantry patrons of Holme's College, one of the two cardinals and the sacristan, took their supervisory role seriously. According to Roger Holme's chantry ordinances, it was their responsibility to appoint one of the seven college chaplains to collect all the income from the tenements and rents assigned to the college.[29] That chaplain, the collector, also had to supervise all repairs to the tenements that might be needed and was obliged to show the college accounts to the patrons and provide them with written copies. Within three years, the patrons had to show these copies to the Dean and Chapter if they asked to see them. In c.1400, after inspecting the chantry tenements, the sacristan and junior cardinal made an official complaint to the Dean and Chapter, claiming that the chantry tenements were so dilapidated that their value, originally calculated at £48 per year, was reduced of £4.[30] This deterioration had occurred because of the chaplains' negligence: they had failed to undertake the necessary repair works. The patrons asked the Dean and Chapter to examine the situation and reprimand the chaplains, reminding them of the oath that they had taken to fulfil these tasks.

Chaplains also intervened to secure the financial success of their own chantries. A few years after his appointment to Bukerel's chantry, John Tykhill tried to save his foundation. He wrote two petitions, now kept in the cathedral archives, one in French to the king and one in Latin to the bishop of London, to secure financial help.[31] His efforts were, however, in vain. When he died in 1423, he was not replaced, and Bukerel's chantry was not mentioned again.[32] John de Purle (d.1384) chose to rescue de Chaddleshunt's chantry, which he had been serving at St Paul's, instead of founding his own chantry.[33] He bequeathed various possessions to provide an annual income amounting to a total of twenty marks. From these twenty marks, 100s were to be given annually to the chantry chaplain to increase his stipend, and two marks were to be used to finance the repair of the houses and buildings, part of the original chantry endowment, which were described as *ruinosa et vetustate notorie consumpta*. If 100s per

---

[28] GL Ms 25630/1, fol. 99.

[29] GL Ms 25145.

[30] GL Ms 25121/1966. The complaint is undated, but since Reginald Spaldyng intervened as sacristan, the approximate date of 1400 can be given.

[31] GL Ms 25121/1952; Ms 25121/1976.

[32] GL Ms 25513, fol. 96.

[33] GL Ms 25121/1929.

annum could be spared, then it was to be used to pay for the celebration of masses at the high altar in honour of the body and blood of Jesus and in honour of St Paul, for the welfare of Purle's soul. In 1466, fifty years after the death of John Stokes, his sister bequeathed a quit-rent of 13s 4d to the Dean and Chapter to endow the chantry of Richard and Stephen de Gravesend, which he had served for almost fifteen years.[34] All these interventions by cathedral authorities, chantry patrons and chantry priests contributed to the high survival rate of chantry foundations at St Paul's.[35]

Discipline and Punishment

The quality of the religious services performed by the chantry chaplains was also of concern to the cathedral authorities and chantry patrons. Before being admitted to their positions, chantry priests passed a series of tests in reading, grammar, Latin and singing, which confirmed their competence for their benefices. First, at their ordination to the priesthood, they would have been examined by the bishop, who would have deemed their literary and theological knowledge sufficient for the office.[36] Then, at their induction to chantries at St Paul's, the candidates were examined once more, this time by the succentor of the cathedral, who would evaluate their singing ability.[37] These examinations were not taken lightly.[38] It appears, however, that a failure to meet the requirement did not result in an immediate dismissal from the chantry position. In fact, it seems to have been the norm for the cathedral authorities to grant a year's probation to chaplains who failed their test to enable them to improve their singing skills. It was a second failure of the examination, imposed after this probationary year, that entailed an expulsion. Chaplain Walter Barton resigned in 1418 after a year in office at one of Roger Holme's chantries when he failed

---

[34]   GL Ms 25121/1177.

[35]   The survival rate is discussed in Chapter 6, pp. 152–3. Chapters 1 and 5 contain examples of donations made by a variety of benefactors for the welfare of chantry foundations.

[36]   A.D. Frankforter, 'The Reformation and the Register: Episcopal Administration of Parishes in Late Medieval England', *Catholic History Review*, 63 (1977), pp. 204–24, esp. p. 209.

[37]   The transfer of the precentor's choir duties to the succentor is discussed in Nicholas Orme, 'The Early Musicians of Exeter Cathedral', *Music and Letters*, 59 (1978), pp. 395–407, esp. p. 396. The succentor was the real director of the choir music. Edwards, *English Secular Cathedrals*, p. 291.

[38]   Other scholars also reached this conclusion: Haines, *Ecclesia Anglicana*, p. 131.

the examination in singing for a second time.[39] Likewise, in April 1418 William Pynnesthorp, admitted on condition that he improved his singing, resigned from the chantry of de Waltham and Basset, in July of the same year.[40] A couple of years later another chaplain, John Crook, resigned because of his failure in singing, and in 1512 Walter Preston was appointed to the chantry of Ralph de Baldock on condition that he improved his singing.[41] Because of the chaplains' participation in the cathedral choir, St Paul's authorities were strict regarding singing requirements.

Participation in the choir was of paramount importance in chantry positions.[42] Chaplains were expected to fulfil the duties as regulated by chantry founders. If they failed, it was the duty of the chantry patrons and the cathedral authorities to remind them of their obligations. In c.1400 sacristan Reginald Spaldyng complained to the Dean and Chapter about the seven chantry chaplains of Holme's College.[43] The focus of his grievance was their absenteeism: they were neglecting their choir duties. As patron of Holme's College, Spaldyng asked the Dean and Chapter to compel the chaplains to be present at the cathedral's main religious offices, namely intoning psalms and attending matins, vespers, solemn public masses, or at least at two of the principal hours. The Dean and Chapter responded to the complaint by ordering the chaplains to observe the chantry rules as they had sworn to do on their admission day.[44] They were threatened with sanctions, although these were not described. Evidence of the Chapter Act Book and Dean Sampson's register suggests that this was not an unusual incident.[45] In 1441 the Dean and Chapter sentenced chaplain Richard Pepyn to buy a new choir habit by way of penance for his frequent absence from the choir, and in 1447 they instructed John Skawyn to read the Bible for a week, at the beginning of each communal meal in the *Presteshous* in order to punish him for his inappropriate behaviour in the cathedral choir.[46] Proper dress in the choir was also an issue: John Went was refused entry to the cathedral as long as he failed to dress properly, at the risk of losing his chantry.[47] In one case the Dean and Chapter's warnings were directed not only to an individual or a small group of chaplains, but to a large number of priests. In 1446 the

[39] GL Ms 25513, fol. 62.

[40] GL Ms 25513, fols 60–61v.

[41] GL Ms 25630/1, fols 73v., 93v.

[42] See Chapter 2, pp. 46–51.

[43] GL Ms 25147.

[44] GL Ms 25148.

[45] GL Ms 25513, fols 17–18, 249, 254; Ms 25,630/1, fol. 31v.

[46] GL Ms 25513, fols 194v., 254.

[47] GL Ms 25630/1, fol. 116.

Dean and Chapter reprimanded nineteen chaplains and nine minor canons for neglecting their choir duties.[48] One case throws light on what might have led the chaplains to disregard their choir responsibilities. In 1540, the Dean and Chapter warned John Cotton, the chaplain serving de Eure's chantry, that he should be singing with the choir rather than teaching children during divine services.[49] Although the regulations of de Eure's chantry (1411) stipulated that the chantry incumbent was supposed to fund the study of poor choristers, they do not suggest that the chaplain himself was to engage in teaching.[50] It seems therefore that this teaching job was something that John Cotton had developed on the side, to the detriment of his other obligations.

The responsibilities of the cathedral authorities extended to the privileges of excusing chaplains from their choir duties if they were old and infirm. In the late fourteenth century, the Dean and Chapter relieved John Lynton of his choir duties because of his weaknesses and in 1446 Simon Deken was excused from attending the canonical hours because of his old age and his ailments.[51] The Dean and Chapter could also sanction absence from the cathedral. They registered in their Chapter Act Book such licences, which varied from eight days to one month.[52] It would appear that they only sanctioned well-justified leaves of absence, such as that granted to Thomas Nunhous and John Masham, who were allowed three weeks to undertake a pilgrimage to York in 1445.[53] In 1531 John Longford was licensed to be absent for one month, but in exchange he promised to pay a penny for each week he was away from the cathedral.[54] If it was the Dean and Chapter's privilege to authorise leaves of absence, it was also their duty to punish chaplains who left without a proper licence.[55] In 1442 the Dean and Chapter sentenced the same Thomas Nunhous to read from the Bible at the beginning of each meal in the *Presteshous* as a penance after he had absented himself from the cathedral without a proper authorisation.[56] The scarcity of these references suggests, however, that taking unauthorised absence from the cathedral was not a common feature of the working life at St Paul's. Participating in the cathedral choir and performing the liturgical duties linked to the chantries were both expected from, and observed by, the chaplains.

---

48   GL Ms 25513, fol. 237v.
49   GL Ms 25630/1, fol. 93.
50   GL Ms 25138.
51   GL Ms 25121/3029; Ms 25513, fol. 242.
52   GL Ms 25513, fols 43, 99.
53   GL Ms 25513, fol. 230v.
54   GL Ms 25630/1, fol. 30v.
55   GL Ms 25513, fol. 167.
56   GL Ms 25513, fol. 205v.

The Chapter Act Book and Dean Sampson's register allude, however, to a number of difficulties encountered by the Dean and Chapter in imposing the regulations for communal living and in enforcing rulings over matters of discipline. Occasionally the Dean and Chapter had to remind chaplains of their initial oath to observe communal residence. In 1419, they threatened to deprive four of the seven chaplains of Holme's College of their chantries if they failed to observe their obligation to share meals and live together.[57] Because the Dean and Chapter did not carry out this threat, it may be assumed that the chaplains subsequently complied with the obligation to live in the college. Another responsibility of the Dean and Chapter was to ensure harmony among the members of the chantry colleges by arbitrating any personal conflicts between them. For example, in 1447 the Dean and Chapter arbitrated between minor canon William West and chaplain William Marshall, and they were required to exchange a kiss of peace.[58] Entries in the Chapter Act Book between April and September 1447 suggest that relations could sometimes be strained between the chaplains of Thomas More's chantry and other chaplains of the *Presteshous*, perhaps because of the particular status of More's chantry chaplains.[59] In 1447 the Dean and Chapter had to intervene to settle a quarrel when the chaplains of More's chantry refused to pay their contribution towards the common expenses after disputes about a window on the east side of their house arose.[60] This quarrel lasted for several months, but in the end the Dean and Chapter compelled the chaplains of Thomas More's chantry to pay their share.[61]

The Dean and Chapter also acted as judges in cases of misbehaviour. In 1416, the chaplain Thomas Barker was accused of drinking excessively, of fighting and of causing discord among his fellows in the *Presteshous*.[62] The situation presumably did not improve, for he resigned shortly afterwards.[63] Likewise, in 1433 the Dean and Chapter punished Thomas Whiteby of Lancaster College for his misconduct, which had prevented his housemate John Hereford and the other *commensales* from living together peaceably in the college.[64] A year later the situation remained problematic, for the Dean and Chapter were again required to intervene, and again judged Whiteby guilty of misconduct. It is worth noting that the Dean and Chapter recorded in the Chapter Act

---

[57] GL Ms 25513, fol. 66.
[58] GL Ms 25513, fol. 260.
[59] GL Ms 25513, fols 250–257.
[60] GL Ms 25513, fol. 250.
[61] GL Ms 25513, fol. 257.
[62] GL Ms 25513, fol. 47v.
[63] GL Ms 25513, fol. 49v.
[64] GL Ms 25513, fol. 143v.

Book that in this case they had received multiple complaints orally as well as in written form.[65] Animosity between chaplains could provoke physical confrontation. In 1428, after discussion, the Dean and Chapter declared that the wound inflicted by John Gloucester on William Barnaby, another chaplain, was not too serious, although Gloucester nevertheless undertook a penitential pilgrimage.[66] Verbal assaults among chaplains were also severely reproved. In 1540 the dean reprimanded four chaplains for vicious and slanderous talk, and threatened to deprive them of their chantries if they did not desist from persecuting their fellows.[67] In one case the number of chaplains involved seems to imply a division among the community: in 1394 twelve chaplains were accused of bullying three others, one of whom resigned shortly after.[68]

As these examples illustrate, the main accusations brought against the chaplains related to disturbing or breaking the communal peace within the *Presteshous* and the other colleges. But the chaplains also broke college rules. In addition to fighting with his housemates, John Skawyn was punished in 1447 for going to the tavern and drinking wine and ale and then returning to the *Presteshous* late at night.[69] These restrictions underlined the fact that the culture of the chaplains was also a culture of exclusion: drinking was allowed only within limits, socialising with women was forbidden, and late entertainment was also prohibited. Remarkably, perhaps, there is no recorded case of a chaplain serving one of the perpetual chantries at St Paul's being accused of having sexual relationships. But a priest, Miles Tiler, was brought before the mayor and aldermen on 10 August 1415 for having an affair with Margaret, wife of Richard Buntyng, labourer. He was said to serve a 'Brekenhok's chantry' located in St Paul's Churchyard, but such a chantry does not appear in the cathedral archives; nor does Miles Tiler.[70] In 1423, John Hye, one of the vicars choral of the cathedral, had to resign for having had an affair with Margaret Baker.[71] Twenty years later John Gravele, another vicar choral, had to defend himself before the Dean and Chapter when he was accused of spending too much time at the public bath (stews), which was also frequented by women of

---

[65]   GL Ms 25513, fol. 149.
[66]   Possibly to St James of Compostela. GL Ms 25513, fol. 122v. Another conflict occurred in 1444 when John Grymston and Thomas Stafford had an altercation, for which John Grymston was found responsible, GL Ms 25513, fol. 223v.
[67]   GL Ms 25630/1, fol. 93.
[68]   *CCR, 1392–1396*, pp. 262–3.
[69]   GL Ms 25513, fol. 262.
[70]   *Letter-Book I*, pp. 279–80.
[71]   GL Ms 25513, fol. 96.

doubtful reputation.[72] He was to mend his ways under the threat of expulsion. This he apparently did, as a few years later he was promoted to a minor canonry and a chantry.[73]

The Chapter Act Book and Dean Sampson's register shed light not only on the discipline cases with which the Dean and Chapter were faced, but also on the procedures they followed to investigate the cases and deliver judgements. Suspect clerics were summoned for questioning before the Dean and Chapter in the chapter house, when the accused was given the chance to explain himself and justify his conduct. For example, in 1541 Henry Rawlyns was summoned before the dean to explain why he should not be deprived of his chantry after having frequented taverns despite having been forbidden to do so.[74] The Dean and Chapter then proceeded to question witnesses. In the case of the discord between John Skawyn and William West in 1447, the dean summoned nine minor canons and sixteen chantry chaplains to give evidence.[75] Certain cases of misconduct were brought before the Dean and Chapter by denunciation. On Friday and Saturday, the Dean and Chapter opened the doors of the chapter house to any member of the lesser clergy who had a complaint or reproach against a fellow cleric.[76]

Once the Dean and Chapter had delivered their judgements, they had to reprimand offenders and allocate punishments. Threats and warnings seem ordinarily to have been deemed sufficient to prevent the chaplains from repeating an offence. The most common warning consisted of threatening to deprive the chaplains or the minor canons of their benefices if they failed to moderate their behaviour. In 1412 Walter Gomelok, who occupied de Haverhull's chantry, was told that, unless he improved the way he served his chantry, he would be deprived of it.[77] When punishments were given they varied according to the offences. In 1444, having found John Skawyn, chantry priest, guilty of misconduct in the choir, the Dean and Chapter sentenced him to attend every canonical hour in the day and at night for eight days.[78] Should Skawyn be absent at any service, he was to pay 4d each time. Furthermore, as a sign of humility John had to stand with the vicars choral during the service.[79] An element of reparation and

---

[72] GL Ms 25513, fol. 215.

[73] GL Ms 25513, fols 170, 232, 255v.

[74] GL Ms 25630/1, fol. 116v.

[75] GL Ms 25513, fol. 254.

[76] GL Ms 25513, fol. 260.

[77] GL Ms 25513, fol. 23.

[78] GL Ms 25513, fol. 223.

[79] *Degragatio*, being deposed from a stall and placed below with inferior clerks, was also the penalty for severe misconduct according to the custom of Old Sarum; see Diana

reconciliation was often prominent in the punishments. John Skawyn was forced to make a public apology to William West, minor canon, whom he had accused of having a woman in his room, when the Dean and Chapter who had investigated the charges among the minor canons found that John's accusation was unfounded, and he had to ask forgiveness, on his knees, from William West.[80] Since in mid-June 1447 John Skawyn was also accused of failing to fulfil his choir duties, the dean also required him to read the first lesson at matins until the feast of St John the Baptist and the Bible in the *Presteshous* at meals. In addition, he was forbidden to celebrate mass until he had served his sentence. A few months later John Skawyn was yet again summoned before the Dean and Chapter for disobedience and for a breach of discipline.[81] This time he was deprived of his chaplain's garb, a symbol of his status, and prevented from participating in the choir. In order to be re-admitted to his chantry, he had to promise not to instigate conflict with his peers, nor to frequent taverns, but to remain sober and well behaved. He also agreed to observe a curfew by returning to the *Presteshous* not later than 9 pm in summer or 8 pm in winter, and he undertook not to absent himself from the church during the canonical hours of the day or the night without obtaining a licence from the dean or the subdean. Communal meals would have been the main occasions when all the chaplains met together, and it is possible that the cathedral authorities used these times to notify the chaplains of new directives, or to reprimand them if necessary. Punishments carried out in the company of peers may have been seen by the Dean and Chapter as a means of ensuring that the guilty chaplain would not commit further offences, and of discouraging other chaplains from emulating such transgressions.

The persistent offences of John Skawyn highlight the kind of difficulties encountered by the Dean and Chapter in matters of discipline, and also the kind of punishments to which they resorted in order to resolve such cases. Disobedience, mischief and immorality were punished with monetary fines, acts of repentance and, only in cases of repeated offences or severe transgressions, with temporary suspension from the benefice. Although the Dean and Chapter frequently threatened deprivation, it appears that they used it only with extreme reluctance.[82] Although John Martyn, chantry chaplain, disappeared from

---

Greenway, 'Orders and Rank in the Cathedral of Old Sarum', in Sheils and Wood, *Ministry: Clerical and Lay*, pp. 55–63, esp. p. 62.

[80] GL Ms 25513, fol. 254.

[81] GL Ms 25513, fols 260–262.

[82] Ecclesiastical authorities resorted to deprivation only in cases of non-residence, when no other solution seemed possible; see Heath, *English Parish Clergy*, p. 134. Same conclusion in Thomson, *Early Tudor Church*, p. 150.

St Paul's Cathedral and failed to respond to all summons for judgement, it took the Dean and Chapter nine months, from July 1411 to April 1412, to decide finally to dismiss him and allocate his chantry to another chaplain.[83] The case of William Diolet also illustrates the reluctance on the part of cathedral authorities to resort to deprivation. Admitted in 1442 to the chantry of William de Everdon and to a minor canonry, William Diolet had his first confrontation with a fellow minor canon, John Clerk, in July 1447.[84] Since a resolution could not be reached in house, the case was presented to the Dean and Chapter, who summoned all the minor canons to the chapter house. They obviously judged William to be responsible for the discord, for he was compelled to ask forgiveness from John Clerk. The dean not only castigated William but also rebuked the warden of the college of minor canons for failing in his duty to judge any case of misconduct and deliver an appropriate sentence. The dean's reproach did not have the desired effect, for only a few months later the situation recurred. In November 1447, the minor canons were summoned yet again to deal with the behaviour of William Diolet.[85] The two parties, the warden and all the minor canons on one side and William Diolet on the other, agreed to accept the arbitration of the Dean and Chapter. The latter found Diolet guilty not only of provoking discord with his fellow minor canons, but also of failing to show appropriate respect towards the major canons.[86] In March 1448 he was presented with a series of injunctions, which he had to swear to observe faithfully according to cathedral rules and his chantry regulations (that of de Everdon) at risk of being deprived.[87] These injunctions focused as much on his flouting of his superiors' authority in the church hierarchy as with ensuring the due observance of his chantry and choir duties, for four of the seven injunctions concerned the respect to be shown to major canons during services. William was given time to amend his conduct and, in July 1448, he appeared before the Dean and Chapter to answer these seven injunctions one by one.[88] In all cases but one he declared that he had fulfilled his obligations as well as possible. He admitted, however, that he had continued to argue with major and minor canons, but only, he claimed, because he was provoked. In turn he complained about particular individuals,

---

[83] GL Ms 25513, fols 5v., 6, 8, 10, 14v., 15, 17, 19v., 22v., 23. During that time his brother appeared before the Dean and Chapter declaring that John was not able and did not dare to come to the cathedral, for fear of death or imprisonment.

[84] GL Ms 25513, fol. 252.

[85] GL Ms 25513, fols 259–260v.

[86] GL Ms 25513, fol. 261.

[87] GL Ms 25513, fol. 262.

[88] GL Ms 25513, fol. 262v.

including the dean, a major canon and a minor canon.[89] Although he expressed his desire to exchange his benefice immediately, he resigned only in November 1448, four months later.[90] His resignation might obscure the fact that the cathedral authorities had withdrawn his benefice, a practice that may have been quite common.[91] William Diolet appears to have been a priest with a particularly bad temper, for after leaving St Paul's he found himself once again in hot water. By 1450, he had secured a position in Canterbury serving the Black Prince's chantry together with one other priest. However, the inability of the two priests to work and live together led the cathedral authorities to draw up a set of regulations to amend their conduct.[92] Among other things, they were asked to: 'restreyn theyr tonges frome all unclene langage, and shamefull word, and unkyndly word, the wych ys rote of all debates betwyx man and man, in payn of 6s 8d at furste tyme, and 13s 8d at the second tyme, and 20s at the thyrde time, and so frome tyme to tyme to multiply the payne aftyr the quantyte of the trepase … '. Apparently Diolet had brought with him his sharp tongue.

In the early sixteenth century, Dean Colet drew up new regulations for all the cathedral clergy.[93] His reformist zeal was especially directed towards the chantry chaplains, who were reminded of their obligations to observe both the cathedral customs and the regulations of their own chantries. These statutes influenced William Sparrow Simpson's negative portrait of the chantry chaplains: 'They had very little duty to perform, and plenty of leisure, and the statutes of the cathedral and common report seems to show that there was really a good deal to be said against them.'[94] The entries in the Chapter Act Book and Dean Sampson's register seem to indicate, however, that misconduct on the part of the chaplains was not a serious problem. There are only few cases of clerks being accused of misbehaviour involving drink or women and, furthermore, the problems were not widespread, but restricted to a few individuals, such as John Skawyn and William Diolet, who failed to integrate into the community. Relations between minor clergy and major canons were also reasonably harmonious. Some isolated incidences of disobedience may be found, but they were not severe, suggesting that the endemic tension observed in other

---

[89]   GL Ms 25513, fol. 263.

[90]   GL Ms 25513, fols 263v.–264.

[91]   Swanson, *Church and Society*, p. 61.

[92]   Joseph Brigstocke Sheppard (ed.), *Literae Cantuarienses. The Letter Books of the Monastery of Christ Church, Canterbury* (Canterbury, 1889), vol. 3, pp. 210–12; N. 182 b.

[93]   E.F. Carpenter, 'The Reformation: 1485–1660', in W.R. Matthews and W.M. Atkins (eds), *A History of St Paul's Cathedral and the Men Associated with it* (London, 1957), pp. 100–171, esp. pp. 106–16; Arnold, 'John Colet, Preaching and Reform', pp. 450–68.

[94]   Simpson, *S. Paul's Cathedral and Old City Life*, p. 103.

cathedrals between different groups of clergy did not affect St Paul's.[95] The next chapter explores the lives and careers of chantry chaplains and examines the ways in which they were able to fashion an integrated community with other members of the cathedral clergy.

---

[95] Cooper, 'Oligarchy and Conflict', p. 51.

Chapter 5

Serving Chantries

As members of the minor clergy, chantry chaplains belonged to a social group that has attracted little historical research.[1] In contrast with the higher clergy of English cathedrals, they have left little evidence of their daily activities and preoccupations.[2] In most cases only their names have been recorded. Nonetheless the rich, but largely unexploited, sources of St Paul's Cathedral allow a clearer understanding of them as a group. In total 810 chantry priests have been identified, although partly as a result of the available material, they are unevenly distributed across the period covered (Table 5.1).[3]

Table 5.1   Number of identified chaplains between 1250 and 1548

Years	Number of chaplains
1250–1299	56
1300–1349	70
1350–1399	157
1400–1449	242
1450–1499	89
1500–1548	196

---

[1] For a general survey of chantry priests of English secular cathedrals, see Edwards, *English Secular Cathedrals*, pp. 285–303. Orme, 'Medieval Clergy: 1. Vicars and Annuellars', pp. 79–102; *idem, Minor Clergy of Exeter Cathedral*. The unbeneficed clergy have been studied by A. McHardy, 'Careers and Disappointments in the Late-Medieval Church: Some English Evidence', in Sheils and Wood, *Ministry: Clerical and Lay*, pp. 111–30.

[2] For a prosopographical study of the higher clergy of secular cathedrals, see David Lepine, *A Brotherhood of Canons Serving God. English Secular Cathedrals in the Later Middle Ages* (Woodbridge, 1995).

[3] For a list of and information on these chaplains, see Rousseau, 'Chantry Chaplains', Table 1. In comparison, Rachel Ward has identified 626 chantry priests for the whole diocese of Norwich in the later Middle Ages: 'Foundation and Functions,' p. 32.

Chaplains' Origins

Were the chaplains serving chantries at St Paul's natives of the city of London, or did they come from small towns or the rural hinterlands of the diocese of London, or from adjacent dioceses, migrating to the capital in the hope of obtaining employment? Determining the geographical origins of the chantry chaplains of St Paul's Cathedral sheds light on the power of the cathedral chantries to attract priests, and the mobility of the lesser clergy in the Middle Ages. Information about the chaplains' geographical origins is taken from the ordination lists in the bishops' registers and the records of induction to chantries.[4] At these two points in their clerical careers, the candidates had to provide evidence of identification to the clerical authorities and, in some cases, details about the origins of the candidates were recorded. Such evidence has been found for 136 chaplains serving St Paul's chantries from 1340 onwards (Table 5.2).

It is important to note, however, that these results may not reflect the true proportion of chaplains from each diocese because irregularities were more likely to be recorded, thus skewing the results. For instance, if, at the ordination, the candidate was not a native of the diocese in which he sought ordination, he was required to produce a letter dimissory from his diocese addressed to the bishop conducting the ceremony.[5] In such cases a note would probably have been made in the records. At the ordination of clerics by the bishop of London the geographical origins of the candidates from dioceses other than London were likely to be specified, but omitted for Londoners. Thus the omission of information about clerics' origins may indicate that they were native to the diocese of London, which would in fact suggest that the majority of chaplains were indigenous to the diocese. Chantry patrons of the diocese of Norwich also favoured local clergy for appointment, while chantry priests of Exeter Cathedral mostly came from Devon and Cornwall, and all chantry priests of York Minster were recruited from rural areas neighbouring the city of York,

---

    [4]   Virginia Davis, *Clergy in London in the Late Middle Ages. A Register of Clergy Ordained in the Diocese of London based on Episcopal Ordination Lists 1361–1539*, Cd-Rom (London, 2000). Evidence can also be provided from wills. For example, the chaplain John Surdevall (d.1522) left a bequest to the parish of Wawne, Yorkshire, where he was born, while Thomas Kent (d.1538) bequeathed money and a vestment to his native parish church of Englefield in Berkshire: TNA PROB 11/20, fol. 228; PROB 11/27, fol. 186.

    [5]   Virginia Davis, 'Episcopal Ordination Lists as a Source for Clerical Mobility in England in the Fourteenth Century', in Nicholas Rogers (ed.), *England in the Fourteenth Century* (Stamford, 1993), pp. 152–70, esp. pp. 154–5.

Table 5.2   Geographical origins of chantry chaplains by diocese[6]

Origin	1300–1349	1350–1399	1400–1449	1450–1499	1500–1548
Canterbury	1	–	1	1	–
Carlisle	–	–	–	–	–
Chichester	–	–	2	–	–
Durham	–	–	3	–	2
Ely	–	–	3	1	1
Exeter	–	1	8	–	1
Hereford	–	–	1	–	–
Lichfield	–	3	1	–	5
Lincoln	–	4	14	2	1
London	–	9	15	2	3
Norwich	–	1	10	1	–
Rochester	–	–	–	–	–
Salisbury	–	–	5	–	2
Wells	–	–	1	–	1
Winchester	–	–	–	–	–
Worcester	–	–	1	–	2
York	–	1	12	1	10
Wales	–	–	1	–	2
Total	1	19	78	8	30

usually within a radius of forty miles.[7] What is therefore surprising about the chantry chaplains of St Paul's Cathedral is not that the majority came from the mother diocese, but rather that a significant minority came from dioceses other than that of London.[8] The geographical origins of the chantry chaplains were extremely varied, the priests coming both from surrounding areas and also from more remote dioceses. Because of the uneven survival rate of evidence over the period covered, it is difficult to suggest any chronological patterns in the origins of the chaplains. The predominance of geographically identifiable

---

[6]   The information in this table is based on ordination and induction records.

[7]   Ward, 'Foundation and Functions', p. 33; Nicholas Orme, 'Education and Learning at a Medieval English Cathedral: Exeter 1380–1548', *Journal of Ecclesiastical History*, 31 (1981), pp. 265–83, esp. 267; N.A. Edwards, 'The Chantry Priests of York Minster in the First Half of the Sixteenth Century' (MA dissertation, University of York, 1999), p. 10.

[8]   The percentage of chaplains coming from outside London may have been even greater, for Virginia Davis concluded that most clergy ordained in London were not indigenous to the diocese: Davis, 'Episcopal Ordination Lists', p. 165.

chaplains in the first half of the fifteenth century is primarily the result of the wealth of sources for that period.[9] In contrast, clear evidence of origins from a diocese other than London has survived for only one of the chaplains who served the cathedral prior to 1350: John Love of Canterbury was appointed to de Eyton's chantry in 1340.[10] Thirteen English and two Welsh dioceses produced chaplains serving at St Paul's at one time or another. Unsurprisingly, the distribution of chaplains was not equally spread between all these dioceses. The larger and more populous dioceses, including Lincoln and York, produced the bulk of the chaplains who migrated to London, while smaller dioceses, such as Hereford, and Bath and Wells, had fewer representatives. The reasons behind the decision of these chaplains to leave their native dioceses probably varied according to individual circumstances and social and economic particularities of the dioceses, but the path they took must surely have been influenced by the powerful draw of London, for which chantries of St Paul's may have served as an introduction. Their positions not only as chantries within the mother church of the diocese, but as points of access to the capital, may explain why men from other dioceses wished to serve them. In this respect, the chantries in St Paul's undoubtedly enjoyed an exceptional position, for the diversity of the geographical origins of its chantry chaplains appears to have been unique.

Although exceptional, the power of the chantries to attract priests did not equal that of the major canonries, which extended well beyond the borders of the realm.[11] In contrast, the chantries of St Paul's did not attract alien priests. This observation makes the prohibition of appointing chaplains other than Englishmen to some chantries from 1450 onwards even more intriguing: did the formulation of this prohibition symbolise a nascent nationalism, or did it express a concern by founders about the presence of Welsh chaplains?[12] For the only non-English chaplains for whom we have direct evidence were indeed the chaplains from Welsh dioceses in the sixteenth century.[13]

Formed in the main part by local men, the community of chantry chaplains was, however, broadened by the inclusion of clerics who came from across England and from Wales, who contributed to the cathedral life in the same manner as the priests born in the diocese of London. Although some of these new arrivals stayed at the cathedral for only a few years, probably using their chantries as stepping stones for more prestigious positions in royal

---

[9] GL Ms 25513.

[10] *CPR, 1338–1340*, p. 432.

[11] Some major canons came from France and Italy; *Fasti II*; Lepine, *Brotherhood of Canons*, pp. 43–8.

[12] See Chapter 2, p. 36.

[13] Thomas ap Adam and John David.

or ecclesiastical administrations, others remained at the cathedral all their working life. For instance William Barnaby from York was at St Paul's between 1417 and 1444, while John Andrew, born in the diocese of Lincoln, served de Guldeford's chantry for over thirty-five years between 1506 and 1541.[14] The geographical origins of the chantry chaplains do not appear to have been a factor in determining the length of time they spent at St Paul's Cathedral.

In general, the educational path taken by chaplains serving chantries in St Paul's did not reach the centres of higher learning, but stopped at a more modest level. University attendance was exceptional, although the proportion of chaplains who attended university increased over the centuries. Before the fifteenth century there is only slim evidence of university education for three chaplains, and firm evidence for one chaplain: at his induction in 1384 Thomas Lansel was presented as a bachelor of canon law.[15] The number of chaplains who attended university rose slightly in the first half of the fifteenth century. These chaplains had many characteristics in common; first of all, they appear to have come from particular colleges: three chaplains were linked with Merton College, Oxford, two with New College, Oxford, and two chaplains were members of King's Hall, Cambridge.[16] The fact that Robert Barker and John Grymston were at Merton College at the same time sheds light on potential networks of chaplains.[17] Robert Barker, who had been a chaplain at St Paul's before moving to Oxford, may have suggested to Grymston to seek a chantry at the cathedral, which he did after leaving his post at Oxford. Furthermore, two scholars, William Elot and William Kirkeby, successively served the chantry of William of Ste-Mère-Eglise, which was probably not a coincidence.[18] It may have been the policy of the chantry patrons, the bishops of London, to appoint scholars to that chantry. Generously endowed and located in the bishop's palace in the cathedral precinct, the chantry offered sufficient advantages to attract graduates. Of these graduates, three were at the cathedral for only a very short time: John Wodeward served his chantry for one year, John Tewkesbury completed eight months, while William Kirkeby spent only two weeks at the cathedral.[19] Instead of being the object of their ambitions, their chantries may have been considered a convenient stepping stone to further ecclesiastical preferment. Presumably

---

[14] GL Ms 25513, fols 57, 122v., 134, 148v., 223; LMA, Journal 10, fol. 362v.; Journal 11, fol. 168v.; GL Ms 25205/3; GL Ms 25630/1, fols 82, 116.

[15] GL Ms 25121/1995.

[16] All details are in Rousseau, 'Chantry Chaplains', Table 1.

[17] *BRUO*, vol. 1, p. 109; vol. 2, p. 835.

[18] GL Ms 9531/4, fol. 260v.; Ms 9531/6, fol. 45.

[19] GL Ms 25513, fols 167v., 170; Ms 9531/6, fols 45, 88v., 92.

Table 5.3   University attendance and degrees obtained (chaplains whose attendance is uncertain are represented in *italic*)[20]

	1300– 1349	1350– 1399	1400– 1449	1450– 1499	1500– 1548	Total
BA; MA; *magister, scholar*	*1*	*1*	4 + *1*	8 + *1*	20 + *2*	32 + *6*
Canon and Civil Law	–	1 + *1*	2	3 + *1*	7 + *1*	13 + *3*
Theology	–	–	1	2	5 + *1*	8 + *1*
Medicine	–	–	–	–	–	–
Music	–	–	–	–	1	1
Grammar	–	–	–	–	2	2
Total	*1*	1 + *2*	7 + *1*	13 + *2*	35 + *4*	56 + *10*

because of their higher education, they were well equipped for obtaining better-paid and more highly regarded positions (see Table 5.3).[21]

By the mid-fifteenth centurythe proportion of scholars among chantry chaplains had increased significantly. This dramatic increase in the number of university scholars among the beneficed clerks was not unique to St Paul's. In the diocese of Lincoln the percentage rose from 3.5 per cent in 1421–1431 to 11.5 per cent in 1495–1520.[22] This increase in university-educated chaplains at St Paul's reflects the general rise in university attendance, but was also a result of the particular interest in education among the later chantry founders.[23] The earliest example is found in Walter Sherrington's foundation (1447).[24] Among the chaplains appointed to Sherrington's chantry we find masters in grammar and a bachelor of arts.[25] The chaplains of Dowman's chantry (founded in 1525) were also to be

---

[20]   Information is taken from *BRUO, BRUC,* and from induction records.

[21]   Similarly, the highly educated secular clergy did not take on parish positions in the fifteenth century: see Virginia Davis, 'The Contribution of University-Educated Secular Clerics to the Pastoral Life of the English Church', in Caroline M. Barron and Jenny Stratford (eds), *The Church and Learning in Later Medieval Society: Essays in Honour of R.B. Dobson. Proceedings of the 1999 Harlaxton Symposium* (Donington, 2002), pp. 255–72.

[22]   Bowker, *Secular Clergy*, p. 44.

[23]   See Chapter 2, pp. 36–7.

[24]   Hearne, *History and Antiquities*, p. 183.

[25]   Thomas Batmanson, master in grammar, GL Ms 25630/1 fol. 81v.; John Wylmy, master in grammar; *Alumni*, vol. 4, p. 426; Richard Mors, BA; *BRUO, 1501–1540*, p. 402; David Owen was probably a doctor of theology: *BRUO, 1501–1540*, p. 426.

graduates.[26] Not surprisingly, a high proportion of the graduate chaplains served his chantries.[27] A concentration of scholars can also be observed among chaplains serving chantries other than those where university training was a requirement. Because Kempe's chantry was combined with a major canonry, the chaplains were ranked with the high officers of the cathedral bureaucracy and therefore more likely to be scholars.[28] Furthermore, two graduates served FitzJames's chantry between 1529 and 1548.[29] Likewise, three graduates were appointed to the chantry of William of Ste-Mère-Eglise in the sixteenth century.[30] It is worth noting that for both the chantries of FitzJames and of Ste-Mère-Eglise, the bishops of London were responsible for appointing the chaplains. Undoubtedly these chantry founders and patrons deemed university experience a guarantee of the quality of the incumbents. Nevertheless, a university education did not necessarily guarantee musical or singing ability, unless the chaplains had a degree in music, such as John Draper, appointed to Lovel's chantry in 1517.[31] In 1540 Walter Preston, although holding a BA, was given a few months to improve his singing.[32] Chaplains' skills had to be practical and enable them to fulfil their various tasks: singing in the choir, reading during the celebration of mass, and a certain level of literacy and numeracy for keeping accounts. Chantry chaplains often took on administrative tasks in addition to their chantry obligations, and their education allowed them to fulfil these responsibilities.[33] For example, John Tykhill, who served Bukerel's chantry, was also a rent collector for the cathedral.[34] Although he probably did not attend university, his handwriting has been described as 'confident and professional-looking – the hand of one obviously very used to writing'.[35] He wrote in Latin and in French, and he was the author of a poem in Middle English written on the verso of a roll of accounts

---

[26] GL Ms 25271/73.

[27] Thomas Ashton; Nicholas Barker; Richard Carre; Thomas Dorham; John Harryson; John Thompson; *Alumni*, vol. 1, pp. 47, 86, 296; vol. 2, pp. 77, 314–15; vol. 4, p. 224; Thomas Baker, *History of the College of St John the Evangelist* (Cambridge, 1869), vol. 1, p. 362.

[28] See Chapter 2, p. 39. Lepine, *Brotherhood of Canons*, pp. 54–65; see also *idem*, '"A Long Way from University": Cathedral Canons and Learning at Hereford in the Fifteenth Century', in Barron and Stratford, *Church and Learning*, pp. 178–95.

[29] John Hylle and Richard Pytt, *BRUO, 1501–1540*, pp. 309, 470.

[30] John Wyllarton, GL Ms 9531/12, fol. 161v.; Thomas Burton, *Alumni*, vol. 1, p. 268; John Longe, *BRUO, 1501–1540*, p. 360.

[31] *BRUO, 1501–1540*, p. 175.

[32] GL Ms 25630/1, fol. 93v.

[33] See below, pp. 127–8.

[34] GL Ms 25121/1985; Ms 25121/1076; Ms 25125/31–38; Ms 25513, fol. 78.

[35] Ruth Kennedy, '"A Bird in Bishopswood": Some Newly-Discovered Lines of Alliterative Verse from the Late Fourteenth Century', in Myra Stokes and T.L. Burton (eds),

dating from the mid-1390s.[36] His proficiency in three languages may have been unusual, and perhaps influenced the Dean and Chapter when they granted him the rectory of St Gregory's by St Paul's in 1398.[37]

Another indication of clerical learning, or at least a means by which to evaluate chaplains' intellectual interest, is their possession of books.[38] Henry Welewes inherited a *portiforium* of the Use of Sarum in 1361, which he gave in turn to one of his executors in 1391.[39] Welewes also distributed four collections of sermons [*libros sermonum*] among his executors and friends.[40] In 1399 William Salman left his *portiforium* to another chaplain, John de Colneye.[41] Minor canon Martin Elys (d.1394) bequeathed his *portiforium* with music of the Use of St Paul to the parish church of St Faith by St Paul's, although his collection was in fact more extensive.[42] At his death his heirs inherited several manuscripts, including the *Decretales Summarum*, a book entitled *Racionale Divinorum*,[43] another compilation of various treatises together with a 'Briton',[44] and a Legend of the Saints, presumably the Golden Legend. Chaplain William Palmer, serving one of Holme's chantries in the early 1390s, was probably another book owner, for a William Palmer (d.1400), rector of St Alphage and possibly the same man, left a copy of *Piers Plowman* to a female parishioner, Agnes Eggesfield.[45] Major canon William Storford (d.1416) bequeathed various books to minor canon Nicholas Overton, including a Psalter and a black book with all his treatises and notes,[46] while chaplain John Hecham was bequeathed

---

Medieval Literature and Antiquities. Studies in Honour of Basil Cottle (Cambridge, 1987), pp. 71–87, esp. p. 74.

[36] GL Ms 25121/1952; Ms 25121/1976.

[37] Hennessy, p. 321.

[38] Orme, 'Education and Learning', p. 274; Joel T. Rosenthal, 'Clerical Book Bequests: *A Vade Mecum*, But Whence and Whither?', in Barron and Stratford, *Church and Learning*, pp. 327–43; and Fiona Kisby, 'Books in London Parish Churches before 1603: Some Preliminary Observations', in *ibid.*, pp. 305–26.

[39] Sharpe, vol. 2, pp. 49–50; TNA PROB 11/1, fols 57v.–58.

[40] Welewes was holding the rectory of St Nicholas Olave, London and a chantry at St Paul's in plurality.

[41] GL Ms 9051/1, fol. 86.

[42] Sharpe, vol. 2, pp. 304–6; LMA HC roll 122(39).

[43] The liturgical handbook compiled in the late thirteenth century by William Durandus, Bishop of Mende.

[44] A treatise on law written in French, attributed to John Breton.

[45] Robert Wood, 'A Fourteenth-Century London Owner of Piers Plowman', *Medium Aevum*, 54 (1984), pp. 83–90.

[46] GL Ms 25513, fol. 49.

two books by major canon John Preston (d.1438).[47] In 1436 Thomas Damett, a major canon, bequeathed his book known as '*Le Speculum Curatorum*' to the communal library located near the *Presteshous*.[48] From 1450 onwards book ownership became more common among chantry chaplains and minor canons. Chaplain Nicholas Sabrisford (d.1464) possessed several books, in both Latin and English, and left to his fellow chaplain John Brewster his book called the Journal of Saints [*Jornal Sanctorum*], and to minor canon William Rooke a *parvum librum cum commendatione*.[49] From this small collection of books, it is apparent that his interests were, as we might expect, mostly religious and devotional. John Motram (d.1493) sold his antiphonal, which he had owned since he was chaplain at St Mary at Hill in 1464, to pay for twenty years of intercessions by his fellow chaplains at Holme's College.[50]

There might even have been a 'common profit library' circulating among chantry chaplains at St Paul's.[51] Nicholas Blome alias Bungay (d.1474) recorded that John Wynter, a former chaplain, had granted him some books for his own use during his lifetime, on the condition that at his death they were to be passed to another chaplain who would, in his turn, hand them over to a third, and so the collection was to be transferred from one suitable chaplain to another as long as the books lasted.[52] Blome chose Thomas Causy, his executor and fellow chaplain, to be the second recipient of these books, and his bequest is most revealing about chaplains' literary interests, as well as about their community. In the first half of the sixteenth century book ownership and book distribution continued to shape the chaplains' community. In 1509 John Church left books to three fellow minor canons: his book on the life of Christ [*librum de vita Christi*] to Nicholas Curleus, a *librum de Lira* (possibly of Nicholas of Lyre) in two volumes to George Horne, and a Bible to Edward Gamlyn.[53] Nicholas Curleus also received from the chaplain John Surdevall in 1522 a *booke of Chrownacles*. In addition, John Surdevall (d.1522) bequeathed his book of the life of Christ to

---

[47]　TNA PROB 11/3, fol. 180.

[48]　TNA PROB 11/3, fol. 164.

[49]　TNA PROB 11/5, fols 55v.–56.

[50]　Clive Burgess and Andrew Wathey, 'Mapping the Soundscape: Church Music in English Town, 1450–1550', *Early Music History*, 19 (2000), pp. 1–46, esp. p. 36.

[51]　Jo Ann H. Moran has studied such a case of book-circulation among chantry chaplains of York: see 'A "Common-Profit" Library in Fifteenth-Century England and Other Books for Chaplains', *Manuscripta*, 28 (1984), pp. 17–25. Wendy Scase has looked into a similar case of 'common-profit' books to be used by lay Londoners. Scase, 'Reginald Pecock, John Carpenter and John Colop's "Common-Profit" Books: Aspects of Book Ownership and Circulation in Fifteenth-Century London', *Medium Aevum*, 61 (1992), pp. 261–74.

[52]　TNA PROB 11/6, fols 135–135v.

[53]　TNA PROB 11/16, fol. 213.

John Clark, another chaplain of St Paul's.[54] Thomas Kent (d.1538) also possessed numerous books, which he distributed to his fellow priests.[55] Chaplains who owned service books also bequeathed them to other ecclesiastical institutions: Robert Aslyn (d.1539), minor canon, left to the parish church of St Gregory by St Paul's his 'manuell of written hand and parchement there ever to remayn'.[56] John Buckworth of St Peter's College (d.1541) bequeathed a new mass book to the chapel of St Anne in Pardon Churchyard.[57] Some chantry priests managed to put together large collections. William Carre (d.1537) owned thirty-two books, while in his will Richard Hooper (d.1545) alluded to more than twenty-five books, including an English Bible that he set aside for his sister.[58] These collections could cover wide areas of knowledge. Robert Skammenden, fellow of Holme's College, owned books of Justinian, of Richard de Saint Victor, and of St Bernard.[59] In 1528 Thomas Sewell, major canon and chaplain of Thomas Kempe's chantry, bequeathed all his books of law to his successors at Kempe's chantry to compensate for the dilapidation of the chantry chapel.[60] Impoverished by the dissolution of chantries, chaplain Thomas Wall (d.1550) only possessed books to give to his sister and executrix to recompense her for her labour: 'I have nothing to give you except therebee anny of my books that may do you please then I will that you shall have them.'[61] This example illustrates that book ownership was not the prerogative of the wealthiest clerics, for even a chaplain who appears to have struggled financially had some books of his own. Overall, book ownership seems to have been relatively common among chantry chaplains and minor canons of St Paul's Cathedral. Twenty seven chaplains either owned books or were given books as testamentary bequests, compared with thirty chaplains who died in office and did not mention any books in their wills. About half the chaplains of Norwich diocese and of York Minster also mentioned books

---

[54] TNA PROB 11/20, fol. 228.

[55] TNA PROB 11/27, fol. 186.

[56] TNA PROB 11/27, fol. 234v.

[57] GL Ms 25626/1, fol. 24. Buckworth also bequeathed a book by Erasmus and a French book of philosophy.

[58] GL Ms 25626/1, fols 60v–61.; TNA PROB 2/203B. I am grateful to David Lepine for this reference.

[59] GL Ms 25626/1, fols 49–49v.

[60] TNA PROB 11/22, fol. 136v.

[61] GL Ms 9171/12, fol. 34.

in their wills.[62] Albeit in lesser number, the chantry priests of Exeter Cathedral owned books, particularly service books, which they used for their work.[63]

Chantry chaplains, when they could, also provided for education and learning.[64] John Barvile, himself a bachelor of theology from Oxford University, asked his executors to distribute his goods in exchange for masses to be celebrated by poor scholars at Oxford or Cambridge.[65] Likewise, John Surdevall left monetary bequests to poor scholars of Oxford.[66] Some chaplains, however, played a more active role in promoting education. In his will (1538), Thomas Kent mentioned as his beneficiaries former and current students.[67] Kent also granted money to his nephew for his education. Another chaplain, Edmund Smyth (d.1540), also mentioned his 'scoller' as his executor.[68] These chaplains seem to have received payments for their educational services. Richard Hooper (d.1545) not only remembered his 'schollers' by letting them chose books from his extended collection, but he also gave them back the presents, such as plates, purses and crossbows, that he had received from their parents or tutors.[69]

It would be interesting to determine the average age at which the chaplains were first appointed to their chantries, in order both to understand the dynamic of their community and to illuminate their career patterns. Evidence about ages has, however, proved difficult to obtain, first because the candidate's age was not indicated at his induction, and second because the minimum required age for the different stages of ordination cannot be taken as a reference point for secular priests.[70] Secular priests, having decided to pursue a clerical career, often opted to be ordained in their twenties, moving rapidly through the various stages for ordination.[71] For example, the chaplain William Sleford obtained

---

[62] Ward, 'Foundation and Functions', p. 87. Edwards, 'Chantry Priests', p. 17; see also Claire Cross, 'York Clergy and Their Books in the Early Sixteenth Century', in Barron and Stratford, *Church and Learning*, pp. 344–54. The percentage of wills containing book bequests was smaller among rural priests; see Judith Middleton-Stewart, *Inward Purity and Outward Splendour. Death and Remembrance in the Deanery of Dunwich, Suffolk, 1370–1547* (Woodbridge, 2001), pp. 159–74, esp. p. 160.

[63] Orme, 'Education and Learning', p. 274.

[64] GL Ms 25626/1, fols 80v.–81v.

[65] *BRUO*, vol. 1, p. 125; GL Ms 9531/7, fol. 11.

[66] TNA PROB 11/20, fol. 228.

[67] TNA PROB 11/27, fol. 186.

[68] TNA PROB 11/28, fol. 86.

[69] GL Ms 25626/1, fols 60v.–61.

[70] The minimum age for ordination as subdeacon was seventeen, nineteen for deacon, and twenty-four for priest.

[71] Virginia Davis, 'Medieval Longevity: The Experience of Members of Religious Orders in Late Medieval England', *Medieval Prosopography*, 19 (1998), pp. 111–24; Swanson,

his three major ordinations within three months, becoming subdeacon on 25 February 1363, deacon on 18 March 1363 and finally priest on 27 May 1363.[72] Evidence, however, indicates the wide range of ages at which the chaplains were appointed. In some cases, as for William Sleford, the proximity between the date of ordination and the date of induction suggests that the candidate was in his twenties when he was given a chantry position at St Paul's.[73] Another indication that some chaplains joined the cathedral at an early stage in their career comes from the fact that some of them stayed in their post for over thirty years.[74] During a lengthy service, the chaplains' attitudes towards authority presumably would have varied. For example, in c.1370 Nicholas Wasshingborn *male occupat* his chantry, but twenty years later he was remembered by Dean John de Appelby in his will, which suggests that the turbulence of his youth had passed.[75] In contrast to these chaplains who were appointed in their youth, other chaplains were clearly appointed at a more advanced age. William Hawley was in his fifties at his appointment to Acra's chantry.[76] Furthermore, the high incidence of death in service, especially at some chantries such as that of Bishop William of Ste-Mère-Eglise, suggests that these chantries may have been given to elderly clerics as a retirement job.[77] It has been suggested elsewhere that 'a chantry was much less arduous than a parochial benefice or cure and possibly some of those exchanges which look so sinister, of a rectory or a vicarage for a chantry, may be accounted for by old age on the part of the incumbent'.[78] At the inquiry into pluralism in 1366 a few chantry chaplains were described as *senex presbiter*.[79] Furthermore, some chaplains had to retire from their positions because of old age. In 1444 Thomas Bukby, appointed to replace Richard Pepyn at More's chantry, promised to give his predecessor six marks annually for his pension.[80] Pepyn's first appearance in the cathedral archives had been in 1418.[81] Further evidence of old age comes from the designation of William Barnaby as deputy of John Wenlock in 1431 because of the latter's senility, and the dispensation

---

Church and Society, p. 43.

[72]   Davis, *Clergy*.

[73]   *Sudbury*, vol. 2, p. 148.

[74]   See below, pp. 123–4.

[75]   GL Ms 25121/1954; TNA PROB 11/1, fol. 11.

[76]   GL Ms 9531/7, fols 118v.–119; *BRUO*, vol. 2, p. 892.

[77]   GL Ms 9531/9, fol. 77v.; Ms 9531/10, fol. 8; Ms 9531/12, fol. 161v.

[78]   Heath, *English Parish Clergy*, p. 185.

[79]   Examples include Robert Keteringham and William Godrych; *Sudbury*, vol. 2, pp. 148, 152.

[80]   GL Ms 25513, fol. 227v.

[81]   GL Ms 25513, fol. 62.

from attending the choir given to Simon Deken in 1446 because of his old age.[82] Although the average age of chantry chaplains cannot be established from these examples, they nevertheless imply that both experienced men and novices were serving chantries at the cathedral, and both groups contributed their strengths and weaknesses to the community of chaplains at St Paul's.

Were the chaplains appointed to chantries newcomers, or already members of the cathedral community? It seems that a minority of chantry chaplains had been vicars choral and minor canons before being admitted to a chantry. According to the cathedral hierarchy, the usual pattern would have been for a clerk first to be appointed a vicar choral, because that position required only the order of subdeacon or deacon, and then be appointed to a chantry or a minor canonry once ordained a priest. Only one exception has been found to this usual pattern: William Savage was admitted as vicar choral a month *after* being admitted to de Baldock's chantry in 1433.[83] Yet only a small minority of vicars choral ever became chantry chaplains; seven between 1350 and 1399 and nine between 1400 and 1449.[84] The reduction in the number of vicars choral from thirty to six at some point during the fifteenth century probably explains why there is no evidence of a vicar choral becoming a chantry chaplain in the late fifteenth and early sixteenth centuries. Why did so few choral vicars become chantry chaplains? An obvious explanation could be that these vicars did not reach priesthood, although studies suggest that subdeacons usually became priests within a few years.[85] Priesthood was an absolute requirement in order to obtain a chantry, even if, on occasion, a chantry appointment pre-dated the acquisition of the correct clerical order.[86] John Pembroke, vicar choral, was elected as a minor canon at the same time as being admitted to the chantry of de Drayton and de Chishull on 23 December 1445, while he was ordained deacon on 2 April 1446 and priest on 11 June 1446 – four and six months *after* his promotion to a chantry at St Paul's.[87] Similarly, Henry Rede was ordained subdeacon in 1414 when he was a vicar choral of St Paul's and, ten years later in 1424, he sought the deaconry as a minor canon, although in 1423 he had been

---

82   GL Ms 25513, fols 134, 242. Deken is described as being in his sixties.
83   GL Ms 25513, fols 167–167v., 183v.
84   See Rousseau, 'Chantry Chaplains', Table 1.
85   Virginia Davis, 'Rivals for Ministry? Ordination of Secular and Regular Clergy in Southern England c.1300–1500', in Sheils and Wood, *Ministry: Clerical and Lay*, pp. 99–109, esp. p. 102.
86   Simon Townley, 'Unbeneficed Clergy in the Thirteenth Century: Two English Dioceses', in David M. Smith (ed.), *Studies in Clergy and Ministry in Medieval England* (York, 1991), pp. 38–65, esp. p. 51.
87   GL Ms 25513, fol. 233.

admitted to a chantry, for which he should have been a priest.[88] Rede may have been forced to resign both his chantry and his minor canonry, because he was accepted back among the vicars choral.[89] Rede received another chantry six years later, in 1430, again a few months before being ordained priest in March 1430; he died two years later.[90] On average, however, the delay between obtaining a position and proceeding to the appropriate clerical status was short, as in the case of Thomas Stafford, who was appointed to a chantry and to a minor canonry on 16 September 1443, and ordained a priest on 21 September 1443, five days later.[91]

Some chaplains were minor canons who took on an additional charge, while some minor canons had first been chantry priests. The selection process for minor canonries made it more likely that they would be chaplains first. Two candidates, apparently chosen by the community of minor canons, were presented to the Dean and Chapter, who elected the most eligible candidate to join the ranks of minor canons.[92] The unsuccessful candidate could, however, be short-listed again. In 1417 John Caston and John Scarle were presented to the minor canons, who selected Scarle, but in 1420 it was the turn of Caston to be elected.[93] Either preceding or following the induction to a chantry, the association of a minor canonry with a chaplaincy was common (Table 5.4).

This association nevertheless involved only a minority of chaplains, since there were only twelve minor canonries and a far greater number of chantries. Consequently, the majority of chaplains 'got their foot in the door' of the cathedral by first obtaining a chantry.

In the later Middle Ages it appears that chantry chaplains considered London as a place of opportunity because of the great number of religious foundations where they could find employment. The attraction of the capital was not restricted to the immediate area, but stretched well beyond the borders of the diocese. This sheds light not only on the great mobility of the lesser clergy, but also on the opportunities available to priests who converged on London in the hope of finding better-paid or more prestigious clerical positions. As long as they were properly ordained, their chances of securing a chantry depended on their reputation and on their social networks. In this market, in which potential employers had specified only the moral qualities required of the candidates, the

88 GL Ms 24, 513, fol. 94.
89 GL Ms 24, 513, fol. 95.
90 GL Ms 25513, fol. 137v.
91 GL Ms 25513, fol. 217.
92 Simpson, *Registrum Statutorum*, p. 325.
93 GL Ms 25513, fols 55v., 70v.

Table 5.4   Minor canons serving chantries

Period	Number of chaplains who also served as minor canons
1250–1299	4
1300–1349	10
1350–1399	15
1400–1449	54
1450–1499	10
1500–1548	38

right contacts and patrons were essential for ensuring a chantry position.[94] Indeed, in the absence of any university qualification or other proof of ability, chantry chaplains probably owed their appointment to their circle of benefactors, who either nominated them directly to a chantry position or put them in contact with patrons. In the sixteenth century the situation changed slightly as more chantry chaplains received a university education, although the importance of social networks and patronage should not be underestimated.[95]

Chaplains' Careers

Tracing the careers of 810 priests who occupied a chantry at St Paul's between the late thirteenth and mid-sixteenth centuries sheds light on the integration of the chantries into the clerical job market of medieval England, alongside rectories and vicarages, and on the chantry priests' contribution to the cathedral bureaucracy. The role played by chantries in the chaplains' careers may be

[94]   Same as Swanson's conclusion, in 'Chaucer's Parson and Other Priests', *Studies in the Age of Chaucer*, 13 (1991), pp. 41–80, esp. p. 56.

[95]   Swanson, 'Universities, Graduates', pp. 55–6. Even for graduates, the main difficulty was to establish the initial contacts with ecclesiastical patrons and obtain their first benefices.

Table 5.5   Number of years at St Paul's

Number of years	1250–1299	1300–1349	1350–1399	1400–1449	1450–1499	1500–1548	Total
Less than one	–	–	2	17	2	2	23
1–4	1	3	21	41	14	23	103
5–9	–	1	11	35	9	40	96
10–14	3	2	13	20	5	31	74
15–19	–	1	16	24	7	6	54
20–24	1	3	8	16	6	5	39
25–29	5	–	3	10	1	2	21
30+	–	6	7	10	4	4	31

appreciated by determining the extent and the nature of their association with the cathedral. Although the precise dates of arrival and departure were not recorded for all chaplains, an approximate length of tenure can be estimated for the great majority of them by taking as a rough benchmark the earliest or latest dates at which the chaplains' names appear in the cathedral records (see Table 5.5). These figures are of great interest but they must be treated with caution, for these dates provide only an indication of minimum durations. This kind of calculation also inevitably excludes some shorter stays at St Paul's, since the names of chaplains staying for a shorter duration are less likely to appear in archives. This explains why the brief occupations of chantries, particularly of less than a year, are only recorded in significant number in the first half of the fifteenth century, when the sources are richer. Despite these caveats, some conclusions may be drawn. The first observation concerns the discrepancy in the length of occupancies, which ranges from two weeks to more than forty years.[96] The chaplains of St Paul's were not unique in this range. The occupation of chantries at York Minster varied from three to forty-seven years.[97] Moreover, a fair proportion of chaplains remained at St Paul's for fewer than ten years. These chaplains presumably considered their chantries a springboard for seeking employment elsewhere. In contrast, a significant proportion of chaplains remained at the cathedral for more than twenty years, which suggests that these men spent most of their adult lives at the cathedral. These chaplains must have provided a measure of stability and continuity among a group constantly modified by rapid arrival and departure of a good proportion of its numbers.

---

[96]   Rousseau, 'Chantry Chaplains', Table 1.
[97]   Edwards, 'Chantry Priests', p. 30.

A sense of the chaplains' mobility may also be obtained by investigating their reasons for leaving their chantries. At St Paul's, approximately 45 per cent of the chaplains resigned from their chantries, while 55 per cent of them died in post. The proportion of those who died in office increased over time, ranging from 40 per cent in 1350–1399 and 45 per cent in 1400–1449, to 57 per cent in 1450–1499 and 82 per cent in the first half of the sixteenth century.[98] This increase suggests that there was a reduction in the opportunities available to chantry priests on the eve of the Reformation, linked to the general rise in population in the early sixteenth century. The chaplains who served for a shorter period of time were more likely to resign, while those who served for longer period more frequently died in office.

Once a chaplain was appointed to a chantry at St Paul's, did he retain the same position for the duration of his association with the cathedral, or did he move from one chantry to another? Movement between chantries would hint at the existence of a hierarchical ranking of the chantries, based perhaps on the monetary value or the prestige of the foundation. Evidence of chaplains serving more than one chantry, either concurrently or consecutively, survives for a minority. Seventy-two of them served at least two chantries, twenty-three were associated with three chantries, while four chaplains occupied four different chantries in the course of their employment at St Paul's. The longer chaplains spent at St Paul's, the more likely they were to transfer from one chantry to another. Length of service cannot, however, be the only explanation, for a number of chaplains who stayed at St Paul's for a considerable period of time occupied the same chantry throughout their service at the cathedral. For over twenty years, from 1370 to 1391, John Brewode received a stipend for serving Foliot's chantry, while Ralph Multon was the incumbent of de Bruera's chantry from 1370 to 1391.[99] John Lathebury was appointed to the chantry of John Beauchamp in 1386, and in 1408 his name appears in the chantry account rolls.[100] This constancy was not restricted to the chaplains of the late fourteenth century. Thomas Bramley served de Bruera's chantry for over forty years, from as early as 1477 to c.1517,[101] while Edmund Brograve was the incumbent of the charnel house for over forty-four years, between 1504 and 1548.[102] It appears to have been common for chaplains to occupy the same chantry over an extended

---

[98]   Ward also calculated an increase of the percentage of the chantry chaplains who died in office for the diocese of Norwich: 'Foundation and Functions', p. 36.

[99]   GL Ms 25121/1954; Ms 25125/18–28.

[100]   GL Ms 25121/1925; Ms 25125/27–50.

[101]   GL Ms 25125/94–99; Ms 5872A/1.

[102]   LMA, Journal 10, fol. 313v.; Repertory, vol. 12, fol. 29; *Chamber Accounts*, pp. 107, 09, 12, 14.

period of time rather than to move from one chantry to another. Among those chaplains who served more than one chantry, some occupied two chantries concurrently. In the list of c.1370, nine chaplains were each recorded as serving two chantries simultaneously.[103] Although exchanges of chantries occurred, it is difficult to know the reasons for these exchanges. No general patterns have emerged to provide a simple explanation for chantry exchanges between chaplains. Following the amalgamations of 1391, most chaplains were provided with an income of between eleven and fifteen marks, the majority of chantries being worth twelve marks.[104] For those chantries that were often combined with a minor canonry, the wages were somewhat more modest, varying between eight and thirteen marks. Nor do some chantries appear to have been more prestigious, or desirable, than others.[105] For example, John Mason was first admitted chaplain of the chantry for Basset and St Roger's parents in January 1427. In the following October he resigned from this chantry to be admitted to de Baldock's chantry, which he served until 1436, when he exchanged it for de Northburgh's chantry.[106] The chaplain who agreed to this last exchange, John Brown, had also served the chantry of Basset and St Roger from 1429 to 1432 before taking on de Northburgh's chantry.[107] There are many comparable exchanges between chantry chaplains of St Paul's. Although there does not appear to have been an established order of value and preference, whereby all the cathedral chantries were listed and according to which chantry chaplains were promoted, there is evidence for some kind of informal hierarchy among certain chantries. The chantry of Chigwell and de Swereford appears to have acted as a point of entry for a number of chantry chaplains, perhaps because this chantry had a low income of only eight marks per annum.[108] Of the eleven chaplains who are known to have been connected with the chantry in the first half of the fifteenth century, nine appear to have been assigned to this chantry upon their first appointment. These nine chaplains later moved to other chantries, either after only a few months or after a number of years. No other chantry at the

---

[103] GL Ms 25121/1954.

[104] Simpson, *Registrum Statutorum*, pp. 142–58.

[105] In this respect the chantry of William of Ste-Mère-Eglise in the bishop's palace did have a particular status. As previously noted, it attracted scholars. The chaplains serving that chantry had never previously been members of the cathedral, nor did they ever exchange their own for another chantry at the cathedral. Once, or possibly twice, the chaplain was promoted to a major canonry of the cathedral; see below.

[106] GL Ms 25513, fols 117, 121, 164v.

[107] GL Ms 25513, fols 130v., 137v., 164v., 167.

[108] *CPR, 1388–1392*, pp. 421–2.

cathedral seems to have fulfilled such a role and, perhaps as a result, this chantry was often given to a minor canon who already had other sources of income.

Chantry exchanges were often connected with the promotion to minor canonries. Some chantries were reserved exclusively for minor canons, although they also served ones that were not specifically reserved for them.[109] For example, the minor canon John Batell (d.1448) served the chantry of Walter de Thorp and Aveline of St Olave in 1443–1444, the chantry of Henry de Guldeford in 1444, and then the chantry of de Northburgh and de Idesworth.[110] None of these three chantries was usually associated with a minor canonry. Among the chantries reserved for minor canons, there seems to have been a certain order of precedence in accordance with which a minor canon was promoted from one chantry to another. John Caston, between 1420 and 1448, was consecutively the chaplain of de Drayton and de Chishull's chantry, then of St Dunstan's, and finally of de Hotham's chantry.[111] Similarly John Clerk (d.1447) served Chigwell and de Swereford's chantry, then de Drayton and de Chishull's chantry, then St Dunstan and Roger the Chaplain's chantry and, finally, the chantry of Richard and Stephen de Gravesend.[112] This association of a particular chantry with a specific minor canonry is clearly noted in Dean Sampson's register. In December 1540 John Norrys was admitted to both the ninth minor canonry and Swereford's chantry, while John Waklyn received the eleventh minor canonry in addition to de Newport's chantry.[113] The minor canons tended to change chantries more frequently than other chaplains, and these changes were connected to their progression in the minor canonries' hierarchy.

A minor canonry was not the only additional employment that chaplains might seek at the cathedral, although it was the most common form of promotion. Perhaps to increase their salary, or to make greater use of their abilities, chantry chaplains were also given administrative tasks. They might be employed in the personal service of the dean or of another cathedral dignitary. In the chantry list of c.1370, John Dunhale was described as being 'with the dean' [*cum decano est*], while in 1435 chaplain John Hecham was granted a licence to remain in the service of major canon John Preston for a few months.[114] The accounts of Dean William Worsley, covering the years 1479 to 1499, contain evidence of the

---

[109] See Chapter 2, pp. 38–9.
[110] GL Ms 25513, fols 211v., 225; Ms 9531/6, fol. 232v.
[111] GL Ms 25513, fols 70v.; 104, 166; Ms 25125/72–73.
[112] GL Ms 24513, fols 95, 166v., 212, 251v., 255v.
[113] GL Ms 25630/1 f. 108v.
[114] GL Ms 25513, fols 153v.–154.

service of a dozen chantry chaplains in the dean's household.[115] Chantry chaplains entered the large cathedral bureaucracy and held positions such as sacristan, chamberlain, rent collector, or warden of relics.[116] Their daily presence in the cathedral church would have made them ideal candidates for administrative tasks. While Henry Jolypace may have had an exceptional profile, his various occupations within St Paul's illustrate the range of opportunities offered to chantry chaplains. From 1391 he held the position of chamberlain in addition to his chantry, while in 1424 he was appointed warden of the New Work.[117] The competence and reliability which he demonstrated while holding these positions presumably accounted for the relationships of trust he clearly established with senior members of the cathedral hierarchy. Jolypace was appointed executor of the wills of four cathedral dignitaries, including three deans.[118] The fact, however, that Jolypace never obtained a minor canonry suggests that although a minor canonry appears to have been the goal of many chaplains, such ambition was not universal; some chaplains clearly preferred to maintain their status as chantry priests instead of joining the ranks of the minor canons.

If the association of a minor canonry with a chantry was comparatively common at St Paul's Cathedral, the combination of a major canonry and chantry was rare. There are only few references that may allude to such an association, and they are problematic. William Coloyne, chaplain of Alan and Aveline Basset's chantry in c.1370, may be the major canon of the same name who held the prebend of Reculversland in 1371 and in 1389.[119] John Wyke, who served the chantry of William of Ste-Mère-Eglise from 1386 to 1396, may then have been promoted to a major canonry, for a John Wyke was precentor from 1394 to 1397, as well as major canon from 1398 to 1428.[120] Thomas Pulter had an extraordinary career path. He was successively chantry chaplain, chamberlain and sacristan, before becoming a major canon both at St Paul's and at Lichfield, in 1427 and in 1428 respectively.[121] In the sixteenth century the association

---

[115] GL Ms 25166; Hannes Kleineke and Stephanie R. Hovland (eds), *The Estate and Household Accounts of William Worsley, Dean of St Paul's Cathedral, 1479–1499*, London Record Society, 40 (Donington, 2004), pp. 135, 137–8, 150, 166, 170–71.

[116] See Rousseau, 'Chantry Chaplains', Table 1.

[117] GL Ms 25125/27; Ms 25121/361; Ms 25513, fol. 135.

[118] He was the executor of wills of Dean Thomas de Eure, GL Ms 25138; of Dean Thomas Stowe, MS 25271/62; of Canon Laurence Allerthorp, TNA PROB 11/2A, fol. 88; and of Dean Thomas More, Lambeth Palace Ms 2018.

[119] *Fasti II*, p. 58; GL Ms 25121/1954.

[120] *Fasti II*, pp. 17, 71; GL Ms 9531/3, fols 108, 203.

[121] GL Ms 25125/51–59; Ms 25513, fols 5v., 59v.; 74v., 118v., 222v.; *Fasti II*, p. 53; Hennessy, p. 107; Le Neve, *Fasti Ecclesiae Anglicanae 1300–1541*, vol. X: *Coventy and Lichfield*, compiled by B. Jones (London, 1964), pp. 41, 48.

between a major canonry and a chantry was more frequent because of Kempe's foundation.[122] There was also a case of a chantry chaplain being promoted to the ranks of the major canons. After serving the chantry of Bishop William of Ste-Mère-Eglise for seven years, Robert Higden was made a major canon in 1541.[123] We have already observed that the bishops of London usually chose highly educated and experienced clerks for that chantry. Contrary to the treasurer of Lincoln Cathedral who took up a chantry at Manton to supplement his income, major canons of St Paul's did not appear to have sought chantry positions, at least not at the cathedral.[124]

In addition to the obligation to fulfil the religious duties of their chantries, some chaplains were also employed by the fraternities that met in the cathedral. For example, the chaplain Richard Gates appears in the accounts of the fraternity of the Holy Name of Jesus between 1522 and 1531 as responsible for ensuring that there was sufficient wax in the chapel of Jesus.[125] The minor canon John Church was also paid for celebrating services for the fraternity in the absence of the dean.[126] In 1507 he signed the fraternity's new ordinances on behalf of all the cathedral ministers.[127] In addition to these commemorative and liturgical services within the cathedral, the chantry priests also took part in services held outside the cathedral. For instance, payments were occasionally made at the London parish church of St Mary at Hill to chantry priests of St Paul's to sing in the choir.[128] This participation in additional religious services enabled the chantry priests to increase their wages without taking on the duties of a second benefice. Only one chantry founder, John Dowman, attempted to restrict the additional extra-mural activities of his chantry priests.[129]

Chantry chaplains usually served the same chantry for the duration of their stay at St Paul's, while also undertaking other administrative and liturgical tasks. Nonetheless, the cathedral did not have a monopoly on their services, for chantry chaplains were also associated with other churches before, during and after their time at St Paul's. In fact, chantries at St Paul's formed part of the large job market open to the English clergy in the later Middle Ages. They were,

---

[122] See Chapter 2, p. 39.

[123] He resigned from his chantry a year later, GL Ms 9531/11, fol. 29v.; Ms 9531/12, fol. 148v.; Ms 25630/1, fol. 116; *Fasti II*, p. 36.

[124] Thomson, *Early Tudor Church*, p. 63.

[125] New, 'Cult of the Holy Name', p. 133.

[126] *Ibid.*, p. 135.

[127] David Mateer and Elizabeth New, '"In Nomine Jesu": Robert Fayrfax and the Guild of the Holy Name in St Paul's Cathedral', *Music & Letters*, 81/4 (2000), pp. 507–19, esp. p. 516.

[128] Burgess and Wathey, 'Mapping the Soundscape', p. 16.

[129] GL Ms 25271/73.

in some ways, comparable to vicarages and rectories, to which chaplains could have access depending on market conditions, the stage of their own careers, and the range of their contacts. Overall, employment outside the cathedral can be established for about one-third of the chantry chaplains of St Paul's.[130] It appears that chantries had the same status as, and presumably equivalent income to, vicarages and rectories. Rectors sometimes left their churches to accept chantry positions at St Paul's, while chaplains also resigned from their chantries to take over vicarages. In 1424 John Ragon left the rectory of St John sub Castro, Lewes to take over the chantry of Lovel and de Braynford at St Paul's, and in 1427 John Wade became vicar of Ledecombe in the diocese of Salisbury after spending six years at St Paul's as a chantry chaplain.[131] The traffic went in both directions. In general, surviving information about appointments to chantries outside St Paul's is scarce. Evidence survives for only a few cases. For example, John Martyn resigned from a chantry in the church of St Nicholas Shambles to accept a position at St Paul, while John Ceyton served the chantry of the Black Prince in Canterbury after leaving St Paul's.[132] It may be assumed nevertheless that a proportion of the chaplains without additional career details may have occupied chantries elsewhere before or after their service at the cathedral.

As mentioned in the discussion of the chaplains' ages, a cathedral chantry could have been a first appointment, a post taken up at any time in the course of the chaplains' careers, or indeed granted as a form of retirement pension, particularly to priests who had been in the service of the bishops of London. Chantries may have provided employment between posts in parish churches. With its numerous chantry positions, the cathedral acted as a haven for some chaplains, to which they came and went throughout the course of their careers. For example, Philip Grene resigned from the chantry of Frisell and John le Romeyn in 1421 to accept the vicarage of Nasing, Essex, which he gave up in 1427 to return to St Paul's and serve Wokyndon's chantry.[133] Chantries were also occupied simultaneously with other employment. Although pluralism never reached the same levels as for the privileged higher clergy of the cathedral, it nevertheless affected the lesser clergy. The inquiry into pluralism at St Paul's in 1366 demonstrated that twenty-five out of seventy-four chaplains held a second benefice in addition to their chantry at St Paul's.[134] Among these twenty-five chaplains, nineteen were associated with a London parish church. In a similar

---

[130] See Rousseau, 'Chantry Chaplains', Table 1.

[131] GL Ms 25513, fols 100; 122.

[132] GL Ms 9531/4, fol. 115; Ms 25513, fols 5v.; Hennessy, p. 42; GL Ms 25513, fols 94, 99.

[133] GL Ms 25513, fols 75v., 79; Ms 9531/5, fol. 23.

[134] *Sudbury*, vol. 2, pp. 148–82. For a general discussion on the 1366 inquiry into pluralism, see Godfrey, 'Pluralists', pp. 23–40.

inquiry made into the twelve minor canons of St Paul's at about the same time, nine of them were declared to hold benefices outside the cathedral.[135] Some chantries seem to have been associated with a particular rectory or vicarage, for Robert Hood was admitted to his chantry on the same day (8 July 1365) that he was appointed to the rectory of St Andrew Undershaft by the bishop of London. In a famous passage that has been much discussed, Chaucer suggests that rural rectors abandoned their parishes to the care of 'hirelings' in order to take up a chantry at St Paul's.[136] In fact, it would seem that this was not frequently the case. When the chantry chaplains held rectories in plurality with their chantries, these were often London benefices, which they would have been well able to take care of alongside their chantry duties. As a result of the amalgamations of 1391, when the chaplains' wages were increased by combining the income of two chantries, the incidence of pluralism among the lesser clergy of the cathedral appears to have been somewhat reduced. In contrast to the nineteen chaplains who had served a London parish in addition to their chantries in 1366, no chantry chaplain and only one minor canon was a rector in London on the eve of the dissolution.[137] Pluralism had not totally disappeared, however. In the few years preceding the dissolution, a number of chaplains had requested dispensation licences from the newly established faculty office to hold benefices additional to their cathedral chantries.[138]

While some of St Paul's chantry chaplains remained in the same clerical office outside the cathedral for a considerable length of time, others frequently moved from one benefice to another. For example, John Ceyton served two chantries at the cathedral between 1438 and 1442 in addition to his minor canonry, and then occupied four rectories and one chantry at Canterbury Cathedral between 1442 and 1450.[139] Some chaplains seem to have retained their chantry as their main employment, while changing their second benefice more frequently. William Coupmanthorp had links with St Paul's from at least 1366 to 1381, while at the same time he was associated with three different parishes: Withcall in the diocese of Lincoln, St Alphage in London and in 1381 Ingatestone in the archdeaconry of Essex.[140] What motivated some chaplains to move from one clerical benefice

---

[135] GL Ms 25121/1908.

[136] Chaucer, *Canterbury Tales*, Prologue, ll. 507–10; Hill, '*Chaunterie for Soules*', pp. 242, 255.

[137] John Waklyn, a minor canon, was also rector of St Gregory; see Kitching, no. 10; Hennessy, p. 321.

[138] D.S. Chambers, *Faculty Office Registers, 1534–1549: a Calendar of the First Two Registers of the Archbishop of Canterbury's Faculty Office* (Oxford, 1966) pp. 51, 71, 174, 223.

[139] GL Ms 25513, fols 166, 167v., 170v., 203v., 208; Hennessy, pp. 61, 275, 341.

[140] *Sudbury*, vol. 1, p. 279; Hennessy, p. 86; McHardy, p. 22.

to another, and other chaplains to stay in one place, is hard to determine. Some reasons can, however, be suggested, such as the monetary value of the benefices, the weight of the responsibilities and duties of the incumbents, and the social prestige attached to some positions. In addition to personal motivation, such as the desire for change, any of these reasons may have influenced a chaplain to transfer from one benefice to another. There were two possible ways for the lesser clergy to acquire a benefice: they were either appointed by the patrons who owned the advowson to that specific position; or they agreed to exchange their benefices with another cleric. The first method was more common, although the second also played an important role among the lesser clergy in the later Middle Ages. A wide range of ecclesiastical patrons assisted with the careers of chantry chaplains before, during and after their association with St Paul's.[141] Not surprisingly, the bishop of London and the Dean and Chapter of St Paul's were among the most influential patrons for chantry priests. Not only did they intervene in the appointment to chantries within the cathedral, but they also appointed chaplains to vicarages and rectories under their patronage. For instance, the Dean and Chapter held the advowsons of nineteen churches in London.[142] There was also a series of patrons who sporadically promoted the lesser clergy to clerical benefices. How the lesser clergy initially established contacts with these patrons remains obscure. It appears that priests in search of job opportunities may have advertised their services on the doors of St Paul's.[143] In 1479 William Paston asked his servant if he knew any young priest in London who 'setteth billis vpon Powlys dorre'.[144]

For the chaplains whose first assignment was a chantry at St Paul's, it may be suggested that their association with the Dean and Chapter allowed them to gain access to a circle of potential patrons. For a number of other chaplains, it was clearly their previous association with some prominent benefactor that accounted for their promotion to clerical benefices at the cathedral. Very unusually, a draft letter shedding light on the mechanism by which a priest may have secured a chantry at St Paul's (by relying on the interventions of a benefactor) survives on the verso of an account roll from the reign of Henry VI belonging to the collegiate chapel of St George at Windsor.[145] In this undated,

---

[141]   See Rousseau, 'Chantry Chaplains', Table 1.

[142]   Caroline M. Barron, 'London and St Paul's Cathedral in the Later Middle Ages', in Backhouse, *Medieval English Cathedral*, pp. 126–49, esp. p. 136.

[143]   Westlake, *Parish Gilds*, p. 48; Swanson, 'Chaucer's Parson', p. 70, n.98.

[144]   Norman Davis (ed.), *Paston Letters and Papers of the Fifteenth Century* (Oxford, 1971), vol. 1, p. 184.

[145]   St George's Chapel XV.48.21. I am grateful to Dr Hannes Kleineke for this reference.

unaddressed and unsigned letter, a priest refused a chantry at St Paul's that his patron (unnamed) had secured for him, on the ground that he was 'sick and old' and that the world was 'strange, troubled, uncertain and unstable', and in these circumstances he preferred to remain in the more secure position at St George's Chapel. He urged his patron to secure the chantry position instead for one of his other protégés. Another means of obtaining a clerical benefice, and one that did not entail either waiting for a vacancy or gaining the favour of a potential patron, was to take part in an exchange for benefices.[146] In 1364 William Neel exchanged his chantry with John Estnesten, rector of Ilford-parva in the archdeaconry of Essex, and the abbot of Stratford-Langthorne, patron of this rectory, approved the exchange.[147] How clerks wishing to exchange their benefices contacted each other is, however, rather vague. In one case, a family connection seems to have been key to the exchange. In 1435, William Geek exchanged Holme's chantry for the rectory of Warley, in the archdeaconry of Essex, with a clerk by the name of Richard Geek, perhaps a relative.[148] In another case, the agreement turned sour after the chaplain found out that the parsonage was not worth as much as promised, and refused to go through with the exchange.[149]

St Paul's chantry chaplains are known to have had connections with more than forty parish churches of the city of London. Some associations were sporadic, while others were more long-term. For instance, in the years between 1363 and 1374, three chaplains of St Paul's were associated with St George's Botolph Lane. At St Mary Abchurch, two chantry chaplains, and at St Peter Paul's Wharf, three, succeeded one another as rector.[150] The lesser clergy of St Paul's were particularly closely associated with two parish churches in London, St Faith and St Gregory, both located in the cathedral precinct. The parishioners of St Faith met in the crypt beneath the east end of St Paul's, and the church of St Gregory was attached to the southern wall of the nave.[151] For each church there were at

---

[146] For a discussion on exchange pattern, see A.K. McHardy, 'Some Patterns of Ecclesiastical Patronage in the Later Middle Ages', in David M. Smith (ed.), *Studies in Clergy and Ministry in Medieval England*, Borthwick Studies in History, 1 (York, 1991), pp. 20–37, esp. p. 32. She suggests that the trade was organised in London by professional brokers.

[147] *Sudbury*, vol. 1, p. 242; Newcourt, vol. 2, p. 345.

[148] GL Ms 25513, fol. 154v.

[149] TNA C1/75/73.

[150] At St Mary Abchurch, Henry Gunne was appointed rector in July 1437, followed by John Pound in 1440. This same Henry Gunne had been rector of St Peter Paul's Wharf in 1435 following the death of rector John Davels, who previously had also been chantry chaplain at St Paul's. In 1437 Gunne was replaced by John Good who, the same year, resigned from Husband's chantry, GL Ms 25513, fols 85, 92, 150v.; Hennessy, pp. 296, 351.

[151] For a discussion of these two parishes, see New, 'Cult of the Holy Name', pp. 355–60.

least four appointments of chantry chaplains, but the number was probably higher.[152] The association was particularly strong between the minor canons and the church of St Gregory, where the minor canons had held the advowson since 1445. Chantry chaplains found employment in the churches in the diocese of London, although some churches had closer connections with the cathedral than others. For example, three chantry chaplains had connection with the church of Acton, Middlesex.[153] The chantry chaplains of St Paul's also had connections with churches across the country. The dioceses of Canterbury, Coventry and Lichfield, Exeter, Norwich, Rochester, Winchester, and Worcester, to name just a few, provided clerical benefices for chaplains of St Paul's.[154] One chaplain was even associated with a parish church in the diocese of Armagh in Ireland.[155] It was, however, in the diocese of Lincoln – no doubt because of its size – that the chantry chaplains of St Paul's Cathedral most frequently found employment.

Although chaplains from St Paul's found employment in parishes across the realm, the strongest connections were developed with churches located relatively close to the cathedral, within the diocese of London and, notably, within the city of London itself. The group of chantry priests seem to have been a particularly mobile group, fully integrated into the national job market for the lower clergy. In their careers, the place occupied by the cathedral varied greatly from one individual to another, according to ambition and vocation. It is possible, however, to explore the integration of these chantry priests into the cathedral community, their ties of friendship and family loyalty, their relations with the city of London, and their personal devotion and piety by examining their surviving wills.

Chaplains' Wills

Although some conventions were observed during the writing of wills, they nevertheless reveal some of the chaplains' preoccupations and preferences, and

---

[152] Appointments in the fifteenth century were not systematically recorded; see Hennessy, pp. 99, 320–21.

[153] Hennessy, pp. 70–71; Rousseau, 'Chantry Chaplains', Table 1: 'Barvile', 'Pertenhale' and 'Wyghton'.

[154] See Rousseau, 'Chantry Chaplains', Table 1. Two chantry chaplains, John Coryngdon and Henry Rede, may have been associated with Exeter Cathedral when they were adolescent; see Orme, *Minor Clergy of Exeter Cathedral*, pp. 94, 107.

[155] Richard Hopere, *Sudbury*, vol. 2, p. 162. Hopere may have been native of Ireland, for a number of Irish clerics found employment in London, see Virginia Davis, 'Irish Clergy in late Medieval England', *Irish Historical Studies*, 32 (2000), pp. 145–60.

constitute a unique source of information about these men.[156] Wills have survived for some eighty chaplains working at St Paul's from the late fourteenth to the mid-sixteenth century.[157] In their wills, testators first took care of their souls, usually placing them in the care of God, the Blessed Virgin Mary and the holy company of Heaven, and then turned to the disposal of their bodies. The belief in the resurrection of the body and the value attributed to masses and prayers to accelerate the passage of souls through purgatory gave a special significance to the choice of burial sites, which reflected beliefs, allegiances, financial dispositions and particular affections.[158] The majority specified a particular place where their bodies should be buried, but some of them left it to the discretion of their executors, or to divine will. Whether the chaplains were holding office at the time of writing their wills seems to have been the most important determination for their choice of burial site. Not surprisingly, most chaplains at St Paul's who died in office wished to be buried within the precinct, and in the later Middle Ages, St Paul's offered a choice of burial grounds in the cathedral precinct. The Pardon Churchyard was situated in middle of the north cloister, in the arm formed by the nave and the north transept of the cathedral.[159] This burial place was popular with the chaplains. Even though John Templer (d.1383) had been chaplain at St Paul's for only two years, he requested burial there.[160] A section of the Pardon Churchyard was presumably reserved for members of the cathedral, and it may be to this that Martin Elys, chaplain and minor canon of St Paul's, referred in 1394 when he requested burial in the 'churchyard of the canons', next to Simon Charwelton, also minor canon.[161] Robert Aslyn (d.1539), minor canon, requested a burial site under the wall of his chamber, revealing the proximity of the cloister to the college of the minor canons on the north side of the cathedral precinct, and Edmund Smyth (d.1540) requested burial in the

[156] Burgess, 'Late Medieval Wills', pp. 14–33.

[157] Most of them are listed in Rousseau, 'Chantry Chaplains', Table 1. The list, however, does not include references to the wills of Thomas Heylyn, Robert Dandy, Thomas Brynkbury, John Andrew, John Painter, Edmund Brograve, John Richardson, William Streket and Henry Rawlyns; see GL Ms 25626/1, fols 11v., 51–51v., 80v.–82v., 83v., 87v.–88, 106–107, 109v., 110–110v.

[158] Burial sites in London have been studied by Vanessa Harding, 'Burial Choice and Burial Location in Later Medieval London', in Basset, *Death in Towns*, pp. 118–35; eadem, *The Dead and the Living in Paris and London, 1500–1670* (Cambridge, 2002), Chapters 3, 4 and 5.

[159] See Chapter 3, p. 74.

[160] GL Ms 9171/1, fol. 109. He had previously been vicar of Little Houghton, in the diocese of Lincoln: *CPR, 1381–1385*, p. 58. Richard Neale (d.1545) also requested to be buried in the Pardon Churchyard, near the tomb of Thomas Becket's father, GL Ms 25626/1, fol. 49.

[161] Sharpe, vol. 2, pp. 304–6.

Pardon Churchyard, next to a late subdean of St Paul's.[162] Thomas Elys asked to be buried next to the tomb of a fellow minor canon, Laurence Damlett, in 1490.[163] A number of chaplains wanted to be buried in the main churchyard of the precinct, which lay to the north-east of the cathedral.[164] This burial site was popular among Londoners, especially for the parishioners of London churches that did not have churchyards.[165] The presence of the famous cross of St Paul's, where people gathered to hear sermons and speeches, probably inspired their choice. Chaplains also often chose specific chapels within the cathedral church or precinct for burial. John Bryggewater (d.1427) expressed the wish to be buried before the altar decorated with the painting of the Last Judgement in the western part of the charnel house chapel.[166] After serving Beyvin's chantry in the charnel house from 1427 until his death in 1443, David Flure asked to be buried in the chapel there in front of the door.[167] Thomas South (d.1534) asked to be buried in the chapel consecrated to SS Anne and Thomas the Martyr.[168] Likewise Peter Watlyngton (d.1458) chose the chapel of the Holy Spirit (Holme's chapel) for his burial.[169] He wanted to be buried before the altar of St James under the marble stone he had already provided. Holme's chapel was also the chosen burial site of Robert Langton (d.1534), while Nicholas Blome alias Bungay asked to be buried in the chapel of St John Baptist in 1474.[170] After serving the chantry of Bishop Kempe, John Barvile (d.1482) expressed his attachment to it by asking to be buried outside the west end of the stone-caged chantry chapel.[171] Members of the cathedral sometimes selected the crypt as a burial place, perhaps in order to express their devotion to the cult of the Holy Name of Jesus.[172] A location near the statue of Christ was particularly prized.[173]

Not all chaplains asked to be buried at St Paul's, particularly if they had moved on to another post. William Salman, who had been chaplain of Chigwell's chantry in 1391, died while rector of St Peter Paul's Wharf in 1400, where he

---

[162] TNA PROB 11/27, fol. 234v.; PROB 11/28, fol. 86.

[163] TNA PROB 11/8, fol. 206v.

[164] See for example, Richard Hooper's will (1545), GL Ms 25626/1, fols 60v.–61; and Thomas Sewell (d.1527), TNA PROB 11/22, fol. 136v.

[165] Harding, 'Burial Choice', pp. 123–5; New, 'Cult of the Holy Name', pp. 346–8.

[166] GL Ms 9171/3, fol. 183.

[167] *Letter-Book K*, p. 60; GL Ms 9531/6, fol. 74; Ms 9171/4, fol. 126v.

[168] TNA PROB 11/25, fol. 93.

[169] GL Ms 25513, fol. 177v.; Ms 9171/5, fol. 238v.

[170] TNA PROB 11/6, fol. 135; PROB 11/25, f. 109v.

[171] GL Ms 9531/7, fol. 11.

[172] New, 'Cult of the Holy Name', pp. 259–60.

[173] John Church (d.1509), TNA PROB 11/16, fol. 213.

had asked to be buried.[174] In 1431 William Wright, by then rector of St Michael Queenhithe, also wished to be buried in the chancel of his church: he had probably left St Paul's some time before, since his last appearance as a chantry chaplain there dates to 1406.[175] He did, however, remember the cathedral in his will and asked that torches be placed in the chapel of SS Anne and Thomas and in the chapel of St Dunstan. He also asked for prayers for Thomas More, his former patron, for whom he had acted as executor.[176] Some chaplains, who were in fact members of the clerical community of St Paul's at the time of their deaths, also chose to be buried elsewhere. These chaplains were concurrently rectors or vicars of a parish church, and their ultimate allegiance seems to have been to their parish church, where they asked to be buried.[177] Henry Bever (d.1386) asked to be buried in the chancel of the parish church of St Peter Broad Street, where he had been rector from 1356 to 1386 while chaplain at St Paul's.[178] Thomas Kendall (d.1390) also preferred his parish church, of St Augustine, where he had been rector for almost thirty years (1362–1390), above the chantry of John Fabel, which he served for more than fifteen years (1366–1381, possibly until 1390).[179] Many of the minor canons who served the church of St Gregory asked to be buried in the chancel there, next to each other, in this way creating a post-mortem community.[180]

The chaplains of St Paul's were brought together by the tasks they had to perform and by the living arrangements they had to observe. The ideals of communal life, promoted by the various colleges, dictated the patterns of their daily lives as members of the lesser clergy, but these regulations seem also to have fostered a collective identity. An *esprit de corps* that bound chaplains together is occasionally revealed in the chaplains' wills through collective donations, and through self-identification as fellows of chantry colleges.[181] Henry Welewes (d.1392), chantry chaplain and rector of St Nicholas Olave, bequeathed 20s to *sociis meis in co(mmun)i aula presbitorum Sancti Pauli*.[182] Until the Reformation, chantry chaplains and other members of the cathedral acknowledged the

---

[174] GL Ms 9051/1, fol. 86.

[175] *Letter-Book I*, pp. 45–6; GL Ms 9171/3, fol. 260v.

[176] Lambeth Palace Ms 2018.

[177] For example, Henry Welewes (d.1392), chantry chaplain and rector of St Nicholas Olave, asked to be buried in the chancel of his parish church, TNA PROB 11/1, fols 57v.–58.

[178] GL Ms 25121/3043; Ms 25121/27; Hennessy, p. 376; McHardy, p. 14; GL Ms 9171/1, fols 144v.–145.

[179] *Sudbury*, vol. 2, p. 155; McHardy, p. 1; Hennessy, p. 98; GL Ms 9171/1, fol. 203.

[180] GL Ms 25626/1, fols 1, 18, 51; TNA PROB 11/18, fol. 8; PROB 11/25, fol. 99.

[181] GL Ms 25626/1, fols 8v.–9, 11v., 24, 31, 49.

[182] TNA PROB 11/1, fols 57v.–58.

existence of the community of chaplains, and contributed to the prosperity of the three chantry colleges – Holme's College, Lancaster College and St Peter's College – by leaving them money, books and various domestic goods.[183] Robert Langton (d.1534) bequeathed to Holme's College a newly printed mass book, a basin and a tablecloth, while Richard Neale (d.1545) and Robert Skammenden (d.1545) left money for the construction of a kitchen chimney and a dinner room in the college.[184] The attachment of the minor canons to their communal hall is revealed in testamentary bequests to improve the comfort of the college. John Palmer (d.1532) and Thomas Kent (d.1538) both left money to the repair of the fireplace, and Kent bequeathed to the college his 'sett of chessemen and the table'.[185] Likewise Thomas Sewell (d.1527), major canon and chaplain of Kempe's chantry, gave a hogshead of wine to the priests of St Peter's College.[186] Other bequests displaying an *esprit de corps* include payments to attend the testator's funeral and other commemorative services, such as chaplain Henry Bever's request in 1386 that the minor canons and the chantry chaplains should each receive 12d for attending his funeral.[187] William Godrych (d.1380) also gave the same amount of money to the chantry chaplains of St Paul's and to the clergy of his parish church to attend his funeral.[188] These donations reveal the importance of the experience at St Paul's in a chaplain's life, and the ways in which a sense of a clerical community was developed.

The communal life led to the development of special relations between chaplains and the formation of ties of friendship. Not surprisingly, chaplains asked each other to act as executors, or to witness their wills.[189] David Flure drew up his will in 1443 in the presence of three priests, while Thomas Elys (d.1490) named two fellow minor canons as executors of his will.[190] Two other chaplains, Thomas Graunger and William Botery, were made executors of the will of John Barvile (d.1482), who was a major canon and chantry chaplain, and the sealing of this will was witnessed by three chaplains.[191] William Carre (d.1538) named

---

[183] In 1400 Dean Thomas de Eure left bequests to the communities of the minor canons, the chantry chaplains and the vicars choral; GL Ms 9531/3, fols 418v.–419; Richard Hayman (d.1464), TNA PROB 11/5, fol. 42v.; Thomas Sewell (d.1527), PROB 11/22, fol. 136v.

[184] TNA PROB 11/25, fol. 109v.; GL Ms 25626/1, fol. 49.

[185] TNA PROB 11/24, fol. 93; PROB 11/27 fol. 186.

[186] TNA PROB 11/22, fol. 136v.

[187] GL Ms 9171/1, fol. 144v.

[188] GL Ms 9171/1, fol. 71v.

[189] Edwards reached the same conclusion about the chantry priests of York Minster: 'Chantry Priests', p. 37.

[190] GL Ms 9171/4, fol. 126v.; TNA PROB 11/8, fol. 204v.

[191] GL Ms 9531/7, fol. 11.

six fellow chaplains who were to receive money to pray for his soul, and Robert Langton (d.1534) also bequeathed money to six chaplains of St Paul's, five of whom witnessed his will.[192] More intimate ties of friendship are also revealed in the chaplains' wills: William Salman (d.1399) remembered a chaplain serving at St Paul's and bequeathed him money.[193] This gift suggests that the friendship between chaplains extended beyond the cathedral precinct, for Salman was at that time serving a parish church. Nicholas Sabrisford (d.1464), who left specific bequests to particular clerics from both the higher and lower ranks of the cathedral clergy, demonstrated a sense of community that included all the clergy of St Paul's.[194] Personal gifts, such as 'gold ryng that [he] wore on [his] fynger with a jacynthe', which Robert Aslyn (d.1539) bequeathed to his fellow minor canon Edmund Smyth, reveal the close affinities developed by the clergy.[195]

Although the minor canons were above the chantry chaplains in the cathedral hierarchy and the two groups lived in different colleges, their daily activities and responsibilities appear to have united them as one large community of lesser clergy. Most testators referred to minor canons and chantry chaplains without distinction. They left each other bequests, witnessed their wills, and acted as executors. Exceptionally, Edmund Smyth (d.1540) made a clear distinction between the minor canons and the other lesser clergy: he designated the minor canons as his 'companye', who were each to receive 12d to attend his funeral, while the rest of the choir, including the chantry chaplains, received only 8d.[196] Wills also reveal friendships and associations between minor and major clergy. Thomas Lisieux, dean of St Paul's, remembered two minor canons by name: William Chamberlain and John Good.[197] Major canon John Preston (d.1438) included the three chaplains of More's chantry among his beneficiaries.[198] The confidence that these men had in one another extended in both directions. Chaplains and minor canons were asked to act as executors of the wills of the higher clergy. Major canon Laurence Allerthorp chose two chaplains, John Stokes and Henry Jolypace, as his executors in 1406, and previous collaboration within the cathedral bureaucracy may have been behind these expressions of confidence and respect.[199] Major canon Thomas Damett in 1436 also appointed

---

[192] TNA PROB 11/25, fol. 109v.; PROB 11/27, fol. 162.

[193] GL Ms 9051/1, fol. 86.

[194] TNA PROB 11/5, fols 55v.–56.

[195] TNA PROB 11/27, fol. 234v.

[196] TNA PROB 11/28, fol. 86.

[197] TNA PROB 11/4, fols 56–58.

[198] TNA PROB 11/3, fol. 180.

[199] See above about Jolypace, p. 128.

two chantry chaplains as executors.[200] Even Dean Colet remembered members of the lesser clergy in his will.[201] The exchange of books between members of the lesser and the higher clergy reinforces the view that the division between major and lesser clergy of the cathedral did not prevent them from associating with one another, or from developing ties of friendship.[202]

Chantry chaplains were Londoners, if not all by birth, then by choice. Their involvement with the local population came about through their roles as rectors and vicars of parish churches, but also through their duties as chantry chaplains of St Paul's. They preached, distributed alms and collected rents in London streets.[203] Some of the chaplains owned tenements in the city, such as John le Seneschal, who in 1277 received a house from Peter Pourte 'near the Red Cross' in the parish of St Giles without Cripplegate.[204] Not surprisingly, the chaplains fostered relationships with Londoners, which found expression in their wills. Robert de Walcote, a London goldsmith who died in 1361, made a bequest to the chaplains of St Paul's who lived together in the common hall.[205] Such bequests suggest that the religious ideals promoted by the communal life of the chaplains prompted a response among some Londoners.[206] Some Londoners trusted chantry chaplains with the execution of their wills. In 1462 Johanna Hayworth named John Baron, chaplain of Lancaster College, as the executor of her will.[207] The relationship of trust also went the other way.[208] The main beneficiary of William Carre's will (d.1538) was a woman named Isabelle Clerk, whose debt was to be erased from his book of debts.[209] Many chaplains demonstrated their attachment to the city by leaving bequests to city institutions.[210] Henry Bever

---

[200] TNA PROB 11/3, fol. 164.

[201] TNA PROB 11/19, fols 174v.–176.

[202] See above, pp. 116–18.

[203] See Chapter 2, pp. 62–4.

[204] Sharpe, vol. 1, p. 28.

[205] Sharpe, vol. 2, pp. 24–5.

[206] Chantries at St Paul's as institutions also received donations by Londoners. One example is that of Mathilda de Staunford, who bequeathed a house located in the parish of St Andrew for the maintenance of chantries at the cathedral in 1322: Sharpe, vol. 1, p. 299. In the mid-fifteenth century, Elena Style bequeathed tenements to the chaplains of the chantry of SS Anne and Thomas the Martyr in Pardon Churchyard, Sharpe, vol. 2, p. 560.

[207] GL Ms 9171/5, fol. 350. Similarly, chaplain John de Ware was the will executor of Alice Outpenne: Sharpe, vol. 2, p. 44.

[208] TNA PROB 11/11, fol. 103v.; PROB 11/25, fol. 93.

[209] TNA PROB 11/27, fol. 162

[210] John Church (d.1509) remembered the friars and the prisoners of Newgate: TNA PROB 11/16, fol. 213; John Surdevall left bequests to the parishes of St George Botolph Lane and to St Olave in Southwark: PROB 11/20, fol. 228.

(d.1386) left monetary bequests to a number of religious institutions of the city, including the Priory of St Mary Overy, Southwark, and the parish church of St Benet Fink, as well as to religious guilds such as the fraternity of the Holy Cross of the church of St Peter Broad Street, where he was rector.[211] He wanted alms to be distributed among the poor members of his parish, and he left a pittance for all rectors and vicars in the city of London.

The relationship between chaplains and Londoners was not only personal, but also took an institutional form. In 1418 John Bryggewater, who served the chantry of Roger Beyvin in the charnel house from 1411, was given a gown by the chamberlain at Christmas, similar in style and cloth to the gowns given to the sergeants of the mayor and chamberlain, in recognition of his great services.[212] When Bryggewater died in 1427, he named as his executors Thomas Marleburgh, a London stationer, together with a fellow chantry priest.[213] The London fraternity for poor priests was founded by a chaplain of St Paul's, William Barnaby.[214] With some fellow priests from London in 1442, he organised a fraternity to take care of old priests, in particular by providing them with lodging.[215] Dedicated to the Holy Charity, the fraternity was based at the church of St Augustine Papey; hence its appellation as the fraternity of the Papey. Perhaps because it was founded by one of their number, the cathedral clergy demonstrated enthusiasm for the fraternity.[216] The first warden of the fraternity was John Welles, probably a former chantry chaplain at St Paul's.[217] Chantry chaplains also joined in some numbers the Fraternity of St Nicholas, the brotherhood of the parish clerks of London, for their names appear on the fraternity's bede rolls.[218] Incorporated by royal charters in 1442 and 1449, the fraternity regulated the tasks and wages of lay clerks who assisted the parish

---

[211] GL Ms 9171/1, fol. 144v.

[212] *Letter-Book I*, p. 194; LMA, Journal 1, fol. 14.

[213] GL Ms 9171/3, fol. 183.

[214] By 1431 William Barnaby had became the attorney of John Wenlock, disabled because of his old age, GL Ms 25513, fol. 134.

[215] *CPR, 1441–1446*, pp. 3, 87–8. See account in Barron and Davies, *Religious Houses*, pp. 188–9.

[216] Bequests to the fraternity are found in the wills of Peter Watlyngton (d.1458), GL Ms 9171/5, fol. 238v.; Thomas Pulter (d.1464), TNA PROB 11/5, fol. 59v.; Nicholas Blome (d.1474), PROB 11/6, fol. 135; John Barvile (d.1482), GL Ms 9531/7, fol. 11.

[217] GL Ms 25513, fols 64v., 86; Ms 9531/4, fol. 203; Thomas Hugo, 'The Hospital of Le Papey, in the City of London', *Transactions of the London and Middlesex Archaeological Society*, 5 (1981), p. 198.

[218] See N.W. and V.A. James, *The Bede Roll of the Fraternity of St Nicholas*, London Record Society, 39 (2 vols, London: 2004). Examples are given in Rousseau, 'Chantry Chaplains', Table 1.

clergy during divine services, and included among its members, in addition to lay clerks, other men and women from London and some members of the clergy such as the chantry chaplains at St Paul's.

Although the chantry chaplains had clearly forged links with the religious community within the cathedral and with the larger community of London, they did not forget their biological families. William Salman (d.1399) remembered John Salman, his servant and probably a relative, and left him a bed and 20s.[219] Henry Bever (d.1386) left 20s to each of his sisters, to an Edward Bever of Walton, probably a relative, and also named two nieces, Emme and Elene, suggesting that he still had a strong sense of family identity.[220] Thomas Kent (d.1538) certainly had the welfare of his relatives in mind when writing his will.[221] He left them elaborate articles of clothing, in addition to sponsoring the studies of his nephew and financing the future marriages of his nieces, and he named his cousin, Elisabeth Quyk, as his executrix. He also left money and a vestment to the parish church of Englefield, Berkshire, where he was born, so that his parents would be commemorated for twenty years and their names written in the bede roll. A female relative was executrix of another minor canon, John Church (d.1509), and she was to share the workload with three chantry chaplains.[222] Thomas Hickman (d.1534) gave this responsibility to his father and brother, and Nicholas Barker named his uncle John Boyes, also chantry priest, as his executor.[223] These examples of family involvement illustrate that for the priests of St Paul's Cathedral their two worlds of family and clerical community coexisted. Moreover, they did not hesitate to bring the two together. Robert Aslyn (d.1539) stipulated that his family were to share his funeral dinner with the community of minor canons, so that the people close to him were united for that occasion, and his appointed executors were a minor canon, Thomas Balgay, and his cousin Walter Aslyn, a pewterer.[224] As a result of his family connections, he had a close association with the pewterers: not only were they asked to attend his funeral and received a monetary compensation for their trouble and 'recreation', but he also gave the company some properties to fund an annual payment to the college of minor canons, who in return were to inscribe his name in the table of

---

[219] GL Ms 9051/1, fol. 86.

[220] GL Ms 9171/1, fol. 144v.

[221] TNA PROB 11/27, fol. 186.

[222] TNA PROB 11/16, fol. 213. John Church appointed as executors his sister Elizabeth, Edward Gamlyn, George Horne and Nicholas Curleus.

[223] GL Ms 25626/1, fol. 39v.

[224] TNA PROB 11/27, fol. 234v. For information on the pewterers, see Ronald F. Homer, 'Tin, Lead and Pewter', in John Blair and Nigel Ramsay (eds), *English Medieval Industries* (London, 1991), pp. 57–80.

'moost special benefactors next after the name of Sir John Gotham evermore there to contynu'. At the dissolution in 1548, the pewterers were still paying 6s 8d to the minor canons for the maintenance of Aslyn's obit.[225]

It is perhaps no surprise to find that the wills of the chantry chaplains were profoundly pious. They asked for masses to be said for their souls at their funerals, and established chantries for themselves. Henry Bever (d.1386) asked for a three-year chantry to be established in his parish church of St Peter Broad Street, London.[226] William Salman left ten marks for a one-year chantry in his church of St Peter Paul's Wharf.[227] Chantry chaplains asked fellow chaplains of their respective colleges to celebrate intercessory masses for them.[228] Post-mortem bequests may reflect devotions that the chaplains had practised in their lifetime. Minor canon John Church (d.1509) left money to the statue of Jesus in the cathedral crypt, where the fraternity of the Holy Name of Jesus met, and of which fraternity he had been a member.[229] His Christocentric devotion was also expressed through the endowment of a daily mass of the Five Wounds to be celebrated in the parish of St Gregory by St Paul's, and another one in St Paul's crypt. One chaplain also used post-mortem pious requests to complete a religious duty that he seems to have neglected during his lifetime. In 1543 Nicholas Barker left money to two priests who '*shall say for me yche if them masses of a trentall which I have not fulfilled for the discharge of my conscience*'.[230]

All these bequests and pious foundations revealed in the wills of chantry chaplains and minor canons suggest that the lesser clergy of the cathedral were quite prosperous. The wages they received seem to have been sufficient to meet their living costs as well as to provide for post-mortem arrangements. Nonetheless, the wills also reveal a disparity in wealth. While Robert Aslyn was able to leave properties to the guild of the pewterers to endow commemorative services in the college of minor canons, the former chantry chaplain Geoffrey Warburton (d.1518) died crippled by debts.[231] In Aslyn's case, his prosperity seems in part to have been the result of his family connections. Chantry chaplains had, however, different ways of supplementing their income, by taking on additional responsibilities in the cathedral or by participating in commemorative services

[225] Kitching, no. 201.

[226] GL Ms 9171/1, fol. 144v.

[227] GL Ms 9051/1, fol. 86.

[228] GL Ms 25626/1, fols 11v., 18, 22v., 24.

[229] TNA PROB 11/16 fol. 213; New, 'Cult of the Holy Name', pp. 134–5.

[230] GL Ms 25626/1, fol. 39v.

[231] TNA PROB 11/27, fol. 234v.; Ida Darlington (ed.), *London Consistory Court Wills, 1492–1547*, London Record Society, 3 (London, 1967), p. 38; Thomson, *Early Tudor Church*, p. 177. He was at the time of the writing up of his will priest at St Mary Abchurch, London.

in the city of London. Chaplain Skammenden (d.1545) bequeathed his half-year pension to his brother.[232] Of course some chaplains also faced financial hardship, and were compelled to borrow money. John Templer (d.1383), who had been admitted in 1381 to de Mondene's chantry, acknowledged in his will that he owed money to John Byllyng, another chaplain who had a few months earlier exchanged his chantry for a rectory in the diocese of Lincoln.[233] Templer was planning to pay back his debts with money due to him from a third party, Henry Bever, chaplain of St Roger's chantry.

The chantry chaplains of St Paul's formed a heterogeneous group of clerics. Their place of origin, age at appointment, their level of education and their financial situation varied greatly. The career paths of these chaplains also differed from one individual to another. Although some of them spent their entire working lives at the cathedral, others were there only for a short period, using their chantries as a step to advancement within the Church. The chantries were fully integrated in the clerical job market, and had the power to attract men with a wide range of experience and ambition. It is apparent that these men were well suited to the tasks they were given; they appear both to have met the expectations of the chantry founders and patrons, and to have offered valuable assistance to the cathedral personnel in the daily management of the cathedral. Incidences of misconduct were rare. In fact, chaplains gained the confidence and respect of their peers and superiors. The bad press that the chantry chaplains received through the satirical comments of Chaucer, who alluded to their greedy ambition, deserves to be revised.[234] Not only did the chaplains demonstrate sufficient conscientiousness in their tasks to please their patrons and cathedral authorities, but they also attracted the goodwill of lay men and women from London. Through their dedication, and presumably by their own piety, they made the system of endowed devotion work, but this system itself was brought to an end in the mid-sixteenth century by the upheavals of the Protestant Reformation.

---

[232] GL Ms 25626/1, fol. 49

[233] GL Ms 9171/1, fol. 109; *CPR, 1381–1385*, p. 243.

[234] This conclusion was also reached by Hill, '*Chaunterie for Soules*', pp. 242, 255.

Chapter 6
Dissolving Chantries

For over three hundred and fifty years chantries constituted an integral part of St Paul's Cathedral, and the priests who occupied them formed its largest contingent of clerics. Praying and celebrating masses for the salvation of souls shaped the liturgical services that were performed at the cathedral. In the early sixteenth century, however, belief in purgatory and in the benefits of prayers in attenuating the sufferings of souls was called into question with the reformist ideas that spread across Europe. Within a generation chantries were dissolved in England and elsewhere, while they continued in other parts of Europe that remained loyal to Roman Catholicism.[1]

The Route to Dissolution

In England, the Lollards formed the first religious group to challenge the concept of purgatory and the liturgical practices associated with it.[2] Although Wyclif himself had only denounced the abuses of the system, rather than condemning it entirely, his followers in the fifteenth and sixteenth centuries rejected altogether belief in the efficacy of prayers for the dead and the existence of purgatory.[3] The

---

[1]   For a general discussion on the dissolution of chantries, see Kreider, *English Chantries*; Orme, 'Dissolution of the Chantries', pp. 75–123; Eamon Duffy, *The Stripping of the Altars. Traditional Religion in England c.1400–c.1580* (New Haven/London), Chapters 13–15. On the dissolution of chantries of London, see the introduction Kitching, pp. ix–xxxiv. In recent years, the perception and reception of, and the reaction to, the dissolution of chantries by the English people has been addressed by Ethan H. Shagan, *Popular Politics and the English Reformation* (Cambridge, 2002), Chapter 7, and Peter Marshall, *Beliefs and the Dead in Reformation England* (Oxford, 2002), Chapter 3. Peter Cunich reflects upon the cultural, social and economic impacts of the dissolution on urban communities in 'The Dissolution of Chantries', in Patrick Collinson and John Craig (eds), *The Reformation in English Towns, 1500–1640* (Basingstoke, 1998), pp. 159–74.
[2]   The following discussion on the attack on purgatory is based largely on Kreider, *English Chantries*, Chapters 4 and 5; and on Marshall, *Beliefs and the Dead*, Chapters 2 and 3.
[3]   Kreider, *English Chantries*, pp. 94–5; Susan Brigden, *London and the Reformation* (Oxford, 1989), pp. 86–106, esp. p. 92. On the influence (or the lack of influence) of Lollards on the Reformation, see Richard Rex, *The Lollards* (Basingstoke, 2002), Chapter 5; Margaret

crucial blow against purgatory, however, did not come from dissenters within England, but from overseas. In the 1520s and 1530s Martin Luther was defining his theory of justification by faith.[4] Convinced that men were granted salvation through their faith in God alone, Luther came to deny the existence of purgatory and cast doubt on the worth of any practice attached to it. Englishmen such as William Tyndale contributed to the dissemination and development of these ideas via clandestine book importation, English translations and authorship.[5] In the *Supplicacyon of the Beggers*, published in Antwerp in late 1528–early 1529, the common lawyer Simon Fish openly denigrated the notion of purgatory.[6] Both secular and ecclesiastical authorities, however, were prompt to attack the new in order to defend the old faith.[7] Campaigns were launched against heretics throughout the 1520s, and books were published, such as Thomas More's *Supplycacyon of Soulys*, to validate the notion of purgatory and its liturgical attributes.[8] Many of the fierce denunciations made by church authorities were delivered at Paul's Cross, on the north side of the cathedral precinct. Rebuilt in the late fifteenth century by Bishop Thomas Kempe, the Cross was an open-air pulpit with a covered gallery used for preaching.[9] It was at this public location that John Fisher, bishop of Rochester, fiercely condemned Luther's theses in 1521.[10] Cuthbert Tunstall, Bishop of London, also stood at the Cross to preach against William Tyndale in 1526.[11] Although St Paul's served as a bastion to defend orthodoxy in the early stages of the Reformation, it was also used by those who

---

Aston, *Lollards and Reformers. Images and Literacy in Late Medieval Religion* (London, 1984), Chapter 7; J.F. Davis, 'Lollardy and the Reformation in England', in Marshall, *Impact of the English Reformation*, pp. 37–54.

    4   Kreider, *English Chantries*, pp. 96–7. On the attack and defence of purgatory in polemic writings, see Peter Marshall, *Religious Identities in Henry VIII's England* (Aldershot, 2006), Chapter 3 [First published as 'Fear, Purgatory and Polemic in Reformation England', in William Naphy and Penny Roberts (eds), *Fear in Early Modern Society* (Manchester, 1997), pp. 150–66].

    5   Brigden, *London*, pp. 106–18. On the reception of these ideas, see Susan Brigden, 'Youth and the Reformation', in Marshall, *Impact of the English Reformation*, pp. 55–85.

    6   Marshall, *Beliefs and the Dead*, p. 49.

    7   On this question, see particularly Richard Rex, 'The English Campaign against Luther in the 1520s', *Transactions of the Royal Historical Society*, 5th series, 39 (1989), pp. 85–106.

    8   Duffy, *Stripping of the Altars*, p. 379.

    9   See William Sparrow Simpson, *Chapters in the History of Old St Paul's* (London, 1881), Chapter 9.

    10   G.W. Bernard, *The King's Reformation. Henry VIII and the Remaking of the English Church* (New Haven/London, 2005), p. 102.

    11   Brigden, *London*, p. 159.

had embraced opposing views to expound their positions.[12] Heretical tracts were posted on St Paul's doors for clergy and laity alike to read.[13] Contentious bills also circulated in the cathedral's vicinity, where a market specialising in books had developed.[14] Bishop Tunstall tried to prevent the dissemination of Luther's work in the early 1520s by forbidding printers and booksellers to import or translate his books.[15]

In the early 1530s, as a result of Henry VIII's pressing need for a divorce and his ensuing separation from Rome, the wind changed direction. The king initiated the implementation of a series of policies restricting the independence of the Church and undermining papal authority within the English realm.[16] In 1531 the clergy were accused of violating the *Statute of Preamunire* for 'illegally exercising jurisdiction through the Church courts'.[17] In 1532 the ecclesiastical courts were again under attack as a result of the presentation of the 'Supplications against the Ordinaries' by the House of Commons, criticising the legal procedures in ecclesiastical courts. Finally, with the 'Submission of the Clergy', the king revoked the clergy's right to make canon law without royal consent. In 1533 the Act in Restraint of Appeals abolished the right of appeal to Rome, thus denying the claim for papal jurisdiction in England. Although they may have had some reluctance about denying the pope's authority in England, the chantry priests of St Paul's took an oath acknowledging the king as supreme head of the Church. On June 1534 the Dean and Chapter produced an official submission endorsed unanimously by seventy-eight members of the cathedral, including eight major canons (one of whom, John Royston, was also holding Kempe's chantry), eleven minor canons, forty-three chantry priests, six vicars choral and ten unidentified members.[18] The chantry priests appear to have accepted the change in religious leadership without protest: none joined the Carthusian monks in refusing to deny papal authority.[19] Following the passage of the Act of First Fruits and

---

[12]   Barron and Rousseau, 'Cathedral, City and State', p. 44.

[13]   Brigden, *London*, pp. 153, 194.

[14]   On the connection between St Paul's and the book trade, see James Raven, 'St Paul's Precinct and the Book Trade to c.1800', in Keene, Burns and Saint, *St Paul's. The Cathedral Church of London*, pp. 430–38; C. Paul Christianson, 'The Rise of London's Book-Trade', in Lotte Hellinga and J.B. Trapp (eds), *The Cambridge History of the Book in Britain* (Cambridge, 1999), vol. 3, pp. 128–47.

[15]   Brigden, *London*, p. 159.

[16]   Stanford E. Lehmberg, *The Reformation of Cathedrals. Cathedrals in English Society, 1485–1603* (Princeton, 1988), pp. 67–9.

[17]   The following is based on Peter Marshall, *Reformation England 1480–1642* (London, 2003), pp. 38–9.

[18]   TNA E25/82, part 1.

[19]   Brigden, *London*, pp. 226–8.

Tenths in 1534, and the resulting production of the *Valor Ecclesiasticus* a year later, the clergy were ordered to pay an annual tax to the king, and thereafter the chantry chaplains of St Paul's paid their dues to the king.[20]

Because reformers were more willing to approve the 1534 Act of Supremacy and to reject the authority of the pope, they received royal protection; and because the notion of purgatory was seen as intrinsically linked with the papacy, preachers were now forbidden to speak out in its defence.[21] Overriding the bishops' prerogatives to license preachers in their own dioceses, both Cromwell and Cranmer appointed clerics with reformist views to preach at Paul's Cross from 1534 onwards.[22] So although John Stokesley, who succeeded Tunstall as bishop of London in 1530, and his men still used the Cross and other sites at St Paul's to defend traditional piety, at the same time the doctrine of purgatory and its accompanying liturgy were continuously undermined by official preachers with opposing opinions.[23] For example, while Robert Singleton directly attacked chantries in his sermon at the Cross on April 1534, Stokesley himself preached at St Paul's to recall the virtue of intercessory masses on April 1535.[24] Two years after the formal separation from Rome, in 1536, the new Church of England officially declared its position on purgatory through the adoption of the Ten Articles: although not formally revoked, purgatory had lost the certainty of the traditional teaching, and was excluded from the group of articles presented as 'commanded expressely by God, and be necessary to our salvation'.[25] This doctrinal ambiguity allowed the English government to rationalise in the same year the dissolution of small monastic houses whose main purpose, it was argued, had been to pray for the dead. Within a few years, the English landscape was destitute of all priories and nunneries, and all monastic lands had been transferred into government hands.

In the late 1530s, Thomas Cromwell in his role as vicegerent of the kingdom carried out religious policies that directly affected St Paul's Cathedral, especially his attacks on the use of images.[26] On 23 August 1538, Dean Richard Sampson, informed of Cromwell's intentions, proceeded at night to remove the statue of

---

[20]   J. Caley and J. Hunter (eds), *Valor Ecclesiasticus Temp. Henry VIII, Auctoritate Regia Institutus, 1535* (London, 1810–34), vol. 1, pp. 365–9; P.H. Coulstock, *The Collegiate Church of Wimborne Minster* (Woodbridge, 1993), p. 121.

[21]   Kreider, *English Chantries*, p. 105; Brigden, *London*, pp. 256–61.

[22]   David Crankshaw, 'Community, City and Nation, 1540–1714', in Keene, Burns and Andrew, *St Paul's. The Cathedral Church of London*, p. 46; Brigden, *London*, pp. 233–5.

[23]   *Ibid.*, pp. 258–9.

[24]   Kreider, *English Chantries*, p. 166; Brigden, *London*, p. 234.

[25]   Kreider, *English Chantries*, p. 123.

[26]   Lehmberg, *Reformation of Cathedrals*, p. 76.

St Uncumber, the rood of the north door, and the image of Our Lady of Grace.[27] These were popular objects of devotion for Londoners, particularly the rood of the north door near which many chantries had been established.[28] It appears that the shrine of St Erkenwald, where masses for Bishop Ralph de Baldock (d.1313) were performed daily, survived for a couple of years. The shrine was mentioned in Wriothesley's description of the obit celebrated in memory of Isabella, wife of Emperor Charles in June 1539, and in his account of Bishop Stokesley's elaborate funeral in September 1539.[29] Possibly some objects belonging to the shrine were taken away during the 1538 royal campaign against images, because the image of St Erkenwald, probably from the shrine, was delivered to the master of the king's jewels in October 1538.[30] The fall from grace of St Thomas Becket in 1538 and the accompanying destruction of his shrine at Canterbury Cathedral had repercussions on St Paul's, as elsewhere in London.[31] The chapel located in the Pardon Churchyard dedicated to the twelfth-century saint, as well as to St Anne, became known as St Anne's, and the name of the disgraced saint was crossed out of official documents.[32] In 1541 the king issued a letter commanding that 'the bishops were therefore to begin with their cathedrals and remove from them any shrines, covering of shrine, table, monument of miracles, or other pilgrimages'.[33] Little by little, artefacts connected to traditional religion were taken away from the cathedral, depriving the chantries and their incumbents of objects associated with their intercessory functions. In 1543 Henry VIII delivered a final blow to the doctrine of purgatory.[34] In his *King's Book* he eradicated altogether the world 'purgatory' from the title of the article dealing with prayers for the dead. Although such prayers were encouraged inasmuch as they served the whole community of Christians, dead and alive, they were deprived of their value in helping specific souls.[35] Without being officially condemned, the chantries had lost their theological validity, thus paving the way for their dissolution. In 1545 Parliament endorsed the first Chantries Act, granting the king the

---

[27]   *Ibid.*, p. 72; Barron and Rousseau, 'Cathedral, City and State', p. 44; Crankshaw, 'Community, City', p. 47; *Letters and Papers*, vol. 13, part 2, no. 209; Brigden, *London*, p. 291; Wriothesley, vol. 1, p. 84.

[28]   See Chapter 3, p. 72.

[29]   Wriothesley, vol. 1, pp. 97–8, 106; Crankshaw, 'Community, City', p. 47; Brigden, *London*, p. 308.

[30]   Lehmberg, *Reformation of Cathedrals*, p. 72.

[31]   Brigden, *London*, pp. 291–2.

[32]   Lambeth Palace Ms 2018.

[33]   Duffy, *Stripping of the Altars*, p. 431.

[34]   Marshall, *Religious Identities*, p. 46.

[35]   Kreider, *English Chantries*, p. 151.

right to seize the endowments of chantries and other intercessory institutions such as hospitals, colleges and free chapels on the grounds that many of these foundations had been exploited over the years by private hands, or that their endowments had not been employed to fulfil the charitable purposes requested by their founders.[36] Parliament thus gave the king the authorisation to take possession of all the endowments of chantries unlawfully converted to private use between 1536 and 1545, and to seize the properties of all other chantries in order to put these institutions to better use.[37] The king's death, thirteen months later, nullified the act. The dissolution of chantries was, however, only postponed momentarily. In July 1547 the newly formed government published the book of *Certayne Sermons or Homilies*, which officially denied the existence of purgatory and denounced all observances associated with it.[38] Concurrently, the new king appointed royal agents to travel across the kingdom, armed with a series of injunctions to enforce conformity to the new government's theological positions.[39] When the royal agents set foot in St Paul's, Bishop Bonner tried to resist, but to no avail.[40] Images were taken down from the cathedral's walls, and for the first time parts of the religious services were performed in English.[41] In December 1547, Parliament ratified the Second Chantries Act. This time, the justification based on the misappropriation of chantry lands was omitted from the text.[42] Chantries were to be dissolved, not because their endowments had been misused, but because they were founded on superstitious beliefs. Whereas the First Chantries Act had focused on intercessory institutions of a certain size that could provide significant revenues for a government facing financial difficulties, the Second Chantries Act covered all institutions whose existence was predicated on the doctrine of purgatory and the belief in salvation by prayers, including lamps, lights, obits and other institutions of somewhat limited monetary value. By officially denying the theological rationale supporting them, the act called for the suppression of all these institutions, however unprofitable their confiscation

---

[36]   *The Statutes of the Realm* (London, 1810–1828), vol. 3, pp. 988–93.

[37]   Kreider, *English Chantries*, pp. 169–74. The act for the dissolution of the lesser monasteries dates from 1536.

[38]   *Ibid.*, p. 186.

[39]   *Ibid.*, p. 186; Marshall, *Reformation England*, p. 63.

[40]   Brigden, *London*, p. 433.

[41]   John Gough Nicholas (ed.), *Chronicle of the Grey Friars of London*, Camden Society, vol. 53 (London, 1852), p. 54; John Stow, *The Annales of England, Faithfully Collected out of the Most Autenticall Authors, Records, and Other Monuments of Antiquitie* (London, 1601), p. 594.

[42]   *The Statutes of the Realm* (London, 1810–1828), vol. 4, part 1, pp. 23–33. Both statutes are studied in detail by Kreider, *English Chantries*, Chapters 7 and 8.

to the Crown might prove to be.[43] Following the Henrician Chantries Act, the Edwardian Chantries Act also asserted that the endowments confiscated by the Crown would be converted to better use: funding of schools, enlargement of universities, relief for the poor and other charitable purposes. The Edwardian Chantries Act exempted only some pious institutions that supported as one of their main components a charitable or social function, such as a hospital, school or university college.[44] Although these institutions retained their endowments, they ended their activities associated with the commemoration of the dead. Many chantries had engaged in additional activities of these kinds, but because their main purposes had been to provide prayers and soul-masses, they were dissolved. Justification by faith alone secured human salvation. Less than thirty years after Luther's writings had reached London, the chantries had officially lost their *raison d'être*.

The Dissolution of Chantries

Parliament's endorsement of these two Chantries Acts called for the production of national surveys by royal commissioners. On 14 February 1546 commissioners were sent around the country in twenty-four circuits to investigate the state of intercessory foundations.[45] Parish and church officials were required to complete written questionnaires, now known as original returns, and to present them to the commissioners. At St Paul's Cathedral, the chantries began to be surveyed from 19 May 1546.[46] Since the Chantries Act of 1545 was invalidated by Henry's death, further sets of commissioners were asked two years later to report yet again on chantry foundations. On 14 February 1548, Edward VI appointed the commissioners, and they appear to have surveyed the intercessory foundations of London during the months of March, April and May 1548.[47] For a second time the commissioners would have been presented with original returns completed

---

[43] *Ibid.*, pp. 176–7, 202. Nevertheless, the Edwardian government was also interested in making a profit from the dissolution.

[44] *Ibid.*, pp. 191–2. Colleges at Oxford and Cambridge as well as the schools of Winchester and Eton were exempted from confiscation. And perhaps because their charitable functions were judged more important than their intercessory ones, hospitals were not mentioned in the Edwardian Chantries Act.

[45] Kitching, p. x.

[46] GL Ms 25526.

[47] An entry dated 19 April 1548 in the Calendar of State Papers reported an extract taken from the chantry certificate for the Dean and Chapter of St Paul's Cathedral: *CSPD*, no. 102.

by the ecclesiastical authorities. The copies or abstracts of information that the commissioners produced on these occasions are known as chantry certificates.[48]

The chantry certificate referred to thirty-five chantries or groups of chantries then in existence at St Paul's Cathedral.[49] For each of these groups, the Dean and Chapter diligently listed all the sources of income and the expenses incurred by these chantries.[50] While a few of these chantry groups broke even, several had positive accounting balances. For example the chantry of Ralph de Baldock reported revenues of £45 13s 4d p.a. from its endowments, while its expenses, including the two chaplains' wages, a myriad of quit-rents, the costs of an annual obit, donations to the poor and a scholarship, amounted only to £27 17s 8d. Based on the figures reported by the Dean and Chapter, chantries at St Paul's accounted for a net annual profit of over £200, while their gross annual value was estimated at nearly £650.[51] At Easter 1548 all these chantry endowments became the property of the Crown. A number of ecclesiastical institutions avoided confiscation on the grounds that the chantry endowments were used for the maintenance of religious services. In Elizabeth's reign an inventory of chantry properties that had not been confiscated by the Crown was produced for the Cathedral of Chichester.[52] At Windsor Castle the Chapel of St George was spared.[53] More than twenty years after the dissolution, a salary of £6 0s 9d was paid to John Merbecke, a lay musician, nominally the chaplain of the Hastings chantry in St George's Chapel.[54] At St Paul's, eighteen chantries were also excluded from the original returns and chantry certificate, and their endowments exempted from confiscation. These chantries had been linked with the twelve minor canonries, and the prebend of St Pancras.[55] The minor canons retained these endowments, and in later years those who had endowed these

---

[48]   For those on St Paul's, see Kitching, nos 108–13.

[49]   These thirty-five chantries or groups of chantries referred to forty-six individual chantry foundations, some of which were amalgamated; and employed forty-seven chaplains. *CSPD*, no. 102, mentions forty-seven chantries, presumably referring to the number of chantry positions.

[50]   Kitching, p. xxix. Whereas numerous communities succeeded in concealing chantry lands from the government authorities, St Paul's higher clergy appear to have complied with the demands of the regime. On the various efforts undertaken by local communities to resist the dissolution of chantries, see Shagan, *Popular Politics*, pp. 247–53.

[51]   Kitching, p. xxx. Davis, 'The Lesser Clergy', p. 160.

[52]   Lehmberg, *Reformation of Cathedrals*, p. 107.

[53]   Kreider, *English Chantries*, p. 192.

[54]   Peter J. Begent, 'The Chantry Chapel of John Oxenbridge in St George's Chapel, Windsor Castle', *Antiquaries Journal*, 81 (2001), p. 340.

[55]   The chantry in the charnel house was also omitted, although a chantry priest was serving there in 1548 (see below, p. 153).

linked chantries were remembered as the founders of the minor canons' stalls, rather than as the founders of former chantries.[56] When all these foundations are taken into account, it would seem that sixty-four chantries, whether stand-alone, amalgamated or linked with another office, had survived until the Reformation. Among those that had not survived, ten chantries had disappeared before the 1391 amalgamations, seven were discontinued sometime in the fifteenth or early sixteenth century, and three were mentioned in the 1536 *Valor* but omitted in the chantry certificate. This high survival rate (76 per cent) was the result of the continuous efforts of the cathedral authorities and other chantry patrons to maintain these pious provisions.[57]

The twelve minor canons maintained their positions at the cathedral, while the forty-seven chaplains who were serving chantries not otherwise attached to St Paul's Cathedral were dismissed.[58] Through their participation in the choir, these priests had contributed significantly to the religious services performed at the cathedral, but because their work at St Paul's lay mainly with the chantries they were serving, they were made redundant. Their associations with the cathedral averaged ten and a half years, ranging from a few months to lifelong commitments. The longest recorded service was that of Edmund Brograve, who had been appointed to the chantry of Roger Beyvin located in the charnel house on 15 May 1504, and who was still holding his position in 1548.[59] On the other hand, some chaplains had only worked at the cathedral for a relatively short period of time. The most recent admission officially recorded was made on 28 October 1545, a few months before the First Chantries Act.[60] Furthermore, the fact that, in St Paul's original returns, the names of a couple of incumbents were crossed out and new names added seems to suggest that there had been recent appointments at the cathedral.[61] These references to recent chantry admissions in the 1540s, especially from 1545 onwards, suggest that, despite the religious uncertainties, chantry business went on as usual. In fact, three new chantries

---

[56] John S. Bumpus, *The Organists and Composers of St Paul's Cathedral* (London, 1891), p. 12. In 1578, John Waklyn, minor canon, signed an indenture regarding a tenement that used to belong to de Gravesend's chantry, and was then referred to as 'the portion of Gravesend': TNA E 41/280.

[57] See discussion in Chapters 1 and 4.

[58] A 48th chaplain, Anthony Mason, was serving the second chantry of Roger de Walden in the parish church of Tottenham. He later appeared in royal documents as one of the former cantarists of St Paul's: Kitching, no. 108; TNA E 101/75/21.

[59] LMA, Journal 10, fol. 313v.; Repertory, vol. 12, fol. 29; *Chamber Accounts*, pp. 107, 109, 112, 114.

[60] GL Ms 9531/12, part 1, fol. 161v.

[61] GL Ms 25526, fol. 34v.

were established at the cathedral, two in the 1520s and the last one in 1535. Managed by city companies, these chantries were founded to commemorate three cathedral officials.[62] Regulations were laid down, endowments provided for their maintenance in perpetuity, and chantry priests appointed to serve them. Until the dissolution, priests were assigned to chantries with specific liturgical obligations and were put in charge of managing and maintaining chantry endowments.[63] The dissolution of monasteries in the late 1530s seems not have affected the chantries whose endowments included monastic rents, since the Dean and Chapter received payments from the Court of Augmentations.[64] Periodically the Dean and Chapter met to discuss chantry affairs, sanction appointments, and supervise incumbent priests. In 1540 the dean warned four chaplains that they would be deprived of their chantries if they did not stop bullying fellow priests.[65] In 1541 the Dean and Chapter authorised the chaplain John Baptist to take a three-week leave from the cathedral.[66] These interventions are very similar to those of the Dean and Chapter in the early fifteenth century as recorded in the Chapter Act Book.[67] They suggest that although a couple of individuals may have caused trouble within the cathedral community, in general chantry priests appear to have fulfilled their obligations and conducted themselves appropriately. Until their dismissal in 1548, these chaplains contributed to the daily celebration of more than sixty chantry masses at side altars within the cathedral and in its surrounding chapels, fulfilling the mission their founders had envisaged.

It is difficult to know how the men associated with the cathedral felt about the religious changes. Succeeding Stokesley as bishop of London in 1540, Edmund Bonner complied with royal policies, while also attempting some resistance. When an image of the Virgin was taken away in 1541, Bonner replaced it with the image of St John the Baptist.[68] Throughout the early 1540s, he appointed preachers who struggled to defend the old religion, and he tried to prevent his clergy from reading reformist works.[69] When the House of the Lords met to discuss the Chantries Acts in 1545 and 1547, Bishop Bonner, as well as Tunstall, the former bishop of London, by then bishop of Durham,

---

[62]   Chapters 1, p. 27, and Chapter 2, pp. 34–5.
[63]   GL Ms 25630/1, fols 63, 71, 94, 103, 175.
[64]   GL Ms 25206; TNA E 314/20/4; *Letters and Papers*, vol. 18, part. 1, no. 436, fol. 57; David Johnson, 'Estates and Income, 1540–1714', in Keene, Burns and Saint, *St Paul's. The Cathedral Church of London*, pp. 304–11.
[65]   GL Ms 25630/1, fol. 93.
[66]   GL Ms 25630/1 fol. 116v.
[67]   See Chapter 4, pp. 99–107.
[68]   Crankshaw, 'Community, City', p. 47; Brigden, *London*, p. 338.
[69]   Brigden, *London*, pp. 339, 397.

twice voted against the legislation.[70] Richard Sampson, who held the deanery (1536–1540) in conjunction with the bishopric of Chichester, shared these convictions. Although he had promoted the royal supremacy by writing a book entitled *Oratio de dignitate et potestate Regis*, he was deprived of the deanery as a result of his clash with Cromwell in 1540 due to his conservative views.[71] When accused of treason and sent to the Tower, he testified that he had joined Bishops Tunstall and Stokesley to defend 'the old usages and traditions of the church'.[72] John Incent, a close ally of Cromwell, succeeded him as dean.[73] At Incent's death in 1545, William May, another reformer, took possession of the deanery. Clergy of both persuasions could also be found among the major canons. On the one hand, protégés of Cromwell were given positions in the late 1530s, prompting Stokesley to complain that his surrender, at the king's order, of appointments into Cromwell's hands had left him 'destituted of learned men'.[74] On the other hand, conservative canons retained their prebends at St Paul's throughout the period: one of them, William Leighton, was one of the very few who dared to defend the mass in the late 1540s, while William Ermestede, also a conservative canon, later became chaplain to Queen Mary in 1554.[75]

Surrounded by men of both allegiances, where did the chantry chaplains stand? Testamentary evidence may shed some light on their religious positions. The wills of seventeen chaplains who died in office in the last few years before the passage of the First Chantries Acts (from the late 1530s to 1545) reveal that while the theological ground for their occupations was officially, and radically, being questioned, St Paul's chantry priests remained, not surprisingly, convinced of the validity of good works, posthumous prayers, and intercessions of the saints to ensure the salvation of souls.[76] According to Caroline Litzenberger's

---

[70]   Kreider, *English Chantries*, p. 203.

[71]   Barron and Rousseau, 'Cathedral, City and State', p. 44. Sampson remained bishop of Chichester until 1543, when he was translated to the see of Coventry and Lichfield.

[72]   Bernard, *King's Reformation*, p. 487.

[73]   H. Douglas-Irvine, 'St Paul's Cathedral', in William Page (ed.), *Victoria History of the Counties of England*, vol. 1: *A History of London* (London, 1908), p. 415; reprt in Barron and Davies, *Religious Houses*, pp. 27–50.

[74]   Quotation in Brigden, *London*, p. 237.

[75]   Brigden, *London*, p. 436. *Chronicle of the Grey Friars*, p. 56; *BRUO, 1501–1540*, pp. 13, 349; *Fasti III*, pp. 25, 45. Ermestede's will dated in 1558 clearly demonstrates his adherence to the restored Catholicism: R.M. Fisher, 'The Reformation of Clergy at the Inns of Court 1530–1580', *Sixteenth Century Journal*, 12/1 (1981), pp. 69–91, esp. p. 86.

[76]   Wills have recently been the object of study of much research: see Claire S. Schen, *Charity and Lay Piety in Reformation London (1500–1620)* (Aldershot, 2002), Chapters 2 and 3; Caroline Litzenberger, *The English Reformation and the Laity. Gloucestershire, 1540–1580* (Cambridge, 1997), Appendix A; Christopher Marsh, 'In the Name of God? Will-

classification of will preambles into three groups – traditional, ambiguous and protestant – the great majority of the chaplains' wills, unsurprisingly, fall into the first one.[77] With a few exceptions, they all bequeathed their souls to 'Allmyghtie God, to our Blessed Ladye, and to all the Hollye Companye of Heven'.[78] A traditional variation used by a chantry priest was to commend his soul to 'God, my maker and redeemer, and to all the Blessed Company of Heaven'.[79] The main text of their wills in which testators bequeathed their goods and possessions also reveals a broad adherence to the beliefs in purgatory and in the efficacy of prayers.[80] The priests serving chantries at the cathedral during these critical years provided for post-mortem masses, in quantity and type according to their means and inclination. Richard Turner (d.1540) left money to his fellow minor canons for them to celebrate his obit, while Thomas Woode (d.1540) asked his colleagues at St Peter's College to say a trental of masses for his soul.[81] Both Richard Jackson (d.1543) and Richard Neale (d.1545) established a one-year chantry in London (without specifying the exact location), in addition to requiem masses and anniversaries to be celebrated at the cathedral.[82] Books were also bequeathed in exchange for prayers: John Buckworth (d.1541) left his new mass book bound in white leather to More's chaplains in exchange for prayers.[83] While the majority of chaplains exhibited traditional beliefs, a small minority expressed ambivalent positions towards traditional practices. Three chantry priests drew up wills that could be labelled as ambiguous. In 1540, Christopher Tyngat commended his soul to God, his maker and redeemer, and

---

Making and Faith in Early Modern England', in G.H. Martin and Peter Spufford (eds), *The Records of the Nation* (Woodbridge, 1990), pp. 215–49; Robert Whiting, '"For the Health of my Soul": Prayers for the Dead in the Tudor South-West', in Marshall, *Impact of the English Reformation*, pp. 121–42. Lorraine C. Attreed, 'Preparation for Death in Sixteenth-Century Northern England', *Sixteenth Century Journal*, 13/3 (1982), pp. 37–66. Some historians are sceptical about using will preambles as historical evidence; see J.D. Alsop, 'Religious Preambles in Early Modern English Will as Formulae', *Journal of Ecclesiastical History*, 40/1 (1989), pp. 19–27.

[77]   See Litzenberger, *English Reformation*, Appendix A, pp. 168–78.

[78]   GL Ms 25626/1, fols 1, 3, 11v., 12, 18, 22v., 25, 49, 51; TNA PROB 11/27, fol. 234v.; PROB 11/28, fol. 86. The same conclusions were reached by Schen, *Charity and Lay Piety*, p. 23; by Attreed, 'Preparation for Dead', p. 49; and by Litzenberger, *English Reformation*, p. 54.

[79]   GL Ms 25626/1, fol. 39v.

[80]   Marsh, 'In the Name of God?', p. 225.

[81]   GL Ms 25626/1, fols 18, 22v. Edmund Smyth also left money to the minor canons in exchange for post-mortem prayers: will (1540), TNA PROB 11/28, fol. 86.

[82]   GL Ms 25626/1, fols 39v.; 49.

[83]   GL Ms 25626/1, fols 24–24v.

refrained from requesting any post-mortem prayers, while John David (d.1542) bequeathed his soul to God, his maker and redeemer, 'beseching him to take it to his Mercye when yt shall please him', and also wrote a will in which there were no intercessory demands.[84] The will of Richard Hooper (d.1545), minor canon and chantry priest, also expresses some ambiguity.[85] One the one hand, he commended his 'soule unto Chryst Jesus my maker and redeemer by whom and by the meryth of whos blessed passion is all my hole trust and hope of clere remission and forgevenes of my sins', and bequeathed his Bible in English to his sister, but on the other hand he also left £20 to the minor canons to celebrate his obit at St Gregory's church for twenty years. No chantry priests' wills exhibit clear Protestant sympathies.

The conservative elements among the chantry chaplains were strengthened by the ex-religious who joined the cathedral in the 1540s. Following the dissolution of the monasteries, numerous ex-regular clergy entered the clerical job market.[86] At St Paul's two chantry priests in the 1540s have been identified as ex-religious: one of them was a former member of the Carthusian order. At the time of the dissolution of the chantries (in 1546 and 1548), Thurstan Hickman, the former procurator of Witham Charterhouse, was serving de Roos's chantry.[87] In 1545 he was mentioned in the will of a fellow chantry priest, Robert Skammenden who bequeathed him a Carthusian book on the *Exposition* of *St. Paul's Epistle*.[88] This bequest revealed a certain sensibility on the part of Skammenden, but also testified to the *esprit de corps* that existed between the chaplains of St Paul's. Hickman had not, however, cut all ties with his former spiritual family. Wriothesley reported that in July 1547 Hickman was found guilty of treason at the Guildhall, London.[89] He was convicted of having participated with Thomas Munday, rector of St Leonard's Foster Lane, and formerly prior of Bodmin in Cornwall, in a plot organised by John Fox, a former monk of the Charterhouse of London. Having fled to Louvain, Fox asked Hickman and Munday to fulfil their promises of bringing him the 'left arme of one John Houghton, late Prior of the Charterhowse in London, which suffred death for treason, denying the

---

[84]   GL Ms 25626/1, fols 24, 31–33v. These preambles were not inconsistent with the teachings of pre-Reformation church; see Litzenberger, *English Reformation*, pp. 5, 172.

[85]   GL Ms 25626/1, fols 60v.–61.

[86]   Geoffrey Baskerville, *English Monks and the Suppression of the Monasteries* (London, 1936); G.W.O. Woodward, *The Dissolution of the Monasteries* (New York, 1966), Chapter 10.

[87]   GL Ms 25526, fol. 34v.; Kitching, no. 109; Brigden, *London*, p. 396; Margaret Thompson, *The Carthusian Order in England* (London, 1930) p. 498.

[88]   GL Ms 25626/1, fols 49–49v.

[89]   Wriothesley, vol. 1, pp. 184–5.

Kinges supremacy', as well as other relics.[90] Found guilty of that crime, Hickman and Munday were sentenced to be 'hanged, drawen, and quartered like treason'. Apparently they were spared that gruesome fate, for on 7 February 1548 both Munday and Hickman received royal pardons, and Hickman's name was included in St Paul's chantry certificate of 1548.[91]

William Perryn, an ex-Dominican, was also a chantry chaplain at St Paul's.[92] He had been ordained priest in 1531, and educated at Blackfriars, in Oxford.[93] Following the declaration of the royal supremacy in 1534, he fled the country. He returned to London during the conservative reaction of 1543, and occupied the chantry of Fulk Basset until 1548.[94] He presumably owed his appointment to his connection with Bishop Bonner, to whom he dedicated one of his books.[95] Perryn preached in London against heresy in the early 1530s and in defence of the old faith in the 1540s.[96] The work dedicated to Bonner is in fact a collection of sermons in defence of transubstantiation.[97] In the spring of 1547, he lectured in defence of images of Christ and saints at St Andrew Undershaft, for which he had to recant in June.[98] He went into exile and only returned in c.1553, when he was made prior of the Dominican house of St Bartholomew in Smithfield, re-founded by Queen Mary, and resumed his preaching career.[99] He died in 1558 and was buried in St Bartholomew's church. In addition to Hickman and Perryn, there may perhaps have been a few other ex-religious amongst the priests

---

[90]   *Ibid.*, p. 185.

[91]   *CPR, 1548–1549*, p. 1. Kitching, no. 109. Brigden believes that Hickman left for exile on Edward's accession, *London*, p. 396; Baskerville, *English Monks*, pp. 260–61. Baskerville mentioned the will of Munday, written in 1551.

[92]   Baskerville believed that many friars became chantry priests at St Paul's: *English Monks*, p. 242. However, evidence so far has been found only for Perryn.

[93]   *BRUO, 1501–1540*, p. 444; *ODNB*; Brigden, *London*, pp. 398, 430; also mentioned in Richard Rex, 'The Friars in the English Reformation', in Peter Marshall (ed.), *The Beginnings of English Protestantism* (Cambridge/New York, 2002), pp. 38–59, esp. p. 55.

[94]   GL Ms 25526; Kitching, no. 110. Licences for change of habit for Perryn or Hickman were not recorded in the registers of the archbishop of Canterbury's Faculty Office.

[95]   Rex, 'Friars', p. 55; *ODNB*. The right of nomination to this chantry belonged, however, to the Dean and Chapter.

[96]   *BRUO, 1501–1540*, p. 444.

[97]   Brigden, *London*, p. 398. His other works are *Spirituall exercises and goostly meditacions and a neare waye to come to perfection and lyfe contemplative* (1557), and *De frequenter celebranda missa* (no copy survived for this book).

[98]   F.A. Gasquet and E. Bishop, *Edward VI and the Book of Common Prayer* (3rd edn, London, 1928), p. 25.

[99]   Stow, *Annales*, p. 594. He is mentioned in the chantry certificate of 1548, Kitching, no. 110.

serving chantries at St Paul's in the 1540s, for whom evidence so far remains inconclusive. For example, Thomas Flere alias Maynard, ex-monk of Rochester Cathedral, may have been the priest appointed to one of Holme's chantries in 1545, ten years after receiving his dispensation to change habit, while Richard Martyndale, serving de Northburgh's chantry from 1542 until the dissolution, may have been an ex-monk from the diocese of York, who obtained a dispensation to change habit in May 1537.[100] With the dissolution of chantries, all these men would have once again lost their clerical positions.

The Aftermath of the Dissolution

Following the endorsement of the Second Chantries Act by Parliament in December 1547, all celebrations of intercessory masses, commemorative prayers and annual obits were abolished. Other activities performed by chantry chaplains, such as the distribution of alms and the provision of scholarships, were also halted. Moreover, the furnishings and objects linked to the celebration of soul-masses were removed. These include mass books, candlesticks, chalices, altar hangings and covers, vestments, and tablets listing the names of beneficiaries.[101] Their removal profoundly modified the internal appearance of the cathedral.[102] Other liturgical reforms also took place in the spring of 1548. Following the orders of Dean William May, the cathedral choir began to sing in English at matins, mass and evensong, and communion was received in both kinds.[103] Censing and processions were also abolished.[104] In 1550 portable wooden communion tables replaced fixed stone altars. St Paul's precinct was radically transformed: all the physical manifestations of the cult of the dead, which had for three and a half centuries shaped the area surrounding the cathedral, were either converted to other uses or simply obliterated. First, on the north side of the precinct, the charnel house, which had housed chantries and shielded the bones of hundreds of Londoners, was secularised, the bones were carted away and scattered at Moorfields and Finsbury.[105] According to Stow, the new owner, Reyner Wolfe, an evangelical Dutch printer, paid for the transport of the bones,

---

[100] Chambers, *Faculty Office Register*, pp. 37, 97.
[101] GL Ms 25526, fols 32–33; transcribed in Gear, 'Chantries of St Paul's', Appendix C.
[102] Cunich, 'Dissolution of Chantries', pp. 169–70.
[103] Wriothesley, vol. 2, p. 2; *Chronicle of the Grey Friars*, p. 55.
[104] *Ibid.*, p. 56.
[105] See below, p. 163.

which amounted to 'some thousands of carrie loades and more to be coveighed'.[106] On 10 April 1549, the cloister of the Pardon Churchyard was razed, 'so that nothing thereof was left but the bare plot of ground', and the stones supplied to Protector Somerset to build his mansion on the Strand.[107] With the cloister, chapel, monuments and tombs, the painted panels of the *Danse Macabre*, which depicted 'death leading all estates' on the cloister walls, also disappeared.[108] In 1552, the Pardon Churchyard was granted to the twelve minor canons who took over the responsibility for repairing the 'residue of the cloister between the library and the church, and the wall on the west of the churchyard adjoining the bishop's palace'.[109] The cemetery remained, but the place where once stood the cloister was converted into a garden.[110]

By triggering an extensive transfer of properties, the dissolution of chantries contributed to the reshaping of the cathedral precinct and at the same time reduced the Dean and Chapter's landownership. The Second Chantries Act called for the confiscation of all chantry and other intercessory endowments into the king's hands. Facing financial hardships as a result of the wars against the Scots, the Crown intended to use the proceeds from the sale of chantry endowments to fill up the royal chests, as the Privy Council's minutes ordering the sale on 17 April 1548 made very clear.[111] As with the dissolution of monasteries, as soon as rumours started to circulate about the possibility of the suppression of chantries, prospective purchasers sent enquiries to members of the king's household and the officials of the Court of Augmentations.[112] First established in 1536 for the sale of monastic lands, the Court of Augmentations was complemented by a second court in 1546 to deal with the overload of lands in their hands.[113] All

---

[106] Stow, *Survey of London*, vol. 1, pp. 293–330; *Chronicle of the Grey Friars*, p. 57; Barrett L. Beer, 'John Stow and the English Reformation, 1547–1559', *Sixteenth Century Journal*, 16 (1985), pp. 257–71, esp. p. 261.

[107] Stow, *Survey of London*, vol. 1, p. 328; *Chronicle of the Grey Friars*, p. 58.

[108] Stow, *Survey of London*, vol. 1, p. 327; see Chapter 3, p. 74. Only Sherrington's library was spared: Gordon Higgott, 'The Fabric to 1670', in Keene, Burns and Saint, *St Paul's. The Cathedral Church of London*, pp. 170–89, esp. p. 171.

[109] *CSPD*, no. 615.

[110] Stow, *Survey of London*, vol. 1, p. 328.

[111] Kreider, *English Chantries*, p. 202.

[112] Christopher J. Kitching, 'The Disposal of Monastic and Chantry Lands', in Felicity Heal and Rosemary O'Deal (eds), *Church and Society in England: Henry VIII to James I* (London, 1977), pp. 119–36, esp. p. 131–2.

[113] For a brief explanation of the Court's operating mechanisms, see Sybil Jack. 'First and Second Courts of Augmentations', in Ronald H. Fritze (ed.), *Historical Dictionary of Tudor England, 1485–1603* (New York/London, 1991), pp. 37–9.

transactions regarding chantry endowments took place in these courts.[114] Not all lands were sold directly; in some cases they were leased; but because of the king's severe monetary needs, considerable efforts were deployed for their sale in return for ready cash.[115] Individuals wishing to buy chantry lands first had to obtain the particulars for the specific chantry endowments they were seeking.[116] These particulars were drawn up by county auditors and surveyors in charge of the up-keep of the retained lands. Once the particulars for grants were in hand, the potential buyers were obliged to have them approved by the commissioners for sale, who also fixed the sale conditions and price. The sale was then conducted in the Court of the Augmentations and the payment had to be paid in cash to the treasurer. Subsequently the particulars were revised by two Crown's lawyers, and only then was the transaction finalised and recorded in the patent rolls. Patents referred to at least fifty of the eighty-four chantries established at St Paul's Cathedral. These transactions occurred over a span of twenty-four years, between June 1548 and August 1572. The bulk of the transactions, however, took place in the early part of Edward VI's reign, in 1548, 1549 and 1550.[117] The transaction in 1572 in fact recorded a deal made by the Dean and Chapter of St Paul's with Queen Elizabeth regarding chantry rents amounting to £110 p.a., at that time payable to the Crown, that were issuing from lands owed by them.[118] In return for the surrender of quit-rents of equivalent value payable to them by the Crown, the Dean and Chapter were released from their financial obligation.[119]

---

[114] In 1554 the Augmentations courts were merged to the Court of Exchequer, but they continued to administer alienated lands under the name of Augmentations Office of the Exchequer. G.H. Woodward, *Calendar of Somerset. Chantry Grants, 1548–1603* (Somerset Record Society, 1982), p. ix. The courts were responsible for the maintenance of chantry lands, their liquidations, and the payment of pensions to former chantry priests.

[115] For example, in the late 1550s Gilbert Hyll leased for twenty-one years a dozen messuages in St Benet's next to Paul's Wharf, formerly belonging to de Bruera's chantry, *CPR, 1557–1558*, p. 260. For a discussion of the links between royal need of money and sale of monastic lands, see Joyce A. Youings, 'The Terms of the Disposal of the Devon Monastic Lands, 1536–1558', *English Historical Review*, 69/270 (1954), pp. 18–38.

[116] For a description of the sale process, see Woodward, *Calendar of Somerset*, pp. ix–x.

[117] It was similar elsewhere; see *ibid.*, p. viii. However, Cunich has calculated that only a little more than 40 per cent of all chantry lands were sold in Edward VI's reign: 'Dissolution of Chantries', pp. 172–3.

[118] Johnson, 'Estates and Income', p. 305. *CPR, 1569–172*, pp. 335–8. At the same time, Dean Alexander Newell secured the endowment for a grammar school in Middleton, Co. Lancaster, with former chantry rents; *ODNB*; *CPR, 1569–172*, pp. 334–5.

[119] A similar arrangement was concluded at Exeter Cathedral, where the cathedral maintained most of the chantry endowments in exchange for an annual payment evaluated at £145 to the Crown: Orme, 'Dissolution of the Chantries', p. 84.

Those who secured royal patents were seldom the final owners of the properties. As with monastic property, chantry endowments were subject to a number of transactions before being finally purchased.[120] Instead of being speculators, as it was once believed, these men, to whom the patents were granted, were probably agents acting on behalf of clients.[121] Because the grants had to be paid in ready money, it would have been a hazardous business for someone not living or working in London to carry the necessary sums to cover the transactions. Therefore potential purchasers relied on agents located in London, who were probably well connected to undertake these transactions. Eighty per cent of grants in Somerset were acquired in this manner by Londoners or royal officers.[122] The transactions relating to St Paul's chantry endowments are similar. The patents were granted to merchant tailors, drapers and mercers, but also to cloth workers and coopers. In total, members of thirteen city crafts were involved in the purchase of tenements, marsh and gardens that once supported St Paul's chantries.[123] Royal officials, aldermen, city officers and county gentlemen also acquired former chantry lands. More than two-thirds of all the grants involving St Paul's chantry endowments were assigned to partnerships of two or more grantees.[124] Partnerships were required because of the large sums of money involved. Chantry endowments were not sold individually but were packaged into bundles of properties: two-thirds of these bundles cost more than £1,000.[125] In a few cases grantees purchased chantry tenements of which they had been tenants. For example, in June 1548 Nicholas Bacon, mercer, and John Crymes, cloth worker, bought among other tenements two messuages in the parish of St Laurence Old Jewry that had been in tenure 'of the said Crymes'.[126] Likewise, in April 1549 Robert Kyng, merchant tailor, and his brother John Kynge were granted two messuages in the parish of St Matthew Friday Street, which had been leased by John.[127] Instead of acting as agents, these grantees probably

---

[120] Kitching, 'The Disposal', p. 131.

[121] Jordan presented the idea of speculators for monastic and chantry lands: W.K. Jordan, *Edward VI*, vol. 2: *The Threshold of Power* (Cambridge, Mass., 1970); for opposing view, see Kitching, 'The Disposal', p. 131; for a discussion on the danger of giving too much credit to the patent rolls as a method of identifying the owners, see Youings, 'Terms of the Dispersal', p. 26.

[122] Woodward, *Calendar of Somerset*, p. xvi.

[123] These were the merchant tailors, leathersellers, mercers, clothworkers, fishmongers, drapers, scriveners, founders, haberdashers, grocers, coopers, goldsmiths and skinners.

[124] G.H. Woodward came up with the same ratio for Somerset: 'The Dispersal of Chantry Lands in Somerset', *Southern History*, 5 (1983), pp. 95–114, esp. p. 96.

[125] The ratio was the same for Somerset land: Woodward, 'Dispersal', p. 96.

[126] *CPR, 1548–49*, pp. 16–17.

[127] *CPR, 1548–49*, p. 406.

undertook these transactions on their own behalf. Although in both cases these chantry endowments were incorporated in assortments of chantry lands, their relatively low prices, of £291 6s 8d and £458 5s 10d respectively, may reinforce the hypothesis that these grantees bought these tenements for their own use. In most cases, however, no links could be established between the grantees and the former tenants of chantry lands.[128]

Chantry endowments took a variety of forms: marshes in Essex as well as farming lands in Middlesex.[129] Most of these tenements, however, were messuages and shops located in the city of London or its suburbs. Far from being grouped in particular neighbourhoods, these former St Paul's chantry tenements were dispersed in forty London parishes, including St Faith and St Gregory located in the cathedral precinct. It is probably the sale of tenements situated in these two parishes that had the greatest impact on the cathedral community. In addition to the loss of properties, these sales considerably increased the numbers of lay men and women living in the precinct, by transferring into lay hands the three chantry colleges established in the cathedral precinct. St Peter's College, alias the *Presteshous*, was sold to John and Richard Keyme of Lewes, Sussex, in November 1548.[130] They took possession of the college site, which consisted of houses, buildings, halls, chambers, a dining room (*cenacula*), storehouses (*prompturia*), kitchens, shops, cellars, solars, wells and lands. The deal also comprised the sale of the outer garden and of the inner garden, and all buildings enclosed in that garden. The site was eventually sold on to the company of the stationers, and became the Stationers' Hall.[131] The stationers were not the only book craft established near the cathedral. In the fifteenth century, the scriveners had also taken up residence near St Paul's, and it was a scrivener, John Hulson, acting in partnership with William Pendred, a founder, who acquired Holme's College in August 1548.[132] A few years later the college and its appurtenances were in the hand of Gregory Idwyn, a cutler.[133] The buildings of Lancaster College were also sold in September 1548 to lay buyers: William Gunter, gentleman of London, and William Hobson, haberdasher.[134] In the same transaction, Gunter and

---

128 In other places, former chantry priests purchased lands that have been part of their chantry endowments. See for an example, M.A. Clark, 'Reformation in the Far North: Cumbria and the Church, 1500–1571', *Northern History*, 32 (1996), pp. 75–89, esp. p. 83. No examples as such exist for St Paul's.

129 *CPR, 1548–1549*, p. 229–231; *CPR, 1563–66*, pp. 63–6.

130 *CPR, 1547–48*, pp. 361–3.

131 Raven, 'St Paul's Precinct', p. 432.

132 Christianson, 'Rise of London's Book-Trade', p. 129; *CPR, 1548–1549*, pp. 35–7.

133 GL Mss 25121/1098, 1099.

134 *CPR, 1547–1548*, pp. 394–6.

Hobson also bought the charnel chapel 'built with stones and roofed with tiles', with a chamber and 'les sheddes'.[135] All these former chaplains' housings were now not only owned by members of the laity but also occupied by lay men and women. Undoubtedly, the Second Chantries Act had a considerable impact on the demography of the cathedral precinct by enlarging the numbers of the laity while reducing the number of priests who worked and lived there.

Wriothesley recorded that the priests occupying chantries at St Paul's Cathedral remained attached to the cathedral for a year after the dissolution of chantries. On Whitsunday (9 June) 1549, while the major and minor canons modified their ceremonial attires, 'all the chauntre priestes were putt to their pencions and to be at libertie'.[136] However, since the chantry endowments had been surrendered to the Crown by the spring of 1548, and the three chantry colleges sold to lay people in the autumn, it seems unlikely that the Dean and Chapter kept the chantry chaplains employed at the cathedral at their own expense. Moreover, the chantry priests in fact began receiving their pensions in June 1548.[137] These were calculated on a sliding scale according to the salary attached to the chantries they last occupied.[138] Eleven ex-chantry priests obtained a pension of ten marks, thirty-six a pension of £6 and another one a pension of £5.[139] Ex-cantarists collected their pensions as long as they lived, unless they took up other clerical benefices with a higher income than their pensions.[140] In Devon, accounts show that a number of pensioners received their dues from the Crown until their death.[141] The same is probably the case for the ex-chaplains of the cathedral. In 1556, thirty-four of them were still

---

[135]   Raven, 'St Paul's Precinct', p. 432; the site was then acquired by Reyner Wolfe.

[136]   Wriothesley, vol. 2, p. 14. The *Chronicle of the Grey Friars* reported the change of clothing, but made no mention of the chantry priests, p. 59.

[137]   TNA E 101/75/21. Major Canon Royston, who had occupied Kempe's chantry, was also a pensioner: TNA E 315/247.

[138]   C.J. Kitching, 'The Chantries of East Riding of Yorkshire at the Dissolution in 1548', *Yorkshire Archaeological Journal*, 44 1972), pp. 178–94, esp. p. 183; *CPR, 1547–48*, p. 417. Chantry chaplains with annual wages of more than £10 received pensions of £6 13s 4d, with annual wages of £6 13s 4d to £10 received pensions of £6, with wages of £5 to £6 13s 4d received pensions of £5, while all salaries below £5 were matched at the same amount by the Crown. Cunich, 'Dissolution of Chantries', p. 171; the majority of ex-chantry priests received annual pensions between £4 and £6.

[139]   Chaplain Anthony Mason was included; see above p. 153 note 58.

[140]   Kitching, 'East Riding', p. 184.

[141]   Orme, 'Dissolution of the Chantries', p. 85; A.G. Dickens, 'The Edwardian Arrears in Augmentations Payments and the Problem', *English Historical Review*, 55/219 (1940), pp. 384–418.

collecting the pensions allocated to them in 1548.[142] The ex-chaplains missing from the list had probably died, or had lost their pensions as a result of advancement.[143] Before the dissolution, several chaplains had held their chantry benefices at St Paul's in conjunction with other clerical positions, and among the chaplains dismissed at the Reformation three had received dispensation from the Faculty Office of Canterbury to hold benefices in plurality: Maurice Gryffyth, chaplain of More's chantry, also chaplain of Arthur Bulkeley, bishop of Bangor, was granted a dispensation in 1543.[144] Robert Garrett, also serving More's chantry, made the same request in 1544.[145] He was given permission to hold another benefice or a chaplaincy to a nobleman. Being in the service of ecclesiastical or lay aristocrats seems to have been fairly common. In 1546 Edward Turner, in addition to serving de Northburgh's chantry, was presented as the chaplain of Henry, earl of Cumberland, when he was granted the right to hold a third benefice.[146] These connections with influential patrons would surely have helped these priests to find employment after their dismissal from the cathedral.[147] Like their predecessors, many found employment in London parish churches.[148] The Dean and Chapter of St Paul's and the bishops of London helped them to enter the post-dissolution job market.[149] Thomas Abbot was appointed in 1550 by the Dean and Chapter to the rectory of St Pancras' church, Middlesex, while they secured the rectory of St Botolph Billingsgate, London for Thomas Barnade.[150] Thomas Banester was appointed to Hoddesdon Chapel, thanks to the patronage of the bishop of London, in 1549.[151] Some ex-chaplains appear to have remained associated to the

---

[142] TNA E 164/31.

[143] Evidence suggests, however, that among the thirty-four pensioners, some were employed at the time. For example, Thomas Acrigge was also a priest of St Nicholas Cole Abbey, London: GL Ms 9171/13, fol. 121.

[144] Chambers, *Faculty Office Register*, p. 234. These three priests were still receiving their pensions in 1556.

[145] *Ibid.*, p. 252.

[146] *Ibid.*, p. 283.

[147] In Cumbria, 80 peer cent of ex-cantarists found employment after the dissolution: Clark, 'Reformation in the Far North', p. 83. It has not been possible to calculate the ratio for St Paul's chaplains.

[148] GL Ms 9171/13, fols 7, 35v., 121; Ms 9051/3, fol. 21v.; Hennessy, p. 111.

[149] Barrett L. Beer, 'London Parish Clergy and the Protestant Reformation, 1547–1559', *Albion: A Quarterly Journal Concerned with British Studies*, 18/3 (1986), pp. 375–93, esp. p. 380.

[150] Hennessy, pp. 108, 358.

[151] GL Ms 25630/1, first folio; Newcourt, vol. 1, p. 812; vol. 2, p. 548.

cathedral: John Richardson was the chaplain of Gabriel Dunne, major canon; and Alexander Smyth became the cathedral's gospeller.[152]

Whereas one minor canon clearly converted to the new religion, most of the ex-chantry priests stayed faithful to the old faith.[153] They used traditional will preambles, and/or requested intercessions for the salvation of their souls.[154] One of them, John Richardon (d.1556), left money for the maintenance of the Jesus mass in the chapel of St Faith, and 'to a priest fore one yeare to syng for my soule'.[155] Ex-chantry priests also remained close to their former clerical family. John Andrew (d.1549) asked to be buried within the Pardon Churchyard, and remembered three chantry priests by name, one of whom he referred to as William of Holme's College (William Streket).[156] Thomas Wall (d.1550) referred to himself as 'late chantry priest of St Paul's' and asked to be buried in St Paul's Churchyard 'nyghe the crosse as may bee', and left his best jacket to another former cantarist, Richard Nelson.[157] Six years after the dissolution, Thomas Acrigge, then priest of St Nicholas Cole Abbey, requested that eight ex-fellow priests of St Peter's College attend his funeral, and he had his will witnessed by another one.[158] William Streket (d.1557) asked to be buried in the chapel where he used to worship as a chantry chaplain, and made bequests to two ex-colleagues, whom he identified as 'late chauntry priest in Lancaster College', and as 'late chauntry priest in Holmes College'.[159]

Mary's accession to the throne led to a short-lived revival of Catholicism. At St Paul's the old service with masses in Latin was revived in August 1553, while the Dean and Chapter restored the high altar and began the reconstruction of the upper sanctuary.[160] In April 1554, the Apostles' mass was celebrated, while in November the clergy introduced prayers for the pope and celebrated the Feast of St Erkenwald's translation.[161] This re-introduction of elements of traditional worship went hand in hand with a reshuffle of the cathedral's clerical community.

---

[152] GL Ms 25626/1, fol. 106; Ms 9171/13, fol. 121.

[153] John Painter (d.1549) bequeathed his soul 'into the hands and pour of the evelastyng God trusting onlye to be saved through faythe in christes death and passion refusing and forsaking all my work and deade as thyng unperfect and of suche imperfection that they can not merit or deserve anye parte of my salvacion'. At the time of his death Painter had married, and he named his wife his sole heir and executrix: GL Ms 25626/1, fol. 83.

[154] GL Ms 25626/1, fols 80v.–81v., 87v.–88, 110, 106; Ms 9171/13, fol. 121; TNA PROB 11/34, fols 23–24.

[155] GL Ms 25626/1, fol. 106.

[156] GL Ms 25626/1, fols 80v.–81v.

[157] GL Ms 9171/12, fol. 34.

[158] GL Ms 9171/13, fol. 121.

[159] GL Ms 25626/1, fols 109v.–110.

[160] Wriothesley, vol. 2, pp. 101–2.

[161] *Ibid.*, p. 88; *Chronicle of the Grey Friars*, p. 84; Crankshaw, 'Community, City', p. 50.

Released from imprisonment, Bonner regained the bishopric of London, and John Feckenham, a former monk, replaced May at the deanery. While some members of the chapter had gladly welcomed the accession of a devout Catholic as the head of state, several major canons resigned or were deprived of their prebends because of their adherence to Protestant beliefs.[162] For a few years, St Paul's Cathedral became once again associated with Catholic practices. The priests who for years had been connected with post-mortem masses and prayers for the dead did not, however, return. Whereas the Marian restoration witnessed the founding of a number of perpetual chantries, none was established at St Paul's, nor were the old ones revived.[163] The plea made by Dean Feckenham that the former ecclesiastical lands be returned to the Church fell upon deaf ears.[164] The assaults of the Edwardian regime on the cult of the dead had been fatal.[165] The endowments that had for centuries supported these intercessory activities were lost; lay owners now occupied the buildings in the cathedral precinct that had housed the chantry priests. Compared to other Catholic practices such as clerical processions and the burning of incense, which could be easily restored, chantries were a capital-intensive form of spirituality that, once their endowments were dissipated, would have needed major investments to be reinstated. The short duration of Mary's reign did not allow it. Chantries and the chaplains who had served them were gone forever. Nevertheless, their memory survived for awhile. Fifty years after it had been sold, the house where the chaplains occupying John of Gaunt's chantries had lived was still referred to as 'Lancaster College'.[166] The stationers who took possession of the buildings that once belonged to St Peter's College held their election feast on the Sunday following St Peter's Day, presumably alluding to the original occupants.[167] However, whereas in other English cathedrals surviving chantry chapels remind modern visitors of the former functions performed by the cathedral clergy for the salvation of souls, at St Paul's Cathedral the Great Fire of London in 1666 obliterated even that link with the past.

---

[162] Wriothesley, vol. 2, p. 97; Crankshaw, 'Community, City', p. 50. Three members of St Paul's, John Rogers, John Cardmaker and John Bradford, became martyrs for the Protestant cause for denying the mass.

[163] Marshall, *Beliefs and the Dead*, p. 116.

[164] Crankshaw, 'Community, City', p. 50.

[165] Duffy, *Stripping of the Altars*, p. 495; Marshall, *Reformation England*, p. 100. In his discussion on the dissolution of chantries, Shagan argues that the Edwardian dissolution could not have been successful if it had not been for the fact that so many profited from it: *Popular Politics*, pp. 267–9.

[166] GL Ms 25121/1096. In 1597, the dean sold a piece of ground to Edward Barker and his wife Susan, dwelling in a house commonly called 'Lancaster College'.

[167] Raven, 'St Paul's Precinct', p. 438.

Conclusion

With at least eighty-four chantry foundations established in its midst, St Paul's Cathedral was undoubtedly a pacesetter in this matter. While the earliest foundations date from the late twelfth century, numerous chantries were established in the thirteenth and first half of the fourteenth centuries. At the outbreak of the Black Death more than sixty chantry founders had chosen to be commemorated at St Paul's. The demographic decline and the economic depression that followed the Black Death considerably reduced the foundation rate, although chantries maintained their popularity as intercessory tools. From the mid-fourteenth century onwards, fewer, but more elaborate, pious enterprises were established at St Paul's. The majority of these chantries constituted post-mortem enterprises on the part of clerics who had been members of the cathedral. Not surprisingly, these men aimed to glorify the institution where they had worked and worshipped. This was particularly true for the members of the minor clergy, who endowed perpetual masses at the altars where they had themselves served as chantry chaplains. Londoners also accounted for a significant number of chantry foundations, as well as endowing existing ones. Although founders regulated their chantries to emphasise their own devotions and priorities, they also had to adapt them to the environment in which they were being established. As a result, most endowments were placed in the hands of the Dean and Chapter, and the cathedral authorities and personnel inherited large responsibilities in the selection of chaplains and in supervising the management of these endowments. In turn, these chantries had a considerable impact on the cathedral: they enhanced the liturgical life of St Paul's by expanding the choir, multiplying the masses to be celebrated daily and increasing the number of anniversaries to be observed annually. In time chantries led to the construction of new altars and chapels and to the foundation of colleges for housing the chantry chaplains in the precinct. Chantries also strengthened the links connecting the cathedral to the city of London. They increased the cathedral's investment in the city as most chantries were endowed with quit-rents and tenements within London. In return, the city benefited from the ancillary services offered by chantries: alms were delivered in the streets of London and local boys were taught by chantry priests. Chantry founders also intensified the lay involvement with St Paul's by appointing city and company officials as chantry patrons. These appointments demonstrate the trust that clerics had in the competence of the merchant class, and their acknowledgement that their foundations would benefit from such a division of responsibilities.

The chantry chaplains were fully integrated into the life of the cathedral. At their induction they joined the ranks of the minor clergy and were placed under the jurisdiction of the Dean and Chapter. Although a majority of them seem to have been natives of the diocese of London, a significant minority came from across the country to sing soul-masses at St Paul's. Their appointment depended on their social networks and on their contacts with chantry patrons. The experience of individual chaplains at St Paul's varied from one individual to another: some chaplains only spent a few years at St Paul's before re-entering the clerical job market, while others spent all their working lives at the cathedral, participating in the cathedral bureaucracy as well as serving its chantries. Their professional and social association with the cathedral personnel and with Londoners, as well as the rare incidences of misconduct, suggest that these chaplains were conscientious in fulfilling the various tasks they were given. Likewise, additional endowments allocated to chantries, together with the strategies adopted by the cathedral authorities to assist chantries in jeopardy, demonstrate that the fate of these pious foundations was of concern. Chantries did not fall into oblivion. They attracted resources because they were seen as serving the interests of the many rather than the few. Over time only a small minority disappeared, while the great majority, although amalgamated or associated with a cathedral minor canonry, survived until the Reformation, when they were swept away. Then the new belief in justification by faith deprived them of their purpose in labouring for the salvation of souls.

St Paul's Cathedral in the medieval period was a magnificent building that led the city in liturgical practice, music, learning and visual splendour, but it was also a spiritual factory where intercessory prayers were offered on a massive scale for the living and the dead. Such prayers were an essential part of the life and service of the cathedral, and the essential agents of salvation were the numerous, often obscure, chantry priests.

APPENDIX

Founders	Foundation date	No. of chaplains	Altar or chapel (burial)	Organisers	Original endowment	Amalgamation/ augmentation	Last mention
Richard Foliot, Archdeacon of Colchester[1]	Died c.1181	One	Altar of St Katherine	–	Properties in London	1391 with de Gloucester's Association with a minor canonry	1548
Richard Fitz Neal, Bishop of London[2]	1189 × 1198	One	Altar of St Radegund	–	Donations to the altar of St Radegund	Transfer to a Chapel in the Crypt	c.1370
Chesthunt, for the Kings of England and the Bishops of London[3]	1189 × 1198	Two	Altars of St Thomas the Martyr and of St Denis	Bishop Richard Fitz Neal	Income from the church of Chesthunt	Not part of the 1391 amalgamations	1438
William of Ste-Mère-Eglise, Bishop of London[4]	1199	One	Chapel in the bishop's palace	–	Income from churches and manors in Essex and Hertfordshire	Not part of the 1391 amalgamations 1408 with Braybroke, Boyes'	1548
Roger the Chaplain, Major Canon[5]	Before 1204	One	Altar of St Radegund	–	Properties in London	In 1391 with St Dunstan's Association with a minor canonry	1548
Richard de Umfraville, Major Canon[6]	1189 × 1212	One	Altar of St John the Evangelist	Will executors	Properties in London	1275 with de Braynford's	c.1320

Founders	Foundation date	No. of chaplains	Altar or chapel (burial)	Organisers	Original endowment	Amalgamation/ augmentation	Last mention
John of London, Major Canon[7]	d.1212	One	Altar of St James	–	Properties in London	c.1320 with de Acra's	c.1320
Alice, Countess of Pembroke[8]	1215 × 1219	Two	Unidentified altar (burial)	William Marshall (Husband)	Income from the manor of Luton	–	–
William Angevin, Major Canon[9]	d.1222	One	Altar of St James	–	–	–	1271
Eustace de Fauconberg, Bishop of London[10]	d.1228	One	Altar of St Michael	–	Income from Shadwell	1391 with de Haverhull and Grantham's	1548
Hugh of London, Archdeacon of Colchester[11]	d.1238	One	At different altars	–	Income from Stebbing, Essex	–	c.1370
Martin of Pattishall, Dean of St Paul's[12]	1239	Two	Altar of the Apostles	Margaret de Bigott	Marsh in Bures, Essex	1391 with Grene/de Gravesend's	1548
Geoffrey de Lucy, Dean of St Paul's[13]	d.1241	One	Altar of St Stephen	Will executors	Properties in Acton, Middlesex	1391 with de Eyton's	1548

Note to reader: See pp. 189–92 for notes to this Appendix.

Founders	Foundation date	No. of chaplains	Altar or chapel (burial)	Organisers	Original endowment	Amalgamation/ augmentation	Last mention
Parents of Roger Niger, Bishop of London[14]	d.1241	One	At different altars	–	–	1391 Basset's parents	1483/84
Richard of St Alban, Cleric[15]	1241 × 1242	One	–	Himself	Quit-rents in London	–	c.1370
William de Sanctae Mariae Ecclesia, Dean of St Paul's[16]	d.1243	One	Altar of St Stephen (burial)	Will executors	Sum of money to provide stipend in kind and cash	–	c.1370
Alexander de Swereford, Treasurer[17]	1234 × 1244	One	Altar of St Chad (burial)	Himself	Properties in Fobbing, Essex	1391 with Chigwell's Association with a minor canonry	1548
Richard de Wendover, Major Canon[18]	d.1252/3	One	Altar of St Hippolitus	Himself	Quit-rents in London	Before 1391, with de Brandon's 1391 with de Newport's	1548
Alan and Aveline, Bishop Fulk Basset's parents[19]	c.1252	Two	At different altars	Fulk Basset	Incomes from the church of Alcinldeham (Aldenham, Herts?)	1391 with St Roger's parents for one chaplain	1447

Founders	Foundation date	No. of chaplains	Altar or chapel (burial)	Organisers	Original endowment	Amalgamation/ augmentation	Last mention
John le Romeyn, Treasurer of York[20]	d.1256	One	At different altars	Will executors	Quit-rents from the Prior of St Mary's Hospital without Bishopsgate	1391 with Frisell's	1548
William de Haverhull, Major Canon[21]	1253 × 1257	One	Altar of St Chad	Will executors	Quit-rents and properties in London	In 1330 augmentation by John Grantham 1391 with de Fauconberg's	1548
Hugh de Sancto Edmundo, Archdeacon of Colchester[22]	1260/61	One	Altar of St Chad	Himself	Quit-rents in London	In 1295 with St Roger's parents	1295
Fulk Basset, Bishop of London[23]	1261	Three	Altar of St Mary the Virgin	Philip Basset, his brother	Manor of Boyton, Suffolk	1391 with: – Husband's – de Neuport's – de Waltham's	1548
Henry de Wingham, Bishop of London[24]	d.1262	Two	Altar of St Michael	–	Quit-rents from the abbey of Beeleigh by Maldon, Essex	1391 reduced to one chaplain	1451

Founders	Foundation date	No. of chaplains	Altar or chapel (burial)	Organisers	Original endowment	Amalgamation/ augmentation	Last mention
Peter de Neuport, Dean of St Paul's[25]	d.1262	One	Altar of St Thomas the Apostle	–	–	1391 with one chantry of Fulk Basset	1548
Godfrey de Acra, Minor Canon (also for Godfrey de Weseham, Major Canon)[26]	1262 × 1268	One	Chapel of St James	Himself	Properties in London	Not part of the 1391 amalgamations	1548
John de Braynford, Chaplain (also for Richard de Umfraville)[27]	1275	One	Altar of St John the Evangelist in the south transept	Dean	Incomes from the cathedral treasury and a house in London	1391 with Fulk Lovel's	1548
Roger Beyvin and wife Isabelle[28]	1278	One	Charnel house	Will executors	Rents from properties in London	Not part of the 1391 amalgamations In 1436 augmentation by John Carpenter for Richard Whittington	1548
Roger de La Legh, Archdeacon of Essex[29]	1278	One	Altar of Sylvester (burial in St Paul's)	Himself	Rents from properties in London	1391 with Fabel's	1548

Founders	Foundation date	No. of chaplains	Altar or chapel (burial)	Organisers	Original endowment	Amalgamation/ augmentation	Last mention
Henry de Edelmeton[30]	1279	One	Charnel house	Will executors	Rents from properties in London	–	c.1370
Isabelle Bukerel[31]	1280	Two	Altar of St Margaret before the Cross (burial?)	Will executors	Rents from properties in London	1391 reduced to one chaplain	1421
John de Chishull Bishop of London[32]	d.1280	One	Altar of St Mary by the Door	–	–	1302 with de Drayton's Not part of the 1391 amalgamations Association with a minor canonry	1548
Ralph de Dunion, Major Canon[33]	1282	One	Altar of St Mary in the nave	Will executors	Sum of money to buy quit-rents in London	1391 with de Everdon's	1548
Aveline de Basing/of St Olave[34]	1282/83	One	Charnel house	Will executors	Rents from properties in London	1391 with de Thorp's	1548
John de Sancta Maria, Major Canon[35]	d.1285	One	Altar of St Mary in the nave	Will executors	Properties in London	1391 with de Hotham's Association with a minor canonry	1548

Founders	Foundation date	No. of chaplains	Altar or chapel (burial)	Organisers	Original endowment	Amalgamation/ augmentation	Last mention
Fulk Lovel, Archdeacon of Colchester[36]	d.1285 1294?	One	Altar of St John the Baptist	Will executors	Rents from prebend of Portpool	1391 with de Braynford's	1548
Godfrey of St Dunstan, Minor Canon[37]	Before 1295	One	Altar of St Thomas the Apostle (burial)	–	Quit-rents in London	1391 with Roger the Chaplain's Association with a minor canonry	1548
John Lovel, Justice of the King[38]	1297	One	Altar of St Andrew	Himself	Properties in London	1391 with one chantry of Pulteney	1548
William de Hareworth, Rector of West Tilbury[39]	1301	One	New altar?	Will executors	Properties in London	1391 with de Blockele's	1420 Only de Blockele's is mentioned in 1548
Robert de Drayton, Treasurer (also for John de Chishull)[40]	1302	One	Altar of St Mary in the nave	Will executors	Properties in London	Not part of the 1391 amalgamations Association with a minor canonry	1548

Founders	Foundation date	No. of chaplains	Altar or chapel (burial)	Organisers	Original endowment	Amalgamation/ augmentation	Last mention
John de Wengham, Precentor[41]	d.1305	One	–	–	–	c.1390 included with Holme's 1391 with de Everdon's	1391
Reginald de Brandon, Major Canon[42]	1307	One	Altar of St Dunstan in the New Work (burial)	Will executors	Properties in London	Before 1391 with de Wendover's 1391 with de Newport's	1548
Walter de Blockele, Chantry Chaplain[43]	1307	One	Altar of Sylvester	Will executors	Rents and properties in London	1391 with William de Hareworth's	1548
Richard de Newport, Archdeacon of Middlesex[44]	1309	Two	Altar of St Radegund	Himself	Books and properties in London	1391 with de Brandon and de Wendover's Association with a minor canonry	1548
Richard Grene/ de Gravesend, Treasurer[45]	1310	One	Altar of St Sylvester	Himself	Houses in the precinct	1391 with one of Pattishall's	1548
Henry de Guldeford, called the Mareschal, Clerk[46]	d.1313	One	Altar of the Apostles	Will executors	Properties in London	Not part of the 1391 amalgamations	1548

Founders	Foundation date	No. of chaplains	Altar or chapel (burial)	Organisers	Original endowment	Amalgamation/augmentation	Last mention
John de Mondene, Major Canon, and his brother Robert[47]	1318	One	Altar of St John the Baptist in the New Work	Robert de Mondene	Properties in London	In 1330 augmentation by Robert de Mondene 1391 with one chantry of John Pulteney	1548
Ralph de Baldock, Bishop of London[48]	1320	Two	Altar of St Erkenwald	Will executors	Properties in London	1391 reduced to one chaplain, but afterwards two chaplains	1548
Nicholas and Joan de Wokyndon[49]	1320	Two	Altar of St Thomas the Martyr (burial)	Joan his wife	Quit-rents and properties in London	1391 reduced to one	1548
Geoffrey de Eyton, Major Canon[50]	d.1328 1320?	One	Altar of St John the Baptist	–	Properties in London	1391 with de Lucy's	1548
William de Chaddleshunt, Major Canon[51]	1321	One	Altar of St Michael in the New Work	Will executors	Properties in London	Not part of the 1391 amalgamations Linked with de Blockele's & of Pattishall's in 15th century	1548

Founders	Foundation date	No. of chaplains	Altar or chapel (burial)	Organisers	Original endowment	Amalgamation/ augmentation	Last mention
Walter de Thorp, Major Canon[52]	1324	One	Altar of St John in the New Work	Will executors	Properties in London	1391 with of St Olave's	1548
Roger de Waltham, Major Canon[53]	1325	Two	Altar of St John the Evangelist Altar of St Laurence	Himself	Properties in London	1391 with Basset's, for two chantries	1548
Richard de Gloucester[54]	1329	One		Will executors	Properties in London	1391 with Foliot's Association with a minor canonry	1548
Hamo Chigwell, Mayor of London[55]	d.1333	One	Altar of the image of St Mary in the old work (burial)		Properties in London	1391 with de Swereford's Association with a minor canonry	1548
John Fabel of Hatfield Peverel[56]	1334	One	Altar of St Thomas the Martyr in the New Work	Will executors	Properties in London	1391 with Roger de La Legh's	1548

Founders	Foundation date	No. of chaplains	Altar or chapel (burial)	Organisers	Original endowment	Amalgamation/ augmentation	Last mention
Nicholas de Farndone, Mayor of London[57]	1334	One	Altar of St Dunstan in the New Work (burial)	Will executors	Properties in London	1361 with Neel's Not part of the 1391 amalgamations Association with a minor canonry	1548
William de Meleford, Archdeacon of Colchester[58]	1337	One	Altar of St John the Baptist	Will executors	Properties in London	1391 with one chantry of Pulteney	1548
Richard and Stephen de Gravesend, Bishops of London (uncle and nephew)[59]	1338	Two	–	Will executors	Properties in London	Not part of the 1391 amalgamations Association with a minor canonry	1548
James Frisell[60]	1343	One	–	Will executors	Properties in London	1391 with John le Romeyn's	1548
Nicholas Husband, Minor Canon[61]	1347	One	–	Will executors	Quit-rent from the Prior and Convent of St Bartholomew	1391 with Basset's Association with a minor canonry	1548

Founders	Foundation date	No. of chaplains	Altar or chapel (burial)	Organisers	Original endowment	Amalgamation/ augmentation	Last mention
John Pulteney, Mayor of London[62]	1349	Three	Chapel of St John the Baptist in the north transept	Will executors	Quit-rents from the College St Laurence Pountney	1391 with: – de Mondene's – de Meleford's – John Lovel's	1548
William de Everdon, Major Canon[63]	1349	Two	Chapel of St Radegund in the crypt (burial)	Will executors	Sum of money	1391 one with de Wingham's and one with de Dunion's Association with a minor canonry	1548
Henry de Idesworth, Archdeacon of Middlesex[64]	1349	One	Altar of St James	Will executors	Properties in London	1391 with Michael de Northburgh's	1548
Alan de Hotham, Major Canon[65]	1352	One	Altar of St Sebastian in the crypt (burial)	Will executors	Properties in London	1391 with de Sancta Maria's Association with a minor canonry	1548
Gilbert de Bruera, Dean of St Paul's[66]	1354	One	Chapel of St Katherine (burial)	Will executors	Properties in London	Not part of the 1391 amalgamations	1548

Founders	Foundation date	No. of chaplains	Altar or chapel (burial)	Organisers	Original endowment	Amalgamation/ augmentation	Last mention
John Beauchamp, Lord Beauchamp of Warwick[67]	d.1360	One	Small altar next tomb in nave (burial)	Himself and will executors	Properties in London	Not part of the 1391 amalgamations	1548
Michael de Northburgh, Bishop of London[68]	1361	One	–	Will executors	Properties in London	1391 with de Idesworth's	1548
Walter Neel, Sheriff of London, and wife Alice[69]	1361	One	Altar of St John the Evangelist (burial)	John de Ware, minor canon	Properties in London	1361 with de Farndone's Not part of the 1391 amalgamations Association with a minor canonry	1548
John Hiltoft, Sheriff of London, and wife Alice[70]	1370	One	Chapel of St Dunstan in the New Work	Will executors	Sum of money to rebuild part of the precinct	Not part of the 1391 amalgamations	1548
Adam de Bury, Mayor of London and Roger Holme, Chancellor[71]	1386	Seven	Chapel of the Holy Ghost (burial of de Bury and Holme)	Roger Holme	Properties in London	Not part of the 1391 amalgamations In late 15th century, reduction to four chaplains	1548

Founders	Foundation date	No. of chaplains	Altar or chapel (burial)	Organisers	Original endowment	Amalgamation/ augmentation	Last mention
John of Gaunt, Duke of Lancaster[72]	1403	Two	Chapel in the north side of the chancel (burial)	Will executors	Properties in London	–	1548
Roger Albrygton, Treasurer, John Boyes, Gerard de Braybroke, and Edmund Hampden[73]	1403	One	Chapel in the bishop's palace	Themselves	Manor of Lofthall, Essex	1408 with the chantry of William of Ste-Mere-Eglise	1548
Beatrice de Roos[74]	1408	One	Chapel of St John the Baptist	Merchant Tailors	Quit-rents from the Merchant Tailors	–	1548
Thomas de Eure, Dean of St Paul's[75]	1411	One	Altar of St Thomas in the New Work	Will executors	Properties in London	–	1548
Thomas Stowe, Dean of St Paul's[76]	1423	One	Altar of St Mary by the Door	John Westyerd, vintner	Quit-rents from the Prior and Convent of St Bartholomew	–	1548

Founders	Foundation date	No. of chaplains	Altar or chapel (burial)	Organisers	Original endowment	Amalgamation/ augmentation	Last mention
Thomas More, Dean of St Paul's[77]	1424	Three	Chapel of SS Anne & Thomas the Martyr in Pardon Churchyard	Will executors	Tenements in London	1434 increased to four chaplains by Walter Caketon	1548
Walter Sherrington, Major Canon[78]	1447	Two	Chapel of St Nicholas near the north door	Will executors	Properties in Tenterden, Kent	–	1548
Roger Walden, Bishop of London[79]	1457	One	Chapel of All Hallows	John Drayton, goldsmith	Properties in London	–	1548
Thomas Kempe, Bishop of London[80]	1467	One	Altar of St Trinity in the nave	Himself	Properties in Great Clacton, Essex; rectory of Chigwell	Association with the penitentiary and a major canonry	1548
William Say, Dean of St Paul's[81]	1503	One	Chapel in the crypt (burial)	William Vale, cutler	Properties in London	–	1548

Founders	Foundation date	No. of chaplains	Altar or chapel (burial)	Organisers	Original endowment	Amalgamation/ augmentation	Last mention
John Dowman, Major Canon[82]	1525	Two	Chapel of St Katherine, Altar of SS Martha & Mary Magdalene	William Barbe, fishmonger	Quit-rents from the Haberdashers	–	1548
Richard FitzJames, Bishop of London[83]	1529 (1521)	One	Chapel of St Paul, stone-cage chapel (burial)	Henry Hyll, haberdasher	Quit-rents from the Merchant Tailors	–	1548
John Withers, Major Canon[84]	1535	Two	Chapel of the Holy Ghost (burial)	Robert Brokel, baker	Quit-rents from the Saddlers	–	1548

Notes to Appendix

1   *Fasti I*, pp. 16, 19, 43, 86; GL Ms 25121/160, 161; Ms 25501, fol. 22v.; Gibbs, *Early Charters*, no. 213. The chantry was at the altar of St John the Evangelist in c.1253, but in 1271 and c.1320 at the altar of St Katherine, GL Ms 25502, fols 100–101; Ms 25504, fols 93–93v., 127v.

2   *Fasti I*, pp. 2, 41; GL Ms 25504, fols 93–93v.

3   GL Ms 25122/1432; Ms 25513, fol. 170v.

4   *Fasti I*, pp. 2, 48; GL Ms 9531/12, fols 54v.–55; GL Ms 25626, fol. 22.

5   *Fasti I*, p. 68; Gibbs, *Early Charters*, no. 240.

6   *Fasti I*, p. 39; Gibbs, *Early Charters*, nos 295–6; GL Ms 25121/1934.

7   *Fasti I*, p. 46; GL Ms 25121/1209, 1210. The type of founding process could not be determined.

8   Daughter of Baldwin de Betun, Earl of Albemarle, and wife of William Marshall, son of William, Earl of Pembroke, *Early Charters*, nos 221–2.

9   *Fasti I*, p. 62; GL Ms 25504, fol. 127v.

10   *Fasti I*, pp. 2, 54; GL Ms 25502, fols 100–101; Ms 25504, fols 93–93v., 127v. He also endowed the choir, Gibbs, *Early Charters*, no. 202.

11   *Fasti I*, pp. 19, 35; GL Ms 25502, fols 100–101; Ms 25504, fols 93–93v.,127v.; Ms 25121/1954.

12   *Fasti I*, pp. 6, 35; GL M 25157; Ms 25501, fol. 59.

13   *Fasti I*, pp. 6, 11, 58; GL Ms 25501, fols 32, 47. In the 1391 amalgamation, it was referred to as chantry of Philip de Fauconberg, Ms 25121/1953.

14   *Fasti I*, pp. 3, 19, 46; GL Ms 25502, fols 100–101; Ms 25504, fol. 127v.; Ms 25121/880–81, 1954.

15   GL Ms 25501, fols 29, 37; Ms 25121/1954.

16   *Fasti I*, pp. 6–7, 35, 91; GL Ms 25121/1947, 1954; Cambridge, St John's College, Ms 272, fols 41v.–42v.

17   *Fasti I*, pp. 22, 43, 89; GL Ms 25501, fols 42–44.

18   *Fasti I*, pp. 46, 64, 76; GL Ms 25504, fols 93–93v. The foundation deed for Bruera's chantry made provision for one chaplain to pray for Richard de Wendover, GL Ms 25121/732.

19   GL Ms 25502, fols 100–101; Ms 25504, fols 93–93v., 127v.; Ms 25513, fol. 258.

20   John Le Neve, *Fasti Ecclesiae Anglicanae 1066–1300*, vol. VI: *York*, compiled by Diana E. Greenway (London, 1999), p. 24. *ODNB*, 'Romanus, John'; GL Ms 25501, fol. 47; GL Ms 25122/1081; Ms 25502, fols 100–101.

21   *Fasti I*, p. 58; GL Ms 25121/534, 535, 710, 1535, 1734.

22   *Fasti I*, pp. 14, 20, 48; GL Ms 25121/613, 1810; Dugdale, p. 333.

23   *Fasti I*, p. 3; GL Ms 25122/286.

24   *Fasti I*, pp. 3, 67.

25   *Fasti I*, pp. 7, 11, 24, 56; GL Ms 25502, fols 100–101.

26   *Fasti I*, p. 92; GL Ms 25121/339; Ms 25523.

27   GL Ms 25121/1482, 1934.

28   Sharpe, vol. 1, pp. 29–30; Ms 25513, fols 156–159; Repertory, vol. 12, fol. 29.

29   Dean of St Paul's in 1283, *Fasti I*, pp. 8, 14, 31; GL Ms 25121/1936

30   GL Ms 25271/79; Ms 25501, fol. 68; Ms 25121/1954; Sharpe, vol. 1, p. 42.

31   Sharpe, vol. 1, pp. 49–50; GL Ms 25513, fol. 78.

32   *Fasti I*, pp. 4, 7, 11, 40; Dugdale, p. 331; GL Ms 25501, fol. 72.

33   *Fasti I*, p. 59; Dugdale, p. 331; GL Ms 25121/251, 252; Ms 25271/7.

34   GL Ms 25121/140.

35   *Fasti I*, p. 87; Sharpe, vol. 1, p. 58.

36   *Fasti I*, p. 4, 20, 34, 58; two chaplains in Dugdale, p. 334; GL Ms 25121/605; Ms 25501, fol. 71.

37   GL Ms 25505, fol. 65v. In 1309/10 Thomas de Bredestrete endowed the chantry for Godfrey of St Dunstan, Sharpe, vol. 1, p. 209.

38   GL Ms 25241/24; GL Ms 25121/427.

39   GL Ms 25121/1935; Ms 25502, fols 100–101; Ms 25513, fol. 73v.; Sharpe, vol. 1, pp. 135–6.

40   *Fasti I*, pp. 22, 82; GL Ms 25501, fol. 72.

41   *Fasti II*, p. 16, 41; GL Ms 25121/1954, 3049; Ms 25145.

42   *Fasti I*, p. 78; GL Ms 25121/1920.

43   GL Ms 25121/1195, 1426; Ms 25271/48; Sharpe, vol. 1, pp. 184–5.

44   Bishop of London (1317–1318), *Fasti II*, pp. 1, 11; GL Ms 25121/741, 1772; Ms 25502, fols 100–101.

45   *Fasti II*, pp. 7, 14, 30; GL Ms 25121/1962, 1963; Ms 25502, fols 100–101.

46   GL Ms 25121/1754.

47   GL Ms 25121/190, 1917, 1918.

48   *Fasti II*, pp. 1, 4, 43, 51; GL Ms 25501, fol. 96.

49   GL Ms 25121/680; Sharpe, vol. 1, p. 290.

50   *Fasti II*, pp. 21, 35, 52; GL Ms 25502, fols 100–101; *CPR, 1334–1338*, p. 259.

51   *Fasti II*, pp. 59, 66; GL Ms 25121/860

52   *Fasti II*, p. 38; GL Ms 25241/15; Ms 25501, fol. 83.

53   *Fasti II*, p. 25; GL Ms 25121/3036–40.

54   Sharpe, vol. 1, pp. 342–3.

55   Beaven, *Aldermen*, vol. 1, p. 18; *ODNB*; Sharpe, vol. 1, pp. 382–3.

56   *CPR, 1334–1338*, p. 22. In 1400 the chantry was located at the altar of St Margaret in the chapel of St Katherine; *CPR, 1399–1401*, p. 390.

57   Beaven, *Aldermen*, vol. 1, p. 143; Sharpe, vol. 1, pp. 397–8; GL Ms 25121/635.

58   *Fasti II*, pp. 13, 47; Sharpe, vol. 1, p. 424.

59   *Fasti II*, pp. 1, 28, 6; *CPR, 1324–1327*, pp. 133, 156–7, 266–7; *CPR, 1345–1348*, pp. 349; 356; GL Ms 25121/1957.

60   Sharpe, vol. 1, p. 469; GL Ms 25139; Ms 25271/29.

61   *CPR, 1307–1313*, p. 557; *CPR, 1314–1317*, p. 366; Sharpe, vol. 1, pp. 496–7.

62   Beaven, *Aldermen*, vol. 1, p. 80; *ODNB*; Sharpe, vol. 1, pp. 609–10; GL Ms 25271/35.

63   *Fasti II*, p. 32; GL Ms 25121/1940, 1969.

64   *Fasti II*, p. 11; Sharpe, vol. 1, pp. 514–15.

65   *Fasti II*, p. 61; Sharpe, vol. 1, pp. 660–61; GL Ms 25264.

66   *Fasti II*, p. 5; Sharpe, vol. 1, pp. 682–3; GL Ms 25121/732.

67   GL Ms 25121/1925.

68   *Fasti II*, pp. 2, 33, 46; Sharpe, vol. 2, pp. 61–2; GL Ms 25526, fol. 30v.

69   Beaven, *Aldermen*, vol. 1, p. 88; GL Ms 25121/635.

70   Beaven, *Aldermen*, vol. 1, p. 286; Dugdale, p. 21; Jefferson, *Wardens' Accounts*, pp. 184–91.

71   Beaven, *Aldermen*, vol. 1, p. 167; *Fasti II*, pp. 11, 19, 27; Sharpe, vol. 2, pp. 254–5; GL Ms 25145; Ms 25146.

72   *CPR, 1401–1405*, pp. 210, 214, 236; GL Ms 251953; Ms 251954.

73   *Fasti II*, p. 15; *CPR, 1401–1405*, p. 239; GL Ms 9531/12, fols 56v.–57v.; Ms 9531/4, fol. 111.

74   *CPR, 1408–1413*, p. 40; Dugdale, pp. 354–7.

75   *Fasti II*, p. 6; *CPR, 1408–1413*, p. 170; GL Ms 25138; Sharpe, vol. 2, pp. 503–4.

76   *Fasti II*, pp. 6, 8, 46; Sharpe, vol. 2, pp. 434–6.

77   *Fasti II*, p. 6; *CPR, 1413–1416*, p. 365; *CPR, 1422–1429*, pp. 179–80, 269; Lambeth Palace Ms 2018; Sharpe, vol. 2, pp. 467–8; GL Ms 25121/1960; Ms 25513, fol. 152v.

78   *Fasti II*, p. 48; *CPR, 1441–1446*, pp. 446, 462; Hearne, *History and Antiquities*, pp. 161–223.

79   *Fasti II*, pp. 2, 70; GL Ms 25526, fol. 5.

80   *Fasti II*, p. 3; *CPR, 1461–1467*, p. 421; *CPR, 1476–1485*, p. 108; TNA PROB 11/8, fols 226v.–228v.

81   *Fasti II*, pp. 6, 44, 51, 69; TNA PROB 11/5, fols 99v.–100v.; GL Ms 25518.

82   *Fasti II*, pp. 57, 65; GL Ms 25271/73.
83   *Fasti II*, pp. 4, 16, 57; Sharpe, vol. 2, pp. 634–5; Chaplains were appointed from 1521 onwards.
84   *Fasti II*, p. 47; Sharpe, vol. 2, pp. 637–8.

Bibliography

Manuscript Sources

Cambridge, University Library

Ms Ee 5.21   *Statuta Ecclesiae Cathedralis S. Pauli*

Cambridge, St John's College

Ms 272   Documents relating to the almoner of St Paul's Cathedral
Ms K54   Copies of deeds of foundation relating to John Dowman

London, Guildhall Library

Ms 5872A/1   Receipt book
Ms 9051   Registers of wills proved in the Archdeaconry Court of London
Ms 9171   Registers of wills proved in the Commissary Court of London
Ms 9531   Registers of Bishops of London
Ms 25121   St Paul's Cathedral, Dean and Chapter, 'London deeds'
Ms 25122   St Paul's Cathedral, Dean and Chapter, 'Country deeds'
Ms 25125   Account rolls for London
Ms 25137–63   Chantry account rolls and deeds
Ms 25206   Account of rent and pensions due to the Cathedral, or to individual chantries
Ms 25241   Original and copy royal charters
Ms 25262–70   Copies and extracts of wills
Ms 25271   Original wills
Ms 25501   Cartulary known as 'Liber A'
Ms 25502   Statute and evidence book
Ms 25503   Copy of a cathedral inventory
Ms 25505   Statute and evidence book
Ms 25509   'Statuta Majora', statute and evidence book
Ms 25513   Chapter Act Book

Ms 25518	Copy of William Vale's will
Ms 25523	Copy of foundation deed for Godfrey de Acra's chantry
Ms 25526	Original Return
Ms 25626/1	Peculiar Court: registers of wills
Ms 25630/1	Dean's register: Sampson
Ms 29418	Copy of statutes of the minor canons of St Paul's cathedral

London, Lambeth Palace

Ms 2018	Foundation deed for Thomas More's chantry

London, London Metropolitan Archives

Husting Rolls of Wills and Deeds
Journals of the Court of Common Council
Repertories of the Court of Aldermen

London, The National Archives

C1	Chancery: Early Proceedings
E25	Exchequer Acknowledgements of Supremacy
E41	Exchequer Ancient Deeds
E101	Exchequer Accounts Various
E164	Exchequer Miscellaneous Books
E314	Exchequer Court of Augmentations and Court of General Surveyors
E315	Exchequer Court of Augmentations and Predecessors and Successors
PROB 11	Prerogative Court of Canterbury and related Probate Jurisdictions: will registers

Windsor Castle, St George's Chapel Archives

SGC XV.48.21	Account Roll

Printed Primary Sources

Calendar of Close Rolls
Calendar of Patent Rolls

Caley, J. and J. Hunter (eds), *Valor Ecclesiasticus Temp. Henry VIII, Auctoritate Regia Institutus, 1535* (6 vols, London: Record Commission of Great Britain, 1810–34)

Chambers, David Sanderson (ed.), *Faculty Office Registers, 1534–1549: a Calendar of the First Two Registers of the Archbishop of Canterbury's Faculty Office* (Oxford: Clarendon Press, 1966)

Chew, Helena M. and William Kellaway (eds), *London Assize of Nuisance 1301–1431*, London Record Society, 10 (London: The Society, 1973)

Darlington, Ida (ed.), *London Consistory Court Wills, 1492–1547*, London Record Society, 3 (London: The Society, 1967)

Davies, Matthew (ed.), *The Merchant Taylors' Company of London: Court Minutes, 1486–1493* (Stamford: Paul Watkins for the Richard III and Yorkist History Trust, 2000)

Davis, Norman (ed.), *Paston Letters and Papers of the Fifteenth Century* (2 vols, Oxford: Clarendon Press, 1971)

Davis, Virginia, *Clergy in London in the Late Middle Ages. A Register of Clergy Ordained in the Diocese of London based on Episcopal Ordination Lists 1361–1539*, CD-ROM (London: Institute of Historical Research, 2000)

Du Boulay, F.R.H. (ed.), *Registrum Thome Bourgchier, Cantuariensis Archiepiscopi, AD 1454–1486*, Canterbury and York Society, 54 (Oxford: Oxford University Press, 1957)

Fitch, Marc (ed.), *Index to the Testamentary Records in the Commissary Court of London (now preserved in the Guildhall Library London)*, vol. 1: *1374–1488* and vol. 2: *1489–1570* (London: HMSO, 1969 & 1973)

— (ed.), *Index to the Testamentary Records in the Archdeaconry Court of London (now preserved in the Guildhall Library London)*, vol. 1: *1363–1649* (London: British Record Society, 1979)

Fowler, Robert C. (ed.), *Registrum Radulphi Baldock, Gilberti Segrave, Ricardi Newport et Stephani Gravesend, Episcoporum Londoniensum, 1304–38*, Canterbury & York Society, 7 (London: The Society, 1911)

— and Claude Jenkins (eds), *Registrum Simonis de Sudbiria Diocesis Londoniensis, AD 1362–75*, Canterbury & York Society, 34, 38 (London: The Society, 1927 & 1938)

Gibbs, Marion (ed.), *Early Charters of the Cathedral Church of St. Paul*, Camden, 3rd series, 58 (London: Royal Historical Society, 1939)

Hackett, Maria (ed.), *Registrum Eleemosynariae S. Pauli Londinensis* (London: J.B. Nichols, 1827)

Harper-Bill, Christopher (ed.), *The Register of John Morton, Archbishop of Canterbury 1486–1500*, vol. 1, Canterbury & York Society, 75 (Leeds:

Privately printed for the Canterbury and York Society by Duffield Printers, 1987)

—(ed.), *The Register of John Morton, Archbishop of Canterbury, 1486–1500*, vol. 2, Canterbury & York Society, 78 (Woodbridge: Boydell Press, 1991)

— (ed.), *The Register of John Morton, Archbishop of Canterbury 1486–1500*, vol. 3, Canterbury & York Society, 89 (Woodbridge: Canterbury & York Society, 2000)

Hearne, Thomas (ed.), *The History and Antiquities of Glastonbury. Added with The Endowment and Orders of Sherington's Chantry, founded in Saint Paul's Church, London* (Oxford: The Theatre, 1722)

Jacob, E.F. (ed.), *Register of Henry Chichele, Archbishop of Canterbury 1414–1443* (4 vols, Oxford: Clarendon Press, 1914–1943)

James, N.W. and V.A. James, *The Bede Roll of the Fraternity of St Nicholas*, London Record Society, 39 (2 vols, London: London Record Society, 2004)

Jefferson, Lisa (ed.), *Wardens' Accounts and Court Minute Books of the Goldsmiths' Mistery of London* (Woodbridge: Boydell Press, 2003)

Kitching, C.J. (ed.), *London and Middlesex Chantry Certificate 1548*, London Record Society, 16 (London: The Society, 1980)

Kleineke, Hannes and Stephanie R. Hovland (eds), *The Estate and Household Accounts of William Worsley, Dean of St Paul's Cathedral, 1479–1499*, London Record Society, 40 (Donington: Richard III and Yorkist History Trust; London Record Society in association with Shaun Tyas, 2004)

Knighton, C.S. (ed.), *Calendar of State Papers, Domestic Series, of the Reign of Edward VI (1547–1553) Preserved in the Public Record Office* (London: HMSO, 1992)

Letters and Papers, Foreign and Domestic, Henry VIII

Lyndwood's Provinciale, Lib. III, tit. 23, cap. 1., reprint in J.V. Bullard and H. Chalmer Bell (eds), *Lyndwood's Provinciale* (London: Faith Press, 1929)

McHardy, Alison K. (ed.), *The Church in London, 1375–1392*, London Record Society, 13 (London: The Society, 1977)

Masters, Betty R. (ed.), *Chamber Accounts of the 16th Century*, London Record Society, 20 (London: Corporation of London and the Society, 1984)

Nicholas, John Gough (ed.), *Chronicle of the Grey Friars of London*, Camden Society, 53 (London: Printed for the Camden Society, 1852)

O'Connor, S.J. (ed.), *A Calendar of the Cartularies of John Pyel and Adam Fraunceys*, Camden, 5th series, 2 (London: Royal Historical Society, 1993)

Riley, H.T. (ed. & trans.), *Memorials of London and London Life in the XIIIth, XIVth and XVth Centuries* (London: Longmans, 1868)

Sharpe, R.R. (ed.), *Calendar of Wills Proved and Enrolled in the Court of Husting, London, 1250–1688* (2 vols, London: J.C. Francis, 1889–1890)

— (ed.), *Calendar of Letter-Books Preserved among the Archives of the Corporation of the City of London at the Guildhall* (11 vols, London: J.E. Francis, 1899–1912)

Sheppard, Joseph Brigstocke (ed.), *Literae Cantuarienses. The Letter Books of the Monastery of Christ Church, Canterbury*, Rerum Britannicarum Medii Aaevi Scriptores, 85 (3 vols, London: Printed for H.M. Stationery off., by Eyre and Spottiswoode, 1887–1889)

Simpson, William Sparrow, 'Charter and Statutes of the College of the Minor Canons in St. Paul's Cathedral', *Archaeologia*, 43 (1871): 165–200

— (ed.), *Registrum Statutorum et Consuetudinum Ecclesiae Cathedralis Sancti Pauli Londinensis* (London: Nichols, 1873)

— *Documents Illustrating the History of St Paul's Cathedral*, Camden Society, ns, 26 (London: The Society, 1880)

— 'On a Newly-Discovered Manuscript Containing Statutes Compiled by Dean Colet for the Government of the Chantry Priests and Other Clergy in St Paul's Cathedral', *Archaeologia*, 52 (1890): 145–74

Smith, David M., *Guide to Bishops' Registers of England and Wales: A Survey from the Middle Ages to the Abolition of Episcopacy in 1646* (London: Royal Historical Society, 1981)

Statutes of the Realm (11 vols, London: G. Eyre and A. Strahan, 1810–1828)

Stow, John, *The Annales of England, Faithfully Collected out of the Most Autenticall Authors, Records, and Other Monuments of Antiquitie* (London: Ralfe Newbery, 1601)

— *A Survey of London.* Reprinted from the text of 1603, with introduction and notes by Charles L. Kingsford (2 vols, Oxford: Clarendon Press, 1908)

Wood, A.C. (ed.), *Registrum Simonis Langham, Cantuariensis Archiepiscopi* (Oxford: Oxford University Press, 1956)

Wood-Legh, Kathleen L., *A Small Household of the XVth Century being the Account Book of Munden's Chantry, Bridport* (Manchester: Manchester University Press, 1956)

Woodward, G.H., *Calendar of Somerset. Chantry Grants, 1548–1603*, Somerset Record Society Series, 77 (Taunton: Somerset Record Society, 1982)

Wriothesley, Charles, *A Chronicle of England during the Reigns of the Tudors from A.D. 1485 to 1559.* Edited by William Douglas Hamilton, Camden, ns 11, 20 (2 vols, Westminster: Nichols, 1875–1877)

Secondary Works

Alsop, J.D., 'Religious Preambles in Early Modern English Will as Formulae', *Journal of Ecclesiastical History*, 40/1 (1989): 19–27

Appleford, Amy, 'The Dance of Death in London: John Carpenter, John Lydgate, and the Daunce of Poulys', *Journal of Medieval and Early Modern Studies*, 38 (2008): 285–314

Archer, Ian, *The History of the Haberdashers' Company* (Chichester: Phillimore, 1991)

Arnold, Jonathan, 'John Colet, Preaching and Reform at St Paul's Cathedral, 1505–19', *Historical Research*, 76/194 (2003): 450–68

— 'John Colet and a Lost Manuscript of 1506', *History*, 89 (2004): 174–92

— *Dean John Colet of St Paul's: Humanism and Reform in Early Tudor England*, International Library of Historical Studies, 49 (London: I.B. Tauris, 2007)

Aston, Margaret, *Lollards and Reformers. Images and Literacy in Late Medieval Religion* (London: Hambledon Press, 1984)

Attreed, Lorraine C., 'Preparation for Death in Sixteenth-Century Northern England', *Sixteenth Century Journal*, 13/3 (1982): 37–66

Bailey, Terence, *The Processions of Sarum and the Western Church* (Toronto: Pontifical Institute of Mediaeval Studies, 1971)

Baker, Thomas, *History of the College of St John the Evangelist* (2 vols, Cambridge: Cambridge University Press, 1869)

Bannister, A.T., *The Cathedral Church of Hereford. Its History and Constitution* (London: Society for Promoting Christian Knowledge, 1924)

Barrett, Philip, 'The College of Vicars Choral', in Gerald Aylmer and John Tiller (eds), *Hereford Cathedral. A History* (London: Hambledon Press, 2000): 441–60

Barron, Caroline M., *The Medieval Guildhall of London* (London: Corporation of London, 1974)

— *Revolt in London: 11th to 15th June 1381* (London: Museum of London, 1981)

— 'The Parish Fraternities of Medieval London', in Caroline M. Barron and Christopher Harper-Bill (eds), *The Church in Pre-Reformation Society: Essays in Honour of F.R.H. Du Boulay* (Woodbridge: Boydell Press, 1985): 13–37

— 'The Later Middle Ages, 1200–1520', in Mary D. Lobel (ed.), *The City of London. From Prehistoric Times to c.1520*, The British Atlas of Historic Towns, 3 (Oxford: Oxford University Press, 1989): 42–56

— 'The Expansion of Education in Fifteenth-Century London', in John Blair and Brian Golding (eds), *The Cloister and the World. Essays in Medieval History in Honour of Barbara Harvey* (Oxford: Clarendon Press, 1996): 219–45

— 'London 1300–1540', in D.M. Palliser (ed.), *The Cambridge Urban History of Britain*, vol. 1: *600–1540* (Cambridge: Cambridge University Press, 2000): 395–440

— 'London and St Paul's Cathedral in the Later Middle Ages', in Janet Backhouse (ed.), *The Medieval English Cathedral. Papers in Honour of Pamela Tudor-Craig. Proceedings of the 1998 Harlaxton Symposium* (Donington: Shaun Tyas, 2003): 126–49

— *London in the Later Middle Ages: Government and People, 1200–1500* (Oxford: Oxford University Press, 2004)

— and Matthew Davies (eds), *The Religious Houses of London and Middlesex* (London: Institute of Historical Research, 2007)

— and Marie-Hélène Rousseau, 'Cathedral, City and State, 1300–1540', in Derek Keene, Arthur Burns and Andrew Saint (eds), *St Paul's. The Cathedral Church of London, 604–2004* (New Haven/London: Yale University Press, 2004): 33–44

Barrow, Julia, 'Vicars Choral and Chaplains in Northern European Cathedrals 1100–1250', in W.S. Sheils and Diana Wood (eds), *The Ministry: Clerical and Lay. Papers Read at the 1988 Summer Meeting and the 1989 Winter Meeting of the Ecclesiastical History Society*, Studies in Church History, 26 (Oxford/Cambridge, Mass.: Published for the Society by B. Blackwell, 1989): 87–97

Baskerville, Geoffrey, *English Monks and the Suppression of the Monasteries* (London: J. Cape, 1936)

Beaven, Alfred, *The Aldermen of the City of London* (2 vols, London: E. Fisher & Co., 1908–1913)

Beer, Barrett L., 'John Stow and the English Reformation', *The Sixteenth Century Journal*, 16/2 (1985): 257–71

— 'London Parish Clergy and the Protestant Reformation, 1547–1559', *Albion: A Quarterly Journal Concerned with British Studies*, 18/3 (1986): 375–93

Begent, Peter J., 'The Chantry Chapel of John Oxenbridge in St George's Chapel, Windsor Castle', *Antiquaries Journal*, 81 (2001): 337–50

Bennett, E.K., 'Notes on the Original Statutes of the College of St John Evangelist of Rushworth, co. Norfolk; founded by Edmund Gonville AD 1342', *Norfolk Archaeology*, 10 (1888): 50–64

Bennett, Nicholas, 'Clerical Non-Residence in the Diocese of Lincoln in the Fourteenth Century', in Nicholas Bennett and David Marcombe (eds), *Thomas de Aston and the Diocese of Lincoln. Two Studies in the Fourteenth-Century Church* (Lincoln: Lincoln Cathedral, 1998): 4–31

Bernard, G.W., 'Vitality and Vulnerability in the Late Medieval Church: Pilgrimage on the Eve of the Break with Rome', in John L. Watts (ed.), *The*

End of the Middle Ages? England in the Fifteenth and Sixteenth Centuries (Stroud: Sutton, 1998): 199–233

— *The King's Reformation. Henry VIII and the Remaking of the English Church* (New Haven/London: Yale University Press, 2005)

Binnal, Peter B.G., 'Notes on the Medieval Altars and Chapels in Lincoln Cathedral', *The Antiquaries Journal*, 42 (1962): 68–80

Binski, Paul, *Medieval Death, Ritual and Representation* (London: British Museum, 1996)

Blair, John, 'Clerical Communities and Parochial Space: The Planning of Urban Mother Churches in the Twelfth and Thirteenth Centuries', in T.R. Slater and Gervase Rosser (eds), *The Church in the Medieval Town* (Aldershot: Ashgate, 1998): 272–94

Bolton, James L., *The Medieval English Economy, 1150–1500* (London: J.M. Dent, 1980)

— '"The World Upside Down": Plague as an Agent of Economic and Social Change', in W.M. Ormrod and P.G. Lindley (eds), *The Black Death in England* (Stamford: Paul Watkins, 1996): 17–78

Bossy, John, 'The Mass as a Social Institution 1200–1700', *Past and Present*, 100 (1983): 29–61

— *Christianity in the West 1400–1700* (Oxford/New York: Oxford University Press, 1985)

Boucheron, Patrick, 'À qui appartient la cathédrale? La fabrique et la cité dans l'Italie médiévale', in Patrick Boucheron and Jacques Chiffoleau (eds), *Religion et société urbaine au Moyen Âge. Études offertes à Jean-Louis Biget par ses anciens élèves* (Paris: Publications de la Sorbonne, 2000): 81–94

Bove, Borris, 'Espace, piété et parenté à Paris aux XIIIe–XIVe siècles d'après les fondations d'anniversaires des familles échevinales', in Patrick Boucheron and Jacques Chiffoleau (eds), *Religion et société urbaine au Moyen Âge. Études offertes à Jean-Louis Biget par ses anciens élèves* (Paris: Publications de la Sorbonne, 2000): 253–81

Bowers, Roger, 'The Lady Chapel and its Musicians, c.1210–1559', in John Crook (ed.), *Winchester Cathedral: Nine Hundred Years* (Chichester: Phillimore, 1993): 247–56

— 'Music and Worship to 1640', in Dorothy Owen (ed.), *A History of Lincoln Minster* (Cambridge: Cambridge University Press, 1994): 47–76

— 'The Liturgy of the Cathedral and its Music', in Patrick Collinson, Nigel Ramsay and Margaret Sparks (eds), *A History of Canterbury Cathedral* (Oxford/New York: Oxford University Press, 1995): 408–50

— *English Church Polyphony. Singers and Sources from the 14th to the 17th Century* (Aldershot: Ashgate, 1999)

Bowker, Margaret, *The Secular Clergy in the Diocese of Lincoln, 1495–1520* (Cambridge: Cambridge University Press, 1968)

— 'The Henrician Reformation and the Parish Clergy', in Christopher Haigh (ed.), *The English Reformation Revised* (Cambridge/New York: Cambridge University Press, 1987): 75–93

— 'Historical Survey, 1450–1750', in Dorothy Owen (ed.), *A History of Lincoln Minster* (Cambridge: Cambridge University Press, 1994): 164–209

Boyle, Leonard E., *Pastoral Care, Clerical Education, and the Canon Law, 1200–1400* (London: Variorum Reprints, 1981)

Brett, Martin, 'The Church at Rochester, 604–1185', in Nigel Yates (ed.), *Faith and Fabric. A History of Rochester Cathedral 604–1994* (Woodbridge: Boydell Press, 1996): 1–27

Brigden, Susan, 'Youth and the Reformation', in Peter Marshall (ed.), *The Impact of the English Reformation 1500–1640* (London: Arnold, 1997): 55–85 [first published in *Past and Present*, 95 (1982)]

— 'Religion and Social Obligation in Early Sixteenth-Century London', *Past and Present*, 103 (1984): 67–112

— *London and the Reformation* (Oxford: Clarendon Press, 1989)

Britnell, R.H., 'The English Economy and the Government, 1450–1550', in John L. Watts (ed.), *The End of the Middle Ages? England in the Fifteenth and Sixteenth Centuries* (Stroud: Sutton, 1998): 89–116

Brooke, C.N.L., 'The Deans of St Paul's c.1090–1499', *Bulletin of the Institute of Historical Research*, 29 (1956): 231–44

— 'The Earliest Times to 1485', in W.R. Matthews and W.M. Atkins (eds), *A History of St Paul's Cathedral and the Men Associated with it* (London: Phoenix House, 1957): 1–99

— *Medieval Church and Society. Collected Essays* (London: Sidgwick & Jackson, 1971)

Brown, Andrew, *Popular Piety in Late Medieval England. The Diocese of Salisbury 1250–1550* (Oxford: Oxford University Press, 1995)

Bumpus, John S. *The Organists and Composers of St Paul's Cathedral* (London: Bowden, Hudson & Co., 1891)

Burgess, Clive, 'For the Increase of Divine Service: Chantries in the Parish in Late Medieval Bristol', *Journal of Ecclesiastical History*, 36 (1985): 46–65

— 'A Service for the Dead: The Form and Function of the Anniversary in Late Medieval Bristol', *Transaction of the Bristol and Gloucestershire Archaeological Society*, 105 (1987): 183–211

— '"By Quick and by Dead": Wills and Pious Provision in Late Medieval Bristol', *English Historical Review*, 102 (1987): 837–58

— '"A Fond Thing Vainly Invented": An Essay on Purgatory and Pious Motive in Later Medieval England', in S.J. Wright (ed.), *Parish, Church and People: Local Studies in Lay Religion, 1350–1700* (London: Hutchinson, 1988): 56–84

— 'Late Medieval Wills and Pious Convention: Testamentary Evidence Reconsidered', in Michael Hicks (ed.), *Profit, Piety and the Professions in Later Medieval England* (Gloucester: Sutton, 1990): 14–33

— 'Strategies for Eternity: Perpetual Chantry Foundation in Late Medieval Bristol', in Christopher Harper-Bill (ed.), *Religious Belief and Ecclesiastical Careers in Late Medieval England* (Woodbridge: Boydell Press, 1991): 1–32

— 'The Benefactions of Mortality: The Lay Response in the Late Medieval Urban Parish', in David M. Smith (ed.), *Studies in Clergy and Ministry in Medieval England*, Borthwick Studies in History, 1 (York: University of York, 1991): 65–86

— 'Shaping the Parish: St Mary at Hill, London, in the Fifteenth Century', in John Blair and Brian Golding (eds), *The Cloister and the World. Essays in Medieval History in Honour of Barbara Harvey* (Oxford: Clarendon Press, 1996): 246–86

— 'London Parishes: Development in Context', in Richard Britnell (ed.), *Daily Life in the Late Middle Ages* (Stroud: Sutton, 1998): 151–74, 217–19

— 'St George's College, Windsor: Context and Consequence', in Nigel Saul (ed.), *St George's Chapel, Windsor, in the Fourteenth Century* (Woodbridge: Boydell Press, 2005): 63–96

— 'An Institution for All Seasons: The Late Medieval English College', in Clive Burgess and Martin Heale (eds), *The Late Medieval College and Its Context* (Woodbridge: Boydell Press, 2008): 3–27

— 'London, the Church and the Kingdom', in Matthew Davies and Andrew Prescott (eds), *London and The Kingdom. Essays in Honour of Caroline M. Barron. Proceedings of the 2004 Harlaxton Symposium* (Donington: Shaun Tyas, 2008): 98–117

— and Beat Kümin, 'Penitential Bequests and Parish Regimes in Late Medieval England', *Journal of Ecclesiastical History*, 44 (1993): 610–30

— and Andrew Wathey, 'Mapping the Soundscape: Church Music in English Towns, 1430–1550', *Early Music History*, 19 (2000): 1–46

Bussby, Frederick, *Winchester Cathedral 1079–1979* (Southampton: Paul Cave, 1979)

Carpenter, Christine, 'The Religion of the Gentry in Fifteenth-Century England', in D. Williams (ed.), *England in the Fifteenth Century* (Woodbridge: Boydell Press, 1987): 53–74

Carpenter, E.F., 'The Reformation: 1485–1660', in W.R. Matthews and W.M. Atkins (eds), *A History of St Paul's Cathedral and the Men Associated with it* (London: Phoenix House, 1957): 100–171

Carter, Patrick R.N., 'The Fiscal Reformation: Clerical Taxation and Opposition in Henrician England', in Beat A Kümin (ed.), *Reformations Old and New. Essays on the Socio-Economic Impact of Religious Change, c. 1470–1630* (Aldershot: Ashgate, 1996): 92–105

Chew, Helena M., 'Mortmain in Medieval London', *English Historical Review*, 60 (1945): 1–15

Chiffoleau, Jacques, *La comptabilité de l'Au-delà: Les hommes, la mort et la religion dans la région d'Avignon à la fin du Moyan Âge, 1320–1480* (Rome: École française de Rome 1980): 448–53

Christianson, C. Paul, 'The Rise of London's Book-Trade', in Lotte Hellinga and J.B. Trapp (eds), *The Cambridge History of the Book in Britain*: vol. 3: *1400–1557* (Cambridge/New York: Cambridge University Press, 1999): 128–47

Clark, J.M., *The Dance of Death in the Middle Ages and Renaissance* (Glasgow: Jackson, 1950)

Clark, M.A. 'Reformation in the Far North: Cumbria and the Church, 1500–1571', *Northern History*, 32 (1996): 75–89

Clark, Margaret, 'Northern Light? Parochial Life in a "Dark Corner" of Tudor England', in Katherine L. French, Gary G. Gibbs and Beat Kümin (eds), *The Parish in English Life 1400–1600* (Manchester/New York: Manchester University Press, 1997): 56–73

Collinson, Patrick, 'The Late Medieval Church and its Reformation, 1400–1600', in J. McManners (ed.), *The Oxford illustrated History of Christianity* (Oxford: Oxford University Press, 1990): 233–66

Colvin, Howard, *Architecture and the After-Life* (New Haven/London: Yale University Press, 1991)

— 'The Origin of Chantries', *Journal of Medieval History*, 26 (2000): 163–73

Cook, G.H., *Medieval Chantries and Chantry Chapels* (London: Phoenix House, 1947)

— *Old St Paul's Cathedral. A Lost Glory of Medieval London* (London, Phoenix House, 1955)

Cooper, T.N., 'Children, the Liturgy and the Reformation: the Evidence of the Lichfield Cathedral Choristers', in Diana Wood (ed.), *The Church and Childhood. Papers Read at the 1993 Summer Meeting and the 1994 Winter Meeting of the Ecclesiastical History Society*, Studies in Church History, 31 (Oxford/Cambridge, Mass.: Published for the Ecclesiastical History Society by Blackwell, 1994): 261–74

— 'Oligarchy and Conflict: Lichfield Cathedral Clergy in the Early Sixteenth Century', *Midland History*, 19 (1994): 40–57

Cornides, A. and R. Snow, 'Requiem Mass', in Thomas Carson and Joann Cerrito (eds), *New Catholic Encyclopedia*, 12 (Washington, DC: Catholic University of America, 2003): 134–6

Coulstock, P.H., *The Collegiate Church of Wimborne Minster* (Woodbridge: Boydell Press, 1993)

Cozens-Hardy, B., 'Chantries in the Duchy of Lancaster in Norfolk, 1548', *Norfolk Archaeology*, 29 (1946): 201–10

Cragoe, Carol Davidson, 'Fabric, Tombs and Precinct, 1087–1540', in Derek Keene, Arthur Burns and Andrew Saint (eds), *St Paul's. The Cathedral Church of London, 604–2004* (New Haven/London: Yale University Press, 2004): 127–142

Crankshaw, David, 'Community, City and Nation, 1540–1714', in Derek Keene, Arthur Burns and Andrew Saint (eds), *St Paul's. The Cathedral Church of London, 604–2004* (New Haven/London: Yale University Press, 2004): 45–70

Crawford, Anne, 'The Charter of Shiryngton's Chantry in the Chapel of St. Margaret, Uxbridge, 1459', *Journal of the Society of Archivists*, 4 (1973): 588–92

Cross, Claire, *Church and People, 1450–1660: The Triumph of the Laity in the English Church* (Hassocks: Harvester Press, 1976)

— 'The Later Middle Ages, 1215–1500', in Gerald Aylmer and Reginald Cant (eds), *A History of York Minster* (Oxford: Clarendon Press, 1977): 193–232

— 'York Clergy and Their Books in the Early Sixteenth Century', in Caroline Barron and Jenny Stratford (eds), *The Church and Learning in Later Medieval Society: Essays in Honour of R.B. Dobson. Proceedings of the 1999 Harlaxton Symposium* (Donington: Shaun Tyas, 2002): 344–54

Crouch, David, 'The Origin of Chantries: Some Further Anglo-Norman Evidence', *Journal of Medieval History*, 27/2 (2001): 159–80

Cunich, Peter, 'The Dissolution of Chantries', in Patrick Collinson and John Craig (eds), *The Reformation in English Towns, 1500–1640* (Basingstoke: Palgrave Macmillan, 1998): 159–74

Davies, Matthew and Ann Saunders, *The History of the Merchant Taylors' Company* (Leeds: Maney Publishing, 2004)

Davies, Richard G., 'The Episcopate', in Cecil Clough (ed.), *Profession, Vocation and Culture in Later Medieval England. Essays Dedicated to the Memory of A.R. Myers* (Liverpool: Liverpool University Press, 1982): 51–89

Davis, J.F., 'Lollardy and the Reformation in England', in Peter Marshall (ed.), *The Impact of the English Reformation 1500–1640* (London: Arnold, 1997): 37–54 [first published in *Archiv für Reformationsgeschichte*, 73 (1982)]

Davis, Virginia, 'Rivals for Ministry? Ordinations of Secular and Regular Clergy in Southern England c.1300–1500', in W.J. Sheils and Diana Wood (eds), *The Ministry: Clerical and Lay. Papers Read at the 1988 Summer Meeting and the 1989 Winter Meeting of the Ecclesiastical History Society*, Studies in Church History, 26 (Oxford/Cambridge, Mass.: Published for the Society by B. Blackwell, 1990): 99–109

— 'Episcopal Ordination Lists as a Source for Clerical Mobility in England in the Fourteenth Century', in Nicholas Rogers (ed.), *England in the Fourteenth Century. Proceedings of the 1991 Harlaxton Symposium* (Stamford: Paul Watkins, 1993): 152–70

— *William Waynflete. Bishop and Educationalist* (Woodbridge: Boydell Press, 1993)

— 'Medieval Longevity: The Experience of Members of Religious Orders in Late Medieval England', *Medieval Prosopography*, 19 (1998): 111–24

— 'Irish Clergy in Late Medieval England', *Irish Historical Studies*, 32 (2000): 145–60

— 'The Contribution of University-Educated Secular Clerics to the Pastoral Life of the English Church', in Caroline Barron and Jenny Stratford (eds), *The Church and Learning in Later Medieval Society: Essays in Honour of R.B. Dobson. Proceedings of the 1999 Harlaxton Symposium* (Donington: Shaun Tyas, 2002): 255–72

— 'The Lesser Clergy in the Later Middle Ages', in Derek Keene, Arthur Burns and Andrew Saint (eds), *St Paul's. The Cathedral Church of London, 604–2004* (New Haven/London: Yale University Press, 2004): 157–61

Dickens, A.G. 'The Edwardian Arrears in Augmentations Payments and the Problem', *English Historical Review*, 55/219 (1940): 384–418

Dinn, Robert, 'Death and Rebirth in Late Medieval Bury St Edmunds', in Steven Bassett (ed.), *Death in Towns. Urban Responses to the Dying and the Dead, 100–1600* (Leicester/London/New York: Leicester University Press, 1992): 150–69

Dobson, R.B., 'The Foundation of Perpetual Chantries by the Citizens of Medieval York', in G.J. Cuming (ed.), *The Province of York. Papers Read at the Fifth Summer Meeting of the Ecclesiastical History Society*, Studies in Church History, 4 (Leiden: Brill, 1967): 22–38

— 'The Later Middle Ages, 1215–1500', in Gerald Aylmer and Reginald Cant (eds), *A History of York Minster* (Oxford: Clarendon Press, 1977): 44–109

— 'The Residentiary Canons of York in the Fifteenth Century', *Journal of Ecclesiastical History*, 30 (1979): 145–74. Reprt in R.B. Dobson, *Church and Society in the Medieval North of England* (London: Hambledon Press, 1996): 196–224

— 'Cathedral Chapters and Cathedral Cities: York, Durham and Carlisle in the Fifteenth Century', *Northern History*, 19 (1983): 15–44

— 'Recent Prosopographical Research in Late Medieval English History: University Graduates, Durham Monks, and York Canons', in Neithard Bulst and Jean-Philippe Genet (eds), *Medieval Lives and the Historian: Studies in Medieval Prosopography. Proceedings of the First International Interdisciplinary Conference on Medieval Prosopography, University of Bielefield, 3–5 December 1982* (Kalamazoo: Medieval Institute Publications, 1986): 181–200

— 'Citizens and Chantries in Late Medieval York', in D. Abulafia, M. Franklin and M. Rubin (eds), *Church and City, 1000–1500. Essays in Honour of Christopher Brooke* (Cambridge: Cambridge University Press, 1992): 311–32. Reprt in R.B. Dobson, *Church and Society in the Medieval of North England* (London: Hambledon Press, 1996): 267–84

— 'The Monks of Canterbury in the Later Middle Ages, 1220–1540', in Patrick, Collinson, Nigel Ramsay and Margaret Sparks (eds), *A History of Canterbury Cathedral* (Oxford/New York: Oxford University Press, 1995): 69–153

— '"Mynistres of Saynt Cuthbert": The Monks of Durham in the Fifteenth Century', in R.B. Dobson, *Church and Society in the Medieval North of England* (London: Hambledon Press, 1996): 47–82

Dodwell, Barbara, 'The Monastic Community', in Ian Atherton, Eric Fernie, Christopher Harper-Bill and Hassell Smith (eds), *Norwich Cathedral. Church, City and Diocese, 1096–1996* (London: Hambledon Press, 1996): 231–54

Douglas-Irvine, H., 'St Paul's Cathedral', in William Page (ed.), *Victoria History of the Counties of England*, vol. 1: *A History of London* (London: Constable and Co. Ltd, 1908): 409–32

Du Boulay, F.R.H., 'The Quarrel between the Carmelite Friars and the Secular Clergy of London 1464–1468', *Journal of Ecclesiastical History*, 6 (1955): 156–74

Duffy, Eamon, *The Stripping of the Altars. Traditional Religion in England 1400–1580* (New Haven/London: Yale University Press, 1992)

— 'The Parish, Piety and Patronage in Late Medieval East Anglia: The Evidence of Rood Screens', in Katherine L. French, Gary G. Gibbs and Beat Kümin (eds), *The Parish in English Life 1400–1600* (Manchester/New York: Manchester University Press, 1997): 133–62

— *The Voices of Morebath. Reformation and Rebellion in an English Village* (New Haven/London: Yale University Press, 2001)

Dugdale, Sir William, *A History of St. Paul's Cathedral*. With a Continuation and Additions by H. Ellis (London, reprt 1818)

Dyer, Christopher, *Standards of Living in the Later Middle Ages. Social Change in England, c. 1200–1520* (Cambridge/New York: Cambridge University Press, 1989)

— 'Trade, Towns and the Church: Ecclesiastical Consumers and the Urban Economy of the West Midlands, 1290–1540', in T.R. Slater and Gervase Rosser (eds), *The Church in the Medieval Town* (Aldershot: Ashgate, 1998): 55–75

Edwards, Kathleen, *The English Secular Cathedrals in the Middle Ages. A Constitutional Study with Special Reference to the Fourteenth Century* (Manchester: Manchester University Press, 1949)

Emden, A.B., *A Biographical Register of the University of Oxford to 1500* (3 vols, Oxford: Clarendon Press, 1957–1959)

— *A Biographical Register of the University of Cambridge* (Cambridge: Cambridge University Press, 1963)

— *A Biographical Register of the University of Oxford A.D. 1501 to 1540* (Oxford: Clarendon Press, 1974)

Farnhill, Ken, 'Religious Policy and Parish "Conformity": Cratfield's Lands in the Sixteenth Century', in Katherine L. French, Gary G. Gibbs and Beat Kümin (eds), *The Parish in English Life 1400–1600* (Manchester/New York: Manchester University Press, 1997): 217–29

Fisher, R.M., 'The Reformation of Clergy at the Inns of Court 1530–1580', *Sixteenth Century Journal*, 12/1 (1981): 69–91

Ford, Judy Ann, 'Marginality and the Assimilation of Foreigners in the Lay Parish Community: The Case of Sandwich', in Katherine L. French, Gary G. Gibbs and Beat Kümin (eds), *The Parish in English Life 1400–1600* (Manchester/ New York: Manchester University Press, 1997): 203–16

Fowler, R.C. 'The Abbey of Beeleigh By Maldon', in William Page (ed.), *Victoria History of the Counties of England. A History of Essex* (London: Constable and Co. Ltd, 1907), vol. 2: 172–76

Foxell, Maurice Frederic, 'An Account of the College of Minor Canons of St Paul's Cathedral', *Transactions of the St Paul's Ecclesiological Society*, 10 (1931): 7–10

Frankforter, A.D., 'The Reformation and the Register: Episcopal Administration of Parishes in Late Medieval England', *Catholic History Review*, 63 (1977): 204–24

Franklin, Michael, 'The Cathedral as Parish Church: The Case of Southern England', in David Abulafia, Michael Franklin and Miri Rubin (eds), *Church and City, 1000–1500. Essays in Honour of Christopher Brooke* (Cambridge: Cambridge University Press, 1992): 173–98

French, Katherine L., 'Parochial Fund-Raising in Late Medieval Somerset', in Katherine L. French, Gary G. Gibbs and Beat Kümin (eds), *The Parish in English Life 1400–1600* (Manchester/New York: Manchester University Press, 1997): 115–32

Galpern, A.N., 'The Legacy of Late Medieval Religion in Sixteenth Century Champagne', in Heiko A. Oberman (ed.), *The Pursuit of Holiness in Late Medieval and Renaissance Religion* (Leiden: Brill, 1974): 141–75

Gasquet, F.A. and E. Bishop, *Edward VI and the Book of Common Prayer* (3rd edn, London: Sheed and Ward, 1928)

Gee, Eric, 'The Topography of Altars, Chantries and Shrines in York Minster', *The Antiquaries Journal*, 64 (1984): 337–50

Gibbs, Gary, 'New Duties for the Parish Community in Tudor London', in Katherine L. French, Gary G. Gibbs and Beat Kümin (eds), *The Parish in English Life 1400–1600* (Manchester/New York: Manchester University Press, 1997): 163–77

Gilchrist, Roberta, 'Christian Bodies and Souls: The Archaeology of Life and Death in Later Medieval Hospitals', in Steven Bassett (ed.), *Death in Towns. Urban Responses to the Dying and the Dead, 100–1600* (Leicester/London/ New York: Leicester University Press, 1992): 101–18

Gittings, Clare, 'Urban Funerals in Late Medieval and Reformation England', in Steven Bassett (ed.), *Death in Towns. Urban Responses to the Dying and the Dead, 100–1600* (Leicester/London/New York: Leicester University Press, 1992): 170–83

Godfrey, C.J., 'The Chantries of Mere and Their Priests', *The Wiltshire Archaeological and Natural History Magazine*, 55 (1953): 153–60

— 'Pluralists in the Province of Canterbury in 1366', *Journal of Ecclesiastical History*, 11 (1960): 23–40

Goodall, John A., *God's House at Ewelme. Life, Devotion and Architecture in a Fifteenth-Century Almshouse* (Aldershot: Ashgate, 2001)

— and Linda Monckton, 'The Chantry of Humphrey, Duke of Gloucester', in Martin Henig and Phillip G. Lindley (eds), *Alban and St Albans: Roman and Medieval Architecture, Art and Archaeology*, British Archaeological Association, Conference Transactions, 24 (Leeds: Maney Publishing, 2001): 231–55

Greatrex, Joan, 'The Almonry School of Norwich Cathedral Priory in the Thirteenth and Fourteenth Centuries', in Diana Wood (ed.), *The Church and*

Childhood. Papers Read at the 1993 Summer Meeting and the 1994 Winter Meeting of the Ecclesiastical History Society, Studies in Church History, 31 (Oxford/Cambridge, Mass.: Published for the Ecclesiastical History Society by Blackwell, 1994): 169–81

Greenway, Diana, 'Orders and Rank in the Cathedral of Old Sarum', in W.J. Sheils and Diana Wood (eds), *The Ministry: Clerical and Lay. Papers Read at the 1988 Summer Meeting and the 1989 Winter Meeting of the Ecclesiastical History Society*, Studies in Church History, 26 (Oxford/Cambridge, Mass.: Published for the Society by B. Blackwell, 1990): 55–63

Gurevich, A., *Medieval Popular Culture: Problems of Belief and Perception* (Cambridge/New York: Cambridge University Press, 1988)

Haigh, Christopher, 'The Anticlericalism and the English Reformation', in Christopher Haigh (ed.), *The English Reformation Revised* (Cambridge/New York: Cambridge University Press, 1987): 56–71

— 'The Continuity of Catholicism in the English Reformation', in Christopher Haigh (ed.), *The English Reformation Revised* (Cambridge/New York: Cambridge University Press, 1987): 176–208

— 'The Recent Historiography of the English Reformation', in Christopher Haigh (ed.), *The English Reformation Revised* (Cambridge/New York: Cambridge University Press, 1987): 19–33

— *English Reformations: Religion, Politics and Society under the Tudors* (Oxford: Clarendon Press, 1993)

Haines, Roy M., 'The Education of the English Clergy during the Later Middle Ages: Some Observation on the Operation of Pope Boniface VIII's Constitution *Cum Ex Eo* (1298)', *Canadian Journal of History*, 4 (1969): 1–22

— *Ecclesia Anglicana: Studies in the English Church of the Later Middle Ages* (Toronto: University of Toronto Press, 1989)

Hamilton Thompson, A., 'The Early History of the College of Irthlingborough', *Northampton and Oakham Architectural Society*, 35 (1920): 267–85

— *The English Clergy and their Organisation in the Later Middle Ages* (Oxford: Clarendon Press, 1947)

Hannam, U.C., 'The Episcopal Registers of Roger Warden and Nicholas Bubwith', *Transactions of the London and Middlesex Archaeological Society*, 11 (1954): 123–6, 214–26

Harding, Vanessa, 'Burial Choice and Burial Location in Later Medieval London', in Steven Basset (ed.), *Death in Towns. Urban Responses to the Dying and the Dead, 100–1600* (Leicester/London/New York: Leicester University Press, 1992): 118–35

— *The Dead and the Living in Paris and London, 1500–1670* (Cambridge: Cambridge University Press, 2002)

Haren, Michael J., 'Social Ideas in the Pastoral Literature of Fourteenth-Century England', in Christopher Harper-Bill (ed.), *Religious Belief and Ecclesiastical Careers in Late Medieval England. Proceedings of the Conference Held at Strawberry Hill, Easter 1989* (Woodbridge: Boydell Press, 1991): 43–57

Harper-Bill, Christopher, 'Dean Colet's Convocation Sermon and the Pre-Reformation Church in England', *History*, 73 (1988): 191–210

— *The Pre-Reformation Church in England 1400–1530* (London/New York: Longman, 1989)

— 'The English Church and English Religion after the Black Death', in W.M. Ormrod and P.G. Lindley (eds), *The Black Death in England* (Stamford: Paul Watkins, 1996): 79–123

— 'The Medieval Church and the Wider World', in Ian Atherton, Eric Fernie, Christopher Harper-Bill and Hassell Smith (eds), *Norwich Cathedral. Church, City and Diocese, 1096–1996* (London: Hambledon Press, 1996): 281–313

Harvey, Barbara, *Living and Dying in England, 1100–1540: The Monastic Experience* (Oxford: Clarendon Press, 1993)

Harvey, John H., *Henry Yevele c. 1320 to 1400. The Life of an English Architect* (London: Batsford, 1944)

Hatcher, John, *Plague, Population and the English Economy, 1348–1530* (London: Macmillan, 1977)

Heard, Kate, 'Death and Representation in the Fifteenth Century: The Wilcote Chantry Chapel at North Leigh', *Journal of British Archaeological Association*, 154 (2001): 134–49

Heath, Peter, *The English Parish Clergy on the Eve of the Reformation* (London: Routledge & K. Paul; Toronto: University of Toronto Press, 1969)

— 'Urban Piety in the Later Middle Ages: The Evidence of Hull Wills', in Barrie Dobson (ed.), *The Church, Politics and Patronage in the Fifteenth Century* (Gloucester: Sutton, 1984): 209–34

Hennessy, George Leydon, *Novum Repertorium Ecclesiasticum Parochiale Londinense* (London: S. Sonnenschein, 1898)

Hicks, Michael (ed.), 'Chantries, Obits and Almshouses: The Hungerford Foundations 1325–1478', in Caroline Barron and Christopher Harper-Bill (eds), *The Church in Pre-Reformation Society: Essays in Honour of F.R.H. Du Boulay* (Woodbridge: Boydell Press, 1985): 123–42

— 'The Piety of Margaret, Lady Hungerford (d.1478)', *Journal of Ecclesiastical History*, 38 (1987): 19–38

Higgott, Gordon, 'The Fabric to 1670', in Derek Keene, Arthur Burns and Andrew Saint (eds), *St Paul's. The Cathedral Church of London, 604–2004* (New Haven/London: Yale University Press, 2004): 170–89

Hill, Rosalind, *"'A Chaunterie for Soules"*: London Chantries in the Reign of Richard II', in F.R. Du Boulay and Caroline Barron (eds), *The Reign of Richard II. Essays in Honour of May McKisack* (London: Athlone Press, 1971): 242–55

Homer, Ronald F., 'Tin, Lead and Pewter', in John Blair and Nigel Ramsay (ed.), *English Medieval Industries* (London: Hambledon Press, 1991): 57–80

Houts, Elizabeth van, 'Nuns and Goldsmiths: The Foundation and Early Benefactors of St Radegund's Priory at Cambridge', in David Abulafia, Michael Franklin and Miri Rubin (eds), *Church and City, 1000–1500. Essays in Honour of Christopher Brooke* (Cambridge: Cambridge University Press, 1992): 59–79

Hugo, Thomas, 'The Hospital of Le Papey, in the City of London', *Transactions of the London and Middlesex Archaeological Society*, 5 (1981): 183–221

Hutton, Ronald, 'The Local Impact of the Tudor Reformation', in Christopher Haigh (ed.), *The English Reformation Revised* (Cambridge/New York: Cambridge University Press, 1987): 114–38

— *The Rise and Fall of Merry England: The Ritual Year 1400–1700* (Oxford, Oxford University Press, 1994)

Imray, Jean, *The Charity of Richard Whittington. A History of the Trust Administered by the Mercers' Company, 1424–1966* (London: Athlone Press, 1968)

Jack, Sybil, 'First and Second Courts of Augmentations', in Ronald H. Fritze (ed.), *Historical Dictionary of Tudor England, 1485–1603* (New York: Greenwood Press, 1991): 37–9

Jacob, E.F., 'Founders and Foundations in Later Middle Ages', *Bulletin of the Institute of Historical Research*, 35 (1962): 29–46

Jewell, Helen, 'English Bishops as Educational Benefactors in the Later Fifteenth Century', in Barrie Dobson (ed.), *The Church, Politics and Patronage in the Fifteenth Century* (Gloucester: Sutton, 1984): 146–67

Johnson, David: 'Estates and Income, 1540–1714', in Derek Keene, Arthur Burns and Andrew Saint (eds), *St Paul's. The Cathedral Church of London, 604–2004* (New Haven/London: Yale University Press, 2004): 304–11

Jordan, W.K., *Philanthropy in England, 1480–1660* (London: G. Allen & Unwin, 1959)

— *Edward VI*, vol. 2: *The Threshold of Power* (Cambridge, Mass.: Harvard University Press, 1970)

Keene, Derek, 'London from the Post-Roman Period to 1300', in D.M. Palliser (ed.), *The Cambridge Urban History of Britain*, vol. 1: *600–1540* (Cambridge: Cambridge University Press, 2000): 187–216

— 'From Conquest to Capital: St Paul's c.1100–1300', in Derek Keene, Arthur Burns and Andrew Saint (eds), *St Paul's. The Cathedral Church of London, 604–2004* (New Haven/London: Yale University Press, 2004): 17–32

— and Vanessa Harding, *A Survey of Documentary Sources for Property Holding in London before the Great Fire*, London Record Society, 22 (London: London Record Society, 1985)

Kennedy, Kathleen E., 'A, B, C is for Chantry? Fifteenth-Century Provincial Merchant Education', *Medieval Perspectives*, 141 (1999): 125–39

Kennedy, Ruth, '"A Bird in Bishopswood": Some Newly-Discovered Lines of Alliterative Verse from the Late Fourteenth Century', in Myra Stokes and T.L. Burton (eds), *Medieval Literature and Antiquities. Studies in Honour of Basil Cottle* (Cambridge: D.S. Brewer, 1987): 71–87

Kermode, Jennifer, 'Merchants of Three English Towns', in Cecil Clough (ed.), *Profession, Vocation and Culture in Later Medieval England. Essays Dedicated to the Memory of A.R. Myers* (Liverpool: Liverpool University Press, 1982): 7–48

— 'Obvious Observations on the Formation of Oligarchies in Late Medieval English Towns', in John A.F. Thomson (ed.), *Towns and Towns People in the Fifteenth Century* (Gloucester: Sutton, 1988): 87–106

King, Pamela M., 'The Treasurer's Cadaver in York Minster Reconsidered', in Caroline Barron and Jenny Stratford (eds), *The Church and Learning in Later Medieval Society: Essays in Honour of R.B. Dobson. Proceedings of the 1999 Harlaxton Symposium* (Donington: Shaun Tyas, 2002): 196–209

Kisby, Fiona, 'Books in London Parish Churches before 1603: Some Preliminary Observations', in Caroline Barron and Jenny Stratford (eds), *The Church and Learning in Later Medieval Society: Essays in Honour of R.B. Dobson. Proceedings of the 1999 Harlaxton Symposium* (Donington: Shaun Tyas, 2002): 305–26

Kitching, Christopher J., 'The Chantries of East Riding of Yorkshire at the Dissolution in 1548', *Yorkshire Archaeological Journal*, 44 (1972): 178–94

— 'The Disposal of Monastic and Chantry Lands', in Felicity Heal and Rosemary O'Deal (eds), *Church and Society in England: Henry VIII to James I* (London, 1977): 119–36

— 'Church and Chapelry in Sixteenth-Century England', in Derek Baker (ed.), *The Church in Town and Countryside. Papers Read at the Seventeenth Summer Meeting and the Eighteenth Winter Meeting of the Ecclesiastical*

History Society, Studies in Church History, 16 (Oxford: Published for the Ecclesiastical History Society by B. Blackwell, 1979): 279–90

Kleineke, Hannas, 'Carleton's Book: William FitzStephen's "Description of London" in a Late Fourteenth-Century Common-Place Book', *Bulletin of the Institute of Historical Research*, 74 (2001): 117–26

— 'The Schoolboy's Tale: A Fifteenth-Century Voice from St Paul's School', in Matthew Davies and Andrew Prescott (eds), *London and the Kingdom. Essays in Honour of Caroline M. Barron. Proceedings of the 2004 Harlaxton Symposium* (Donington: Shaun Tyas, 2008): 146–59

Knowles, Dom David, *The Monastic Order in England. A History of Its Development from the Times of St Dunstan to the Fourth Lateran Council* (2nd edn, Cambridge: Cambridge University Press, 1963)

Kreider, Alan, *English Chantries: The Road to Dissolution* (Cambridge, Mass.: Harvard University Press, 1979)

Kümin, Beat A., *The Shaping of a Community. The Rise and Reformation of the English Parish c.1400–1560* (Aldershot: Ashgate, 1996)

— 'The English Parish in a European Perspective', in Katherine L. French, Gary G. Gibbs and Beat Kümin (eds), *The Parish in English Life 1400–1600* (Manchester/New York: Manchester University Press, 1997): 15–32

Lander, Stephen, 'Church Courts and the Reformation in the Diocese of Chichester', in Christopher Haigh (ed.), *The English Reformation Revised* (Cambridge/New York: Cambridge University Press, 1987): 34–55

Le Goff, Jacques, *The Birth of Purgatory*, translated by Arthur Goldhammer (Chicago: University of Chicago Press, 1984)

— Le Neve, John, *Fasti Ecclesiae Anglicanae 1066–1300*, vol. I: *St Paul's, London*, compiled by Diana E. Greenway (London: Athlone Press, 1968)

— *Fasti Ecclesiae Anglicanae 1066–1300*, vol. VI: *York*, compiled by Diana E. Greenway (London: Athlone Press, 1999)

— *Fasti Ecclesiae Anglicanae 1300–1541*, vol. V: *St Paul's, London*, compiled by Joyce M. Horn (London: Athlone Press, 1963)

— *Fasti Ecclesiae Anglicanae 1300–1541*, vol. X: *Coventy and Lichfield*, compiled by B. Jones (London: Athlone Press, 1964)

— *Fasti Ecclesiae Anglicanae 1541–1857*, vol. I: *St Paul's, London*, compiled by Joyce M. Horn (London: Athlone Press, 1969)

Leach, A. F., 'St Paul's School before Colet', *Archaeologia*, 62 (1910): 191–238

Lehmberg, Stanford E., *The Reformation of Cathedrals. Cathedrals in English Society, 1485–1603* (Princeton: Princeton University Press, 1988)

— 'Reformation to Restoration', in Gerald Aylmer and John Tiller (eds), *Hereford Cathedral. A History* (London: Hambledon Press, 2000): 87–108

Lepine, David N., 'The Origins and Careers of the Canons of Exeter Cathedral, 1300–1455', in Christopher Harper-Bill (ed.), *Religious Belief and Ecclesiastical Careers in Late Medieval England. Proceedings of the Conference Held at Strawberry Hill, Easter 1989* (Woodbridge: Boydell Press, 1991): 87–120

— *A Brotherhood of Canons Serving God. English Secular Cathedrals in the Later Middle Ages* (Woodbridge: Boydell Press, 1995)

— '"A Long Way from University": Cathedral Canons and Learning at Hereford in the Fifteenth Century', in Caroline Barron and Jenny Stratford (eds), *The Church and Learning in Later Medieval Society: Essays in Honour of R.B. Dobson. Proceedings of the 1999 Harlaxton Symposium* (Donington: Shaun Tyas, 2002): 178–95

— '"Their Name Liveth for Evermore"?: Obits at Exeter Cathedral in the Later Middle Ages', in Caroline M. Barron and Clive Burgess (eds), *Memory and Commemoration in Medieval England. Proceedings of the 2008 Harlaxton Symposium* (forthcoming)

Lindley, Philip, 'The Black Death and English Art. A Debate and Some Assumptions', in W.M. Ormrod and P.G. Lindley (eds), *The Black Death in England* (Stamford: Paul Watkins, 1996): 125–46

Litzenberger, Caroline, *The English Reformation and the Laity. Gloucestershire, 1540–1580* (Cambridge/New York: Cambridge University Press, 1997)

Longman, William, *A History of the Three Cathedrals Dedicated to St Paul in London* (London: Longmans, 1873)

Lyte, H.C. Maxwell, *Ninth Report of the Royal Commission on Historical Manuscripts. Part 1: Report and Appendix* (London: Eyre and Spottiswoode, 1883)

McGuire, Brian Patrick, 'Purgatory, the Communion of Saints, and Medieval Change', *Viator*, 20 (1989): 61–84

McHardy, A.K., 'Clerical Taxation in Fifteenth-Century England: the Clergy as Agents of the Crown', in Barrie Dobson (ed.), *The Church, Politics and Patronage in the Fifteenth Century* (Gloucester: Sutton, 1984): 168–92

— 'Careers and Disappointments in the Late-Medieval Church: Some English Evidence', in W.J. Sheils and Diana Wood (eds), *The Ministry: Clerical and Lay. Papers Read at the 1988 Summer Meeting and the 1989 Winter Meeting of the Ecclesiastical History Society*, Studies in Church History, 26 (Oxford/Cambridge, Mass.: Published for the Society by B. Blackwell, 1990): 111–30

— 'Some Patterns of Ecclesiastical Patronage in the Later Middle Ages', in David M. Smith (ed.), *Studies in Clergy and Ministry in Medieval England*, Borthwick Studies in History, 1 (York: University of York, 1991): 20–37

MacLeod, Roderick, 'The Topography of St Paul's Precinct, 1200–1500', *London Topographical Society*, 26 (1990): 1–14

McRee, Ben R., 'Religious Gilds and Regulation of Behavior in Late Medieval Towns', in Joel Rosenthal and Colin Richmond (eds), *People, Politics and Community in the Later Middle Ages* (Gloucester: Sutton, 1987): 108–22

Marcombe, David, 'Thomas de Aston. The Chantries and Charities of a Fourteenth-Century Archdeacon', in Nicholas Bennett and David Marcombe (ed.), *Thomas de Aston and the Diocese of Lincoln. Two Studies in the Fourteenth-Century Church* (Lincoln: Lincoln Cathedral, 1998): 32–55

Marsh, Christopher, 'In the Name of God? Will-Making and Faith in Early Modern England', in G.H. Martin and Peter Spufford (eds), *The Records of the Nation* (Woodbridge: Boydell Press, 1990): 215–49

Marshall, Peter, *The Catholic Priesthood and the English Reformation* (Oxford: Clarendon Press, 1994)

— 'The Dispersal of Monastic Patronage in East Yorkshire, 1520–90', in Beat A Kümin (ed.), *Reformations Old and New. Essays on the Socio-Economic Impact of Religious Change, c. 1470–1630* (Aldershot: Ashgate, 1996): 124–46

— *Beliefs and the Dead in Reformation England* (Oxford: Oxford University Press, 2002)

— *Reformation England 1480–1642* (London: Arnold, 2003)

— *Religious Identities in Henry VIII's England* (Aldershot: Ashgate, 2006)

Martindale, Andrew, 'Patrons and Minders: The Intrusion of the Secular into Sacred Spaces in the Later Middle Ages', in Diana Wood (ed.), *The Church and the Arts. Papers Read at the 1990 Summer Meeting and the 1991 Winter Meeting of the Ecclesiastical History Society*, Studies in Church History, 28 (Oxford: Published for the Ecclesiastical History Society by Blackwell Publishers 1992): 143–78

Mason, Emma, 'The Role of the English Parishioner, 1100–1500', *Journal of Ecclesiastical History*, 27/1 (1976): 17–29

Mateer, David and Elizabeth New, '"In Nomine Jesu": Robert Fayrfax and the Guild of the Holy Name in St Paul's Cathedral', *Music & Letters*, 81/4 (2000): 507–19

— Mertes, R.G.K.A., 'The Household as a Religious Community', in Joel Rosenthal and Colin Richmond (eds), *People, Politics and Community in the Later Middle Ages* (Gloucester: Sutton, 1987): 123–39

Middleton-Stewart, Judith, 'Singing for Souls in Suffolk 1300–1548', *Suffolk Review*, 16 (1991): 1–19

— *Inward Purity and Outward Splendour. Death and Remembrance in the Deanery of Dunwich, Suffolk, 1370–1547* (Woodbridge: Boydell Press, 2001)

Moorman, John R.H., *Church Life in England in the Thirteenth* Century (Cambridge: Cambridge University Press, 1945)

Moran, Jo Ann H., 'A "Common-Profit" Library in Fifteenth-Century England and Other Books for Chaplains', *Manuscripta*, 28 (1984): 17–25

Morganstern, Anne M., 'The Bishop, the Young Lion and the Two-headed Dragon: The Burghersh Memorial in Lincoln Cathedral', in Wessel Reinink and Jeroen Stumpel (eds), *Memory and Oblivion. Proceedings of the XXIXth International Congress of the History of Art Held in Amsterdam, 1–7 September 1996* (Dordrecht and Norwell, Mass.: Kluwer Academic, 1999): 515–26

Morris, Richard K. 'The New Work at Old St Paul's Cathedral and its Place in English Thirteenth-Century Architecture', in Linda Grant (ed.), *Medieval Art, Architecture and Archaeology in London*, British Archaeological Association, Conference Transactions, 10 (Leeds: Maney Publishing, 1990): 74–100

New, Elizabeth A., 'Fraternities in English Cathedrals in the Later Medieval Period', in Tim Thornton (ed.), *Social Attitudes and Political Structures in the Fifteenth Century* (Stroud: Sutton, 2000): 33–51

— 'The Jesus Chapel in St Paul's Cathedral, London: A Reconstruction of Its Appearance before the Reformation', *The Antiquaries Journal*, 85 (2005): 103–24

Newcombe, D.G., 'John Hooper's Visitation and Examination of the Clergy in the Diocese of Gloucester 1551', in Beat A Kümin (ed.), *Reformations Old and New. Essays on the Socio-Economic Impact of Religious Change, c. 1470–1630* (Aldershot: Ashgate, 1996): 57–70

Newcourt, Richard, *Repertorium Ecclesiasticum Parochiale Londinense* (2 vols, London: Printed by B. Motte, 1708–1710)

Newman, P.R., *The History of St William's College* (York: Dean and Chapter of York, 1994)

Nilson, Benjamin, *Cathedral Shrines of Medieval England* (Woodbridge: Boydell Press, 1998)

Norris, Malcolm, 'Later Medieval Monumental Brasses: an Urban Funerary Industry and its Representation of Death', in Steven Bassett (ed.), *Death in Towns. Urban Responses to the Dying and the Dead, 100–1600* (Leicester/London/New York: Leicester University Press, 1992): 184–209

Oakley, Anne, 'Rochester Priory, 1185–1540', in Nigel Yates (ed.), *Faith and Fabric. A History of Rochester Cathedral 604–1994* (Woodbridge: Boydell Press, 1996): 29–55

Oosterwijk, Sophie, 'Of Corpses, Constables and Kings: The Danse Macabre in Late Medieval and Renaissance Culture', *The Journal of the British Archaeological Association*, 157 (2004): 61–90

Orme, Nicholas, 'The Early Musicians of Exeter Cathedral', *Music and Letters*, 59 (1978): 395–407

— 'The Dissolution of the Chantries in Devon', *Report and Transactions of the Devonshire Association for the Advancement of Science, Literatures and Art*, 111 (1979): 75–123

— *The Minor Clergy of Exeter Cathedral, 1300–1548. A List of the Minor Officers, Vicar Choral, Annuellars, Secondaries and Choristers* (Exeter, 1980)

— 'Education and Learning at a Medieval English Cathedral: Exeter 1380–1548', *Journal of Ecclesiastical History*, 31 (1981): 265–83

— 'The Medieval Clergy of Exeter Cathedral, 1. The Vicars and Annuellars', *Report and Transactions of the Devonshire Association for the Advancement of Science, Literatures and Arts*, 113 (1981): 79–102

— 'Henry de Berbilond, d.1296, a Vicar Choral of Exeter Cathedral', *Devon and Cornwall Notes and Queries*, 34 (1981–1982): 1–7

— 'The Medieval Chantries of Exeter Cathedral, Part 1', *Devon and Cornwall Notes and Queries*, 34 (1981–1982): 319–26

— 'The Medieval Chantries of Exeter Cathedral, Part 2', *Devon and Cornwall Notes and Queries*, 35 (1982): 12–21

— 'The Medieval Chantries of Exeter Cathedral, Part 3', *Devon and Cornwall Notes and Queries*, 35 (1982): 67–71

— 'Schoolmasters, 1307–1509', in Cecil Clough (ed.), *Profession, Vocation and Culture in Later Medieval England. Essays dedicated to the Memory of A.R. Myers* (Liverpool: Liverpool University Press, 1982): 218–41

— 'Sir John Speke and His Chapel in Exeter Cathedral', *Report and Transactions of the Devonshire Association*, 118 (1986): 25–41

— *Education and Society in Medieval and Renaissance England* (London: Hambledon Press, 1989)

— 'The Charnel House of Exeter Cathedral', in Francis Kelly (ed.), *Medieval Art and Architecture at Exeter Cathedral* (Oxford: British Archaeological Association, 1991): 162–71

— 'The Medieval Schools of Herefordshire', *Nottingham Medieval Studies*, 40 (1996): 47–62

Osborne, Kenan, 'Reconciliation', in Richard P. McBrien (ed.), *The Harper-Collins Encyclopedia of Catholicism* (New York: HarperCollins, 1995): 1083–7

Owen, Dorothy, *Church and Society in Medieval Lincolnshire* (Lincoln: Lincolnshire Local History Committee, 1971)

— 'Historical Survey, 1091–1450', in Dorothy Owen (ed.), *A History of Lincoln Minster* (Cambridge: Cambridge University Press, 1994): 112–63

Owen, H. Gareth, 'Parochial Curates in Elizabethan London', *Journal of Ecclesiastical History*, 10 (1959): 66–73

Palliser, D.M., 'Popular Reactions to the Reformation during the Years of Uncertainty, 1530–1570', in Christopher Haigh (ed.), *The English Reformation Revised* (Cambridge/New York: Cambridge University Press, 1987): 94–113

— 'Introduction: The Parish in Perspective', in S.J. Wright (ed.), *Parish, Church and People: Local Studies in Lay Religion, 1350–1700* (London: Hutchinson, 1988): 5–28

— 'Urban Decay Revisited', in John A.F. Thomson (ed.), *Towns and Towns People in the Fifteenth Century* (Gloucester: Sutton, 1988): 11–21

Pantin, W.A., 'Chantry Priests' Houses and Other Medieval Lodgings', *Medieval Archaeology*, 111 (1959): 216–58

Pfaff, R.W., *New Liturgical Feasts in Later Medieval England* (Oxford: Clarendon Press, 1970)

Pogson, R.H., 'Revival and Reform in Mary Tudor's Church: A Question of Money', in Christopher Haigh (ed.), *The English Reformation Revised* (Cambridge/New York: Cambridge University Press, 1987): 139–56

Post, J.B., 'The Obsequies of John of Gaunt', *Guildhall Studies in London History*, 5 (1981): 1–12

Postles, David, 'Lamps, Lights and Layfolk: "Popular" Devotion before the Black Death', *Journal of Medieval History*, 25 (1999): 97–114

Price, J.E., *A Descriptive Account of the Guildhall of the City of London: Its History and Association* (London: Blades, 1886)

Raban, Sandra, *Mortmain Legislation and the English Church 1279–1500* (Cambridge/New York: Cambridge University Press, 1982)

Ramsay, Nigel, 'The Cathedral Archives and Library', in Patrick Collinson, Nigel Ramsay and Margaret Sparks (eds), *A History of Canterbury Cathedral* (Oxford/New York: Oxford University Press, 1995): 341–407

— 'The Library and Archives to 1897', in Derek Keene, Arthur Burns and Andrew Saint (eds), *St Paul's. The Cathedral Church of London, 604–2004* (New Haven/London: Yale University Press, 2004): 413–25

Raven, James, 'St Paul's Precinct and the Book Trade to c.1800', in Derek Keene, Arthur Burns and Andrew Saint (eds), *St Paul's. The Cathedral Church of London, 604–2004* (New Haven/London: Yale University Press, 2004): 430–38

Reddan, M., 'Religious Houses', in William Page (ed.), *Victoria History of the Counties of England*, vol. 1: *A History of London* (London: Constable and Co. Ltd, 1908): 574–81

Redstone, V.B., 'Chapels, Chantries and Gildes in Suffolk', *Proceedings of the Suffolk Institute of Archaeology*, 12 (1906): 1–87

Rex, Richard, 'The English Campaign against Luther in the 1520s', *Transactions of the Royal Historical Society*, 5th series, 39 (1989): 85–106

— 'The Friars in the English Reformation', in Peter Marshall (ed.), *The Beginnings of English Protestantism* (Cambridge/New York: Cambridge University Press, 2002): 38–59

— *The Lollards* (Basingstoke: Houndmills, 2002)

Richmond, Colin, 'Religion and the Fifteenth-Century English Gentleman', in Barrie Dobson (ed.), *The Church, Politics and Patronage in the Fifteenth Century* (Gloucester: Sutton, 1984): 193–208

— 'The English Gentry and Religion, c.1500', in Christopher Harper-Bill (ed.), *Religious Belief and Ecclesiastical Careers in Late Medieval England. Proceedings of the Conference Held at Strawberry Hill, Easter 1989* (Woodbridge: Boydell Press, 1991): 121–50

Rodes, Robert E. Jr., *Ecclesiastical Administration in Medieval England. The Anglo-Saxons to the Reformation* (Notre Dame, IN: University of Notre Dame Press, 1977)

Roffey, Simon, *The Medieval Chantry Chapel. An Archaeology* (Woodbridge: Boydell Press, 2007)

Röhrkasten, Jens, 'The Origin and Early Development of London Mendicant Houses', in T.R. Slater and Gervase Rosser (eds), *The Church in the Medieval Town* (Aldershot: Ashgate, 1998): 76–99

Rosenthal, Joel T., *The Purchase of Paradise. Gift Giving and the Aristocracy 1307–1485* (London, 1972)

— 'Lancastrian Bishops and Educational Benefaction', in Caroline Barron and Christopher Harper-Bill (eds), *The Church in Pre-Reformation society: Essays in Honour of F.R.H. Du Boulay* (London, 1985): 199–211

— 'Clerical Book Bequests: *A Vade Mecum*, But Whence and Whither?', in Caroline Barron and Jenny Stratford (eds), *The Church and Learning in Later Medieval Society: Essays in Honour of R.B. Dobson. Proceedings of the 1999 Harlaxton Symposium* (Donington: Shaun Tyas, 2002): 327–43

Rosser, Gervase, 'Communities of Parish and Guild in the Late Middle Ages?', in S.J. Wright (ed.), *Parish, Church and People: Local Studies in Lay Religion, 1350–1700* (London: Hutchinson, 1988): 29–55

— 'London and Westminster: The Suburb in the Urban Economy in the Later Middle Ages', in John A.F. Thomson (ed.), *Towns and Towns People in the Fifteenth Century* (Gloucester: Sutton, 1988): 45–61

— 'The Anglo-Saxon Gilds', in J. Blair (ed.), *Minsters and Parish Churches: The Local Church in Transition, 950–1200* (Oxford: Oxford University Committee for Archaeology, 1988): 31–4

— 'Parochial Conformity and Voluntary Religion in Late Medieval England', *Transactions of the Royal Historical Society*, 6th series, 1 (1991): 173–89

— 'Conflict and Political Community in the Medieval Town: Disputes between Clergy and Laity in Hereford', in T.R. Slater and Gervase Rosser (eds), *The Church in the Medieval Town* (Aldershot: Ashgate, 1998): 20–42

— 'Urban Culture and the Church 1300–1540', in D.M. Palliser (ed.), *The Cambridge Urban History of Britain*, vol. 1: *600–1540* (Cambridge: Cambridge University Press, 2000): 335–69

Rousseau, Marie-Hélène, 'Chantry Chaplains at St Paul's Cathedral, London c. 1200–1548', *Medieval Prosopography*, 26 (2005): 197–314

Rubin, Miri, *Corpus Christi. The Eucharist in Late Medieval Culture* (Cambridge/ New York: Cambridge University Press, 1991)

— 'Religious Culture in Town and County: Reflections on a Great Divide', in David Abulafia, Michael Franklin and Miri Rubin (eds), *Church and City, 1000–1500. Essays in Honour of Christopher Brooke* (Cambridge: Cambridge University Press, 1992): 3–22

Sadgrove, Michael, 'The Theatre of the Soul – Liturgy Then and Now: Worship in Coventry's Priory Church', in George Demidowicz (ed.), *Coventry's First Cathedral. The Cathedral and Priory of St Mary* (Stamford: Paul Watkins, 1994): 169–80

Sandler, Lucy, 'The Chantry of Roger of Waltham in Old St Paul's', in Janet Backhouse (ed.), *The Medieval English Cathedral. Papers in Honour of Pamela Tudor-Craig. Proceedings of the 1998 Harlaxton Symposium* (Donington: Shaun Tyas, 2003): 168–90

Scarisbrick, J.J., *The Reformation and the English People* (Oxford: Blackwell, 1984)

Scase, Wendy, 'Reginald Pecock, John Carpenter and John Colop's "Common-Profit" Books: Aspects of Book Ownership and Circulation in Fifteenth-Century London', *Medium Aevum*, 61 (1992): 261–74

Schen, Claire S., 'Women and the London Parishes 1500–1620', in Katherine L. French, Gary G. Gibbs and Beat Kümin (eds), *The Parish in English Life 1400–1600* (Manchester/New York: Manchester University Press, 1997): 250–68

— *Charity and Lay Piety in Reformation London (1500–1620)* (Aldershot: Ashgate, 2002)

Schofield, John, 'Medieval Parish Churches in the City of London: the Archaeology Evidence', in Katherine L. French, Gary G. Gibbs and Beat

Kümin (eds), *The Parish in English Life 1400–1600* (Manchester/New York: Manchester University Press, 1997): 35–55

— *St Paul's Cathedral before Wren: an Archaeology and History up to 1675* (English Heritage, forthcoming)

Shagan, Ethan H., *Popular Politics and the English Reformation* (Cambridge: Cambridge University Press, 2002)

Shahar, Shulamith, 'The Boy Bishop's Feast: A Case-Study in Church Attitudes towards Children in the High and Late Middle Ages', in Diana Wood (ed.), *The Church and Childhood. Papers Read at the 1993 Summer Meeting and the 1994 Winter Meeting of the Ecclesiastical History Society*, Studies in Church History, 31 (Oxford/Cambridge, Mass.: Published for the Ecclesiastical History Society by Blackwell, 1994): 243–60

Sherwell, John William, *The History of the Guild of Saddlers of the City of London*, 3rd edn by K.S. Laurie (London: The Company, 1956)

Simpson, James, 'Bulldozing the Middle Ages: The Case of John Lydgate', in Wendy Case, Rita Copeland and David Lawton (eds), *New Medieval Literatures*, vol. 4 (Oxford: Clarendon Press, 2001): 213–42

Simpson, William Sparrow, *Chapters in the History of Old St. Paul's* (London, 1881)

— *Gleanings from Old St. Paul's* (London, 1889)

— 'A Mandate of Bishop Clifford Superseding the Ancient Use of St Paul's Cathedral Church by the Use of Sarum', *Proceeding of the Society of Antiquaries of London*, 2nd series, 14 (1892): 118–28

— *S. Paul's Cathedral and Old City Life: Illustrations of Civil and Cathedral Life from the 13th to the 16th Century* (London: E. Stock, 1894)

Skeeters, Martha, *Community and Clergy. Bristol and the Reformation, c.1530–c.1570* (Oxford: Clarendon Press, 1993)

Slater, T.R., 'Benedictine Town: Planning in Medieval England. Evidence from St Albans', in T.R. Slater and Gervase Rosser (eds), *The Church in the Medieval Town* (Aldershot: Ashgate, 1998): 155–76

Smith, David M., *Guide to Bishops' Registers of England and Wales. A Survey from the Middle Ages to the Abolition of Episcopacy in 1646* (London, 1981)

— 'Thomas Cantilupe's Register: The Administration of the Diocese of Hereford 1275–1282', in Meryl Jancey (ed.), *St Thomas Cantilupe, Bishop of Hereford. Essays in his Honour* (Leominster Friends of the Hereford Cathedral, 1982): 83–101

— 'The Foundation of Chantries in the Chapel of St William on Ouse Bridge, York', in David M. Smith (ed.), *The Church in Medieval York. Records Edited in Honour of Professor Barrie Dobson*, Borthwick Texts and Calendars, 24 (York: University of York, 1999): 51–68

Snell, Laurence S., 'London Chantries and Chantry Chapels', in Joanna Bird, Hugh Chapman and John Clark (eds), *Collectanea Londondiniensia. Studies in London Archaeology and History to Ralph Merrifield*, Special Paper (London and Middlesex Archaeological Society), 2 (London: London and Middlesex Archaeological Society, 1978): 216–22

Southern, R.W., *Western Society and the Church in the Middle Ages* (London: Hodder and Stoughton, 1970)

— 'Between Heaven and Hell', *Times Literary Supplement*, 18 June 1982: 651–2

Steer, Christian, 'The Canons of St Paul's and their Brasses', *Transactions of the Monumental Brass Society* (forthcoming)

Storey, R.L., *Diocesan Administration in the Fifteenth Century* (London: St. Anthony's Press, 1959)

— *Thomas Langley and the Bishopric of Durham, 1406–1437* (London: SPCK, 1961)

— 'Recruitment of English Clergy in the Period of the Conciliar Movement', *Annuarium Historiae Conciliorum*, 7 (1975): 307–10

Swanson, Robert, 'Universities, Graduates and Benefices in Later Medieval England', *Past and Present*, 106 (1985): 28–61

— 'Learning and Livings: University Study and Clerical Careers in Late Medieval England', *Histories of Universities*, 6 (1986–1987): 81–103

— *Church and Society in Late Medieval England* (Oxford: Blackwell, 1989)

— 'Problems of the Priesthood in Pre-Reformation England', *English Historical Review*, 105 (1990): 845–69

— 'Chaucer's Parson and Other Priests', *Studies in the Age of Chaucer*, 13 (1991): 41–80

— 'Standards of Livings: Parochial Revenues in Pre-Reformation England', in Christopher Harper-Bill (ed.), *Religious Belief and Ecclesiastical Career in Late Medieval England* (Woodbridge: Boydell Press, 1991): 151–96

— *Catholic England. Faith, Religion and Observance before the Reformation* (Manchester: Manchester University Press, 1993)

— 'The Priory in the Later Middle Ages', in George Demidowicz (ed.), *Coventry's First Cathedral. The Cathedral and Priory of St Mary* (Stamford: Paul Watkins, 1994): 139–57

— 'Indulgences at Norwich Cathedral Priory in the Later Middle Ages: Popular Piety in the Balance Sheet', *Historical Research*, 16/191 (2003): 18–29

— and David Lepine, 'The Later Middle Ages, 1268–1535', in Gerald Aylmer and John Tiller (eds), *Hereford Cathedral. A History* (London: Hambledon Press, 2000): 48–86

Tanner, Norman, *The Church in Late Medieval Norwich, 1370–1532* (Toronto: Pontifical Institute of Mediaeval Studies, 1984)

— 'The Reformation and Regionalism: Further Reflections on the Church in Late Medieval Norwich', in John A.F. Thomson (ed.), *Towns and Towns People in the Fifteenth Century* (Gloucester: Sutton, 1988): 129–47

— 'The Cathedral and the City', in Ian Atherton, Eric Fernie, Christopher Harper-Bill and Hassell Smith (eds), *Norwich Cathedral. Church, City and Diocese, 1096–1996* (London: Hambledon Press, 1996): 255–80

Tatton-Brown, Tim, 'Medieval Parishes and Parish Churches in Canterbury', in T.R. Slater and Gervase Rosser (eds), *The Church in the Medieval Town* (Aldershot: Ashgate, 1998): 236–71

Taylor, Pamela, 'Foundation and Endowment: St Paul's and the English Kingdoms, 604–1087', in Derek Keene, Arthur Burns and Andrew Saint (eds), *St Paul's. The Cathedral Church of London, 604–2004* (New Haven/London: Yale University Press, 2004): 5–16

Thacker, Alan, 'The Cult of Saints and the Liturgy', in Derek Keene, Arthur Burns and Andrew Saint (eds), *St Paul's. The Cathedral Church of London, 604–2004* (New Haven/London: Yale University Press, 2004): 113–22

Thompson, Benjamin, '*Habendum et Tenendum*: Lay and Ecclesiastical Attitudes to the Property of the Church', in Christopher Harper-Bill (ed.), *Religious Belief and Ecclesiastical Careers in Late Medieval England* (Woodbridge: Boydell Press, 1991): 197–238

Thompson, Margaret, *The Carthusian Order in England* (London: Society for Promoting Christian Knowledge, 1930)

Thomson, John A.F., 'Piety and Charity in Late Medieval London', *Journal of Ecclesiastical History*, 16 (1965): 178–95

— *The Early Tudor Church and Society, 1485–1529* (London: Longman, 1993)

Thrupp, Sylvia, *The Merchant Class of Medieval London* (Chicago, IL: Chicago University Press, 1948)

Townley, Simon, 'Unbeneficed Clergy in the Thirteenth Century: Two English Dioceses', in David M. Smith (ed.), *Studies in Clergy and Ministry in Medieval England*, Borthwick Studies in History, 1 (York: University of York, 1991): 38–64

Veale, Elspeth, *The English Fur Trade in the Later Middle Ages*, London Record Society, 38 (2nd edn, London: London Record Society, 2003)

Venn, John and J.A. Venn, *Alumni Cantabrigienses. A Biographical List of All Known Students, Graduates and Holders of Office at the University of Cambridge from the Earliest Times to 1900* (3 vols, Cambridge: Cambridge University Press, 1922–1954)

Vovelle, M., *La mort et l'Occident de 1300 à nos jours* (Paris: Gallimard, 1983)

Walcott, Mackenzie E.C., 'Old St Paul's', *Transactions of the St Paul's Ecclesiological Society*, 1 (1885): 177–87

Ward, Rachel, 'Chantry Certificates of Norfolk: Towards a Partial Reconstruction', *Norfolk Archaeology*, 43 (1999): 287–306

Watt, J.A., 'The Medieval Chapter of Armagh Cathedral', in David Abulafia, Michael Franklin and Miri Rubin (eds), *Church and City, 1000–1500. Essays in Honour of Christopher Brooke* (Cambridge: Cambridge University Press, 1992): 219–45

Westlake, H.F., *The Parish Gilds of Medieval England* (London: Society for Promoting Christian Knowledge, 1919)

Whatley, E. Gorton (ed.), *The Saint of London. The Life and Miracles of St Erkenwald*, Text and Translation (Binghamton, NY: Medieval & Renaissance Texts & Studies, 1989)

Whiting, Robert, '"For the Health of My Soul": Prayers for the Dead in the Tudor South-West', in Peter Marshall (ed.), *The Impact of the English Reformation 1500–1640* (London: Arnold, 1997): 121–42 [first published in *Southern History*, 5 (1983)]

Wilson, Christopher, *The Gothic Cathedral. The Architecture of the Great Church, 1130–1530* (New York/London: Thames and Hudson, 1990)

— 'The Medieval Monuments', in Patrick Collinson, Nigel Ramsay and Margaret Sparks (eds), *A History of Canterbury Cathedral* (Oxford/New York: Oxford University Press, 1995): 408–50

Wilson, H.B., *A History of the Parish of St Laurence Pountney, including an Account of Corpus Christi (or Pountney) College* (London: Rivington, 1831)

Wood, Robert, 'A Fourteenth-Century London Owner of Piers Plowman', *Medium Aevum*, 54 (1984): 83–90

Wood-Legh, Kathleen L., 'Some Aspects of the History of Chantries in the Later Middle Ages', *Transactions of the Royal Historical Society*, 4th series, 28 (1946): 47–66

— *Perpetual Chantries in Britain* (Cambridge, 1965)

Woodward, G.H., 'The Dispersal of Chantry Lands in Somerset', *Southern History*, 5 (1983): 95–114

Woodward, G.W.O., *The Dissolution of the Monasteries* (New York: Walker, 1966)

Yeo, Geoffrey, 'Record-Keeping at St Paul's Cathedral', *Journal of the Society of Archivists*, 8 (1986): 30–44

Youings, Joyce A., 'The Terms of the Disposal of the Devon Monastic Lands, 1536–1558', *English Historical Review*, 69/270 (1954): 18–38

Unpublished Studies

Boldrick, Stacey, 'The Rise of Chantry Space in England from ca.1260 to ca.1400' (PhD thesis, University of Manchester, 1997)

Butler, Lionel, 'Robert Braybrooke, Bishop of London (1381–1404) and his Kinsmen' (DPhil thesis, University of Oxford, 1951)

Davies, Matthew P., 'The Tailors of London and their Guild, c.1300–1500' (PhD thesis, University of Oxford, 1994)

Edwards, N.A., 'The Chantry Priests of York Minster in the First Half of the Sixteenth Century' (MA dissertation, University of York, 1999)

Eldin, Grégoire, 'Les chapellenies à Notre-Dame de Paris (XIIe–XVIe siècles). Recherches historiques et archéologiques' (3 vols, thesis, École nationale des chartes, 1994)

Fuller, A.R.B., 'The Minor Corporations of the Secular Cathedrals of the Province of Canterbury Excluding the Welsh Sees between the Thirteenth Century and 1585 with Special Reference to the Minor Canons of St Paul's Cathedral from their Origins in the Fourteenth Century to the Visitations of Bishop Gibson in 1724' (MA dissertation, University of London, 1947)

Gear, Nichola, 'The Chantries of St Paul's Cathedral' (MA dissertation, Royal Holloway, University of London, 1996)

Hannam, Una, 'The Administration of the See of London under Bishops Roger Walden (1405–06) and Nicholas Bubwith (1406–07)' (MA dissertation, University of London, 1951)

McManaway, Sarah, 'Some Aspects of the Foundation of Perpetual Chantries in York Minster' (MA dissertation, University of York, 1981)

New, Elizabeth, 'The Cult of the Holy Name of Jesus in Late Medieval England, with Special Reference to the Fraternity in St Paul's Cathedral' (PhD thesis, University of London, 1999)

Rousseau, Marie-Hélène, 'Chantry Foundations and Chantry Chaplains at St Paul's Cathedral, London c.1200–1548' (PhD thesis, University of London, 2003)

Ward, Rachel, 'Chantries and Their Founders in Late Medieval Norwich' (MPhil thesis, University of Cambridge, 1994)

— 'The Foundation and Functions of Perpetual Chantries in the Diocese of Norwich, c.1250–1547' (PhD thesis, University of Cambridge, 1998)

Zadnick, Irene, 'The Administration of the Diocese of London. Bishops William Gray, Robert FitzHugh and Robert Gilbert (1426–1448)' (PhD thesis, University of Cambridge, 1993)

Index

For Product Safety Concerns and Information please contact our EU
representative GPSR@taylorandfrancis.com Taylor & Francis Verlag GmbH,
Kaufingerstraße 24, 80331 München, Germany

Printed and bound by CPI Group (UK) Ltd, Croydon, CR0 4YY
01/05/2025
01858450-0004